DATE DUE			
AUG _ 8 1996			
FEB 13 2003			
MAR 23 2003			
APR 24 2003			
GAYLORD			PRINTED IN U.S.A.

Louis Lowenstein

SENSE
AND
Nonsense
IN
CORPORATE
FINANCE

ADDISON-WESLEY PUBLISHING COMPANY

Reading, Massachusetts   Menlo Park, California
New York   Don Mills, Ontario   Wokingham, England
Amsterdam   Bonn   Sydney   Singapore   Tokyo   Madrid
San Juan   Paris   Seoul   Milan   Mexico City   Taipei

Many of the designations used by manufacturers and sellers to distinguish their products are claimed as trademarks. Where those designations appear in this book and Addison-Wesley was aware of a trademark claim, the designations have been printed in initial capital letters (e.g., Rolex).

Library of Congress Cataloging-in-Publication Data

Lowenstein, Louis.
    Sense and nonsense in corporate finance / Louis Lowenstein.
      p. cm.
    Includes bibliographical references (p. 239) and index.
    ISBN 0-201-52358-2
    ISBN 0-201-63223-3 (pbk.)
    1. Corporations—Finance. I. Title.
    HG4026.L78   1991
    658.15—dc20   91-13027
                                              CIP

Jacket design by Meredith Lightbown
Text design by David Ford
Set in 10-point Caledonia by Shepard Poorman Communications

1 2 3 4 5 6 7 8 9-MA-95949392
First printing, September 1991
First paperback printing, September 1992

T O

Matt

Zack

Russ

Josh

Allison

and Sarabeth

and their (almost) as delicious parents

Contents

Acknowledgments

Given the nature of this book, I am indebted to a substantial number of people who consented to be interviewed, furnished data, or read portions of the manuscript. Among them was a small group who patiently read through drafts of all the chapters, no matter how distantly related to the final product. These especially good friends were Bernie Black, Meredith Brown, Tibor Fabian, Bud Gibbs, Page Hoeper, Seth Klarman, Sam Miller, and Bill Ruane. They forced me to rethink issues and assumptions, found errors, and contributed in a variety of other ways.

Martin L. Liebowitz and his colleagues at Salomon Brothers were remarkably responsive in meeting my requests for data. In virtually every chapter there are data or analyses that Salomon Brothers either provided or were able to substantiate for me. The book would be a lot less accurate and valuable without their help.

Rebecca Gaskin Lawson and Steve Waldman were my research assistants, and very good ones too. Steve in particular brought to the project not just enthusiasm but his valuable experience as a security analyst.

Then there were Charlie and Roger. It was Charles T. Munger who from the very beginning understood what the book should be about, and by giving me a title, "Sense and Nonsense," helped to define the mission. Charlie does not suffer foolishness easily, and those scribbled notes and telephone calls (invariably at dinnertime on the East Coast) changed the analysis of a number of issues and, best of all, saved me from some nonsense of my own.

I doubt that I could describe Roger Lowenstein's contribution objectively. Why try? In part it was editorial. He can spot a weak paragraph or even whole sections with a critical but gentle eye. But it went well beyond that, approaching at times a full (and for Papa, pleasurable) collaboration. Suffice it to say that the book would be much less useful and focused but for his efforts.

Introduction

The sun was in his eyes, and the intercom from his secretary was buzzing gently but persistently. Charles Edward O'Rourke had been asleep at his desk, a catnap he thought, although he was soon to see that it was a nap such as no cat had ever enjoyed.

The phone was buzzing again. He shifted his well-cushioned self into a more upright position in the well-cushioned chair. "Yes, Mrs. Smith?" As O'Rourke listened, he noticed idly that according to the liquid crystal display on his phone it was the morning of January 20, 1989.

CEO, as he was known by his associates, was chairman and chief executive officer of Middle American Corporation, a large, publicly held manufacturer of ethical drugs. This morning, Mrs. Smith said, there were three calls waiting for him. He had a feeling that there was some history to each of them, but try as he would, none of the calls made much sense. One was from Phineas Nance, the company's chief financial officer, with a report on a "defensive restructuring" of the company. "My God," O'Rourke thought, "what's going on?" The second call was from an Alice Tomlinson, the director of the Association of Institutional Shareholders, about a scheduled meeting to discuss the makeup and governance practices of Middle American's board of directors. Alice Tomlinson? The Association of Institutional Shareholders? There was zero recall. The third call was in some respects the worst—something about the company's floating-rate Eurobond offering—but at least it didn't seem to require any response on his part.

"I'll call them all shortly," he told Mrs. Smith, with more than the usual tone of authority in his voice.

1

2 / Sense and Nonsense in Corporate Finance

O'Rourke simply did not remember an Alice Tomlinson. And a restructuring? The company had only recently been awarded an AA bond rating by Standard & Poor's. Would they lose it now? O'Rourke was a thoughtful executive, one who listened carefully, and he prided himself on knowing how and when to act. For a man who was ordinarily in control, he now felt utterly out of control. What was happening? A few beads of sweat trickled down his forehead.

What he did remember was discussing a new drug with the company's chief pharmacologist. The product was being developed under a secret arrangement with the CIA and, so he had been told, at "the request of the White House." Called a time capsule, it was a very powerful sedative, more powerful than any ever known. This was in January 1969. The capsules, which looked like ordinary saccharin, the sugar substitute, induced a dramatic but safe lowering of the body temperature and a deep sleep. In the lab they were known as hibernation pills because of their long-lasting effects.

The time capsule was a minor project. Why was it coming to mind now? There had been no foreseeable market except the government for time capsules. For Middle American, a primary concern, in fact, was keeping the time capsule out of the press. O'Rourke and the pharmacologist had been sitting in the lab discussing just that—how to keep it confidential. If they told the chemists that the project had to be kept under wraps, would that help, or would it excite more interest? Then the two of them had some coffee. The usual . . . no cream . . . definitely no sugar . . . just two brand X sugar substitutes. And back to the office.

WHILE O'ROURKE SLEPT

TAKEOVERS

In the twenty years that O'Rourke slept, the world of corporate finance experienced a series of revolutionary changes. Bright as he was, O'Rourke could not have understood the three phone calls. First, nothing in the late 1960s would have prepared him to deal with an era in which takeovers, leveraged buyouts, and other mergers were running at an annual rate as high as $250 billion; large, well-run companies like Middle American could be targets of a hostile bid. By 1989, when he awoke, the stock exchange had become a market not just for stocks but for whole companies and not simply the small, less-than-$100 million companies that had been the occasional targets of bids in the 1960s.

As he was brought up to date, O'Rourke was puzzled. Looking over some data, he saw that as late as 1975 there had been only $12 billion of mergers in the United States. No enabling laws had been adopted; no significant rules had been changed. Whatever the reason, however, it was now quite clear that takeovers, which once ran counter to the culture and were essentially unknown, and then for a time seemed only a temporary phenomenon, were here to stay. That was why he was now confronted with the prospect of a restructuring.

THE TRANSFORMATION OF FINANCIAL MARKETS

At the end of the 1960s, when O'Rourke "dozed" off, there had been nothing to suggest the transformation of banking and other financial services that was soon to take place. Those Eurobonds, which had come into being just shortly before he fell asleep, were only a small part of it. Computer technology and other innovations had created worldwide trading and funding strategies and a stream of new financial techniques and instruments. The once-clear lines between different types of banks—commercial banks and investment banks, U.S. banks and foreign banks—were rapidly eroding. Other forces were at work too. Deregulation, securitization, a prolonged prosperity, and an explosive growth in trading of financial instruments of all sorts helped to produce an intense competition in financial markets that had not been even hinted at when O'Rourke sipped that bewitched cup of coffee.

While O'Rourke once got money from just a few places and people, with whom Middle American had longstanding relationships, now almost anyone, anywhere with a phone number and money was competing in what had once been such nicely protected businesses as banking and insurance. The president of the Federal Reserve Bank of New York was speaking of "overcrowding" in the financial marketplace.[1]

Competition works. Here it quickly translated into an easier supply of credit and a new tolerance for risk throughout the financial system. For corporate borrowers, it was a picnic of sorts: more money was available, for more companies, and at more competitive rates than at any other time in history. Even in the 1920s credit standards had not been so relaxed. With a few exceptions, notably the public utilities, industry in the 1920s had been conservatively financed. The 1980s, on the other hand, witnessed an extraordinary deterioration in corporate balance sheets. By the end of the decade, the median bond rated by Standard & Poor's was rated "junk." For O'Rourke, this general downgrading was a particularly rude jolt.

THE GROWING IMPORTANCE OF INSTITUTIONAL INVESTORS

In the 1960s O'Rourke also could not have conjured up anyone like Alice Tomlinson. Shareholders had always been a dream come true for corporate managers. They had been like children, only better, being neither seen nor heard. In form, the board of directors was elected by shareholders, but typically it was a handpicked slate of candidates, and the hand was that of an O'Rourke. Here again, however, without any explicit signal, that dream was becoming less tranquil. By 1989 pension funds and other institutional investors had largely replaced individuals as the owners of American industry. On average these institutions owned almost half the shares of public corporations,[2] but in many of the larger, more visible companies, they owned as much as 75 percent.

For years this growing institutionalization had seemed not to matter much. Eventually, of course, something had to give. The amounts of money in institutional hands were simply too large. Pension funds alone had assets of $2 trillion.[3] Public-employee pension funds, in particular, had begun to complain that corporate managements were "entrenching" themselves and that they, the fund managers, were losing the benefit of some valuable tender offers. Trade associations like Alice Tomlinson's helped them to flex their muscles.

Takeovers were the engine pushing the pace of change. Pension plans funded the leveraged buyout (LBO) firms, such as Kohlberg Kravis & Roberts, that had sprung up to engineer and finance leveraged buyouts. In effect, pension funds were instrumental in creating an entirely new kind of institutional investor, one that would buy a public company or a division of one and manage it for a period of time as a privately owned venture. These new LBO banking firms played the lead role in the record $61 billion of going-private transactions and other buyouts announced in 1988.[4]

For decades it hadn't mattered much to corporate leaders how their investors behaved. Typically they ignored them. Stock prices might be high or low, but so what? Corporations didn't issue new shares very often. Shareholders were dispersed, their holdings were fragmented, and, with rare exception, they were meek as lambs.

Since there were very few takeovers or proxy contests, corporations could largely disregard what went on in Wall Street.

As O'Rourke could see, now it mattered.

It was also beginning to matter that he hadn't brushed his teeth in twenty years.

FINANCE IS COMPLEX, BUT THE BASIC RULES ARE NOT

There has been a major metamorphosis, a watershed, in corporate finance. In fact, there have been several watersheds, because no sooner had O'Rourke awakened in January 1989, than many aspects of the new world that greeted him started to unravel. Hostile takeovers began to dry up, not completely, but what remained were the so-called strategic bids by a few well-heeled companies, such as AT&T. The sunlit days when money flowed in the streets, available in billion-dollar handipacks for those who had large ambitions but no money of their own, soon turned into nights when even worthy companies would go begging for funds. Wall Street had almost convinced corporate America that credit would always be available; even for the poor, it would be only a question of the interest rate. But now credit was being rationed, not by price but by the quality of the borrower. The once-deep market turned out to be remarkably shallow and unforgiving. Santa Claus had gone back home, and there was no promise that he would return anytime soon.

It was the end of an era, an end that, once it came, was recognized almost immediately and perhaps with a general sigh of relief. There is no Santa Claus, and down deep we had known it all along. Was it also a return to some normalcy, whatever that might mean? By the beginning of 1991, the prognosis was being muddied by a recession that was not supposed to have happened, and behind the steep declines in production and employment, there appeared some new and alarming questions. For the first time since World War II, many of the usual shock absorbers in the American financial system were themselves out of kilter and therefore less able to cushion a business downturn. In the 1980s the country had borrowed at all levels as it had never borrowed before, and now the bills were coming due. The banking system, which had so enthusiastically embraced leveraged buyouts and the commercial real estate boom of the 1980s, was in disarray. With their own condition impaired, banks, and insurance companies too, had put a lid on credit availability. Foreign investment in the United States, which had also helped to pay for much of the nation's growth during the 1980s, was shrinking. These strains, evident all through the financial system, were visible too in the corporate sector, where the collective industrial balance sheet was weaker at the end of a long boom than it had been at the bottom of any recession during the postwar period. Aggravating these concerns was the fact that despite some congressional budget cuts, the federal deficit was still expected to approach $300 billion in fiscal 1991. Whatever credit was available, therefore, would be subject to fierce competition.

With so much turbulence and uncertainty, it might seem to be a poor time for a book about corporate finance. Let the dust settle, perhaps. That would be true if we were trying to make projections (guesses?) about the likely turn of events in the financial markets. How would a breakdown in the Soviet Union or a major failure in the commercial paper market affect the flow of money? Will there be an implosion of credit, as some have been saying? It is, however, an excellent time for a book that seeks instead to separate what is basic and enduring in corporate finance from what is ephemeral . . . and nonsensical.

The excesses of the 1980s largely grew out of an almost obsessive preoccupation with near-term developments. Companies became so concerned with the prospects for buying and selling assets at inflated prices, or being on the auction block themselves, that they lost sight of the basic factors that determine value. They really began to believe that rather ordinary businesses could routinely be sold for thirteen times their earnings before interest, taxes, and depreciation. They mistook a short-lived bubble for the nature of the universe.

Better results can be had, I believe, by putting much less emphasis on predicting the next turn of the wheel or exploring the latest hedging mechanism or some ingenious form of convertible security. The real lesson of the 1980s is to ignore, or at least not to dramatize, what is new and changing in corporate finance. The problems change, as they always do, but some principles are basic and enduring. Pursued in this way, finance is not the complicated, arcane subject that it sometimes seems to be. And since all markets seem uncertain while we are in them, this is as good a time as any other, perhaps the best, to be writing on these issues.

WHAT IS CORPORATE FINANCE?

Corporate finance is about the ways in which American industry finds the money to do its work and what its capital structures look like as a result. Externally it is about the markets, in the United States and elsewhere, in which corporations raise capital. It is about commercial bankers interested in putting their banks' own money to work and about investment bankers who find other people with money that needs to be put to work. And internally, within corporations, it is about how those funds are put to work, about how projects are selected and monitored, and how managements can use capital efficiently, not letting it sit idle, and still be confident that the cupboard will not someday be bare. In practice it is usually, but not always, about larger, publicly held corporations.

Corporate finance is about a loosely related set of financial transactions, such as mergers and bankruptcies. It is also about the nature and measurement of value. Yardsticks are needed to compare the profitability of projects that in some cases will take years to bear fruit. Corporate finance provides the yardsticks.

In this rather short book, we will deal with some, but by no means all, of the issues that seem particularly important or troublesome. Listed in the Contents, they are issues that should engage business managers, corporate directors, policymakers, bankers, lawyers, and those (relatively few) investors who think of themselves as continuing owners of the business rather than in-and-outers. The governing aim is not to produce a comprehensive text but rather to interest readers in concepts, principles, and, above all, logical reasoning. As a result, some significant issues have been glossed over, either because they are already well understood or because not much of real value can be said on the subject. Others, such as dividend policy and the effects of excessive debt, are given much more attention than in most books on finance. These are issues where there is a contribution to be made.

In sum, corporate finance has four significant aspects: (1) to be sure that those who do the important work of designing, manufacturing, and marketing have the financial flexibility that flows from prudent financial structures and management (prudence is a concept that has fallen out of favor in finance texts, but along with some other bits of old lace, I hope to revive it); (2) as an analytic tool, for use in allocating capital to those who do the designing, manufacturing, and so on and to measure their performance; (3) as an accountability and profit-sharing mechanism to ensure that investors are neither left out of the party nor spoil it. For investors and others on the outside, financial accountability is key; and (4) as a loose catchall for mergers, bankruptcies, and other so-called reorganizations.

Beyond these specific concerns, good corporate policy should be socially responsible. The invisible hand of the financial marketplace is always digging for a profit, but as we have recently seen, it is not always digging in productive ways. Corporate managers are the stewards of other people's money and also of much of the nation's wealth, and we all have a stake in how they perform. We are entitled, for example, to some assurance that financial statements are honest and forthcoming, that seemingly generous dividends are being paid out of current earnings and not out of capital, that a company is using its investors' capital efficiently and yet with a degree of prudence. For those business people who find such talk of good citizenship uncomfortable, the issues can easily be recast in terms of fear of a backlash. Sensitivity to the shareholders' or the public interest today is a practical way to avoid testifying before Congress tomorrow—or worse.

SOME BASIC RULES OR PRINCIPLES

Finance is complex. It analyzes where a business has been and, in financial terms at least, how best to plan for its future and then implement it. My own experience, however, in both business and teaching, suggests the importance of not becoming overly caught up in the complexity of finance. Business people often do lose their way, it is true, but they need not. If the issues are stated properly, most people in industry will solve financial problems in a sensible fashion.

It is most certainly not required that one make precise projections about where a company or the world is headed. Projections are essential planning tools, but good planners recognize their limitations. Astrologers may predict the future; corporate planners merely do their best to provide for a variety of unpleasant as well as pleasant outcomes. They need a skeptical spirit. Not every decision need go against the mood of the industry or the financial marketplace, but the able executive examines them carefully before going along.

Following are some basic rules or principles of finance that were burnished by the speculations and recklessness of the 1980s. They are offered as useful at a time, such as the present, when credit has been running dry, but at other times too. Still, readers will, I hope, bring to them the same skepticism that was suggested for the advice of others.

   1. *Finance does not win industrial ball games.* One of the great errors of the 1980s was to think of financial tools as the cutting

edge that would work speedy and felicitous changes in industrial efficiency. Research, marketing, and manufacturing are what win ball games. Finance should not matter nearly so much as it does, and the people who are in finance should not matter so much either. Unfortunately, bankers have very good dining rooms and are charming salespeople. Or perhaps the fault is that financial transactions are innately appealing for those impatient for results: they bring a quick sense of accomplishment, and they enjoy great visibility. (Just in case you missed their latest triumph, investment bankers take out large advertisements to announce every transaction. The failures, which usually are not recognized for a while, are buried quietly.)

2. *Intricate, bizarre capital structures, such as the pyramided structure of Texas Air (renamed Continental Airlines Holdings and now in Chapter 11), are the hallmark of financially weak or troubled companies.* A balkanized capitalization can rarely be fixed without extraordinary conflict and cost. Public utilities are exceptions, but there are very few businesses with the protected market position and dependable earnings of a power company. Unless the government awards you a monopoly, keep the capital structure simple.

3. *Financial and accounting practices of public companies should essentially mimic those of a privately owned business.* This is not an easy rule to follow, probably because if so many people on Wall Street are watching, it is difficult not to be distracted and to play to the security analysts' thirst for an unbroken string of good news. For a company on Main Street, the proper policy for dividend payments or share repurchases, for example, would be fairly easy to work out. Financial reporting would be forthright. Make believe you're still on Main Street.

4. *Opportunity knocks primarily on the door of the rich.* Junk bond–financed restructurings were an escape hatch for companies targeted for takeover, but they became financial beggars, not choosers. All over the industrial landscape, there are once-strong companies that now must sit on their hands while better-financed competitors use the current recession to seize additional market share. But then, the rich have always had their pick of opportunities.

5. *There is no benefit in owning a good business if the profits are neither distributed to the shareholders nor reinvested wisely.* There are not many very good businesses, in the sense of being able to earn returns on capital that are consistently above average. What is striking is how difficult it has been for the managers to reinvest the earnings well. Undaunted by past failures, many of them insist on buying businesses that are inferior to what they already own and know, buying good ones at excessive prices, or buying ones outside the area of their experience and expertise. Far better to have paid dividends.

6. *Everything else is a poor substitute for cash.* Another version of this rule is that you can run out of anything but cash. True, there are more exciting things for a headstrong executive than to maintain adequate reserves. Why else have so many of them let the corporate bank account run near empty? This may seem like an obvious rule when, as in 1991, the construction, automobile, and other industries are pinched for cash and credit and so many companies are ruefully saying, "But who knew?" That's the point. With few exceptions, no one ever knows.

7. *Projections are usually nothing more than an extrapolation of current trends.* During the recent takeover boom, companies borrowed huge sums on the basis of projections that assumed that the prosperity would continue uninterrupted until the millennium. Wallboard companies would cease to be as cyclical as the construction industry on which they depend. Department store sales would grow steadily at 11 percent, compounded annually. Current trends may be useful, but that does not make them valid as forecasts.

8. *Never issue a bond that you are not firmly confident of repaying out of the ordinary income of the business,* without depending on some sort of "blessed event," such as asset sales or a refinancing. Although it got waylaid in the 1980s, it is a time-tested precept of finance that the earnings of the business should amply cover not just interest charges but also repayment of the principal. Nothing is a certainty, but the confidence should be there.

9. *Because our financial markets have become so active and liquid,*

they encourage a misleading definition of business value. In fact, much of the presumed liquidity is a mirage, being present only when it's needed least. Even at its best, liquidity does not create wealth or substitute for an analysis of fundamental values. Value is measured by the cash that an investment will generate over a sustained period of time. That's it. The only function of liquidity is to enable us to hold an investment for less than its life span. That's useful, but liquidity, or the trading that creates it, can be an expensive indulgence. Worse, the illusion of liquidity may seduce corporate managers into skipping over the fundamentals. Don't.

10. *Risks and reward are not directly related.* Investment bankers and economists will tell you that risk can be precisely measured and that you maximize profits not by reducing risk but by grasping it. Those theories, which helped to foster the debt explosion of the 1980s, brought large fees for bankers and impressive prizes for economists, but they are dangerous fallacies for business people. In finance, it is better to think about the necessity of balancing business risk against financial risk and about the potential pain for not staying on the conservative side of the issue. Young, growing companies and any others in cyclical industries should not layer financial risk on their already considerable business uncertainties. Contrary to economic theory, the window for what someday may be a desperately needed capital infusion is likely to close at the very moment it is most needed.

11. *While stock prices do not matter over the short run (see rule 9), they matter very much over the long run.* Corporate managers are not responsible for short-term stock price fluctuations. But the behavior of a company's stock over a period of years, compared to the rest of the industry and the market as a whole, usually speaks volumes about managerial performance. You may not care for the message it contains, but it is there. To put it differently, after discounting for the manic-depressive behavior of the stock market in the short run, the apparent conflict between shareholder values and business values disappears.

12. *Financial planning should not be keyed to winning the game of inflation, outguessing the currency–exchange rate puzzle, or the like.*

There are too many imponderables, and except for short-term arbitrages and true hedges, the outcome is not predictable by any soundly conceived technique. Leave games of intuition to your mother. But without seeking to profit from them, you should try to protect your business from tidal events over which there is neither control nor any special ability to forecast. In short, in the face of uncertainty be humble, not arrogant.

These rules may seem sensible and even commonplace, but they are at odds with much of the practice in industry and especially with most other books on corporate finance. What one finds in these other books, and what helped to inspire this one, is such intensely scrutinized ideas as the following: risk is something that can be precisely quantified; shareholders will not care if the corporate dividend rate is high or low, and it is better for the corporate pension fund to own five hundred stocks about which it knows nothing rather than twenty that have been carefully studied. By now these ideas, etched in the brains of students, have worked their way through a generation of corporate managers and bankers.

In a real sense, therefore, the purpose of this book is to revive and nourish some old, fundamentalist truths about corporate finance but to do so in the context of a financial environment that is new, more complex, and still evolving. It is worthwhile noting, with respect to corporate management, what Ben Graham once said of investment management. The underlying principles, he wrote, "should not alter from decade to decade, but the application of these principles must be adapted to significant changes in the financial mechanisms and climate."[5]

SENSE AND NONSENSE IN CORPORATE FINANCE

Primarily we will be searching for the good sense in finance—the sense that should not be obscure but often is. As the title indicates, the book is also about nonsense. Although we will not spend much time tilting at other people's windmills, the "sense" of finance can best be understood by seeing some of the traps and pitfalls, as Charles T. Munger, vice-chairman of Berkshire Hathaway, who suggested the title, correctly understood.

We will look at nonsense in the boardroom and the marketplace and also from economists on Wall Street and in academia. Marketplace nonsense takes many forms, but underlying most of them is the enormous attention paid to guessing the next tiny piece of financial news—at the Federal Reserve Board, in the trade deficit, Zinger Company's sales for the next quarter—focusing on all the details of the immediate picture and almost none of the larger, longer-term mosaic. Stocks are a very long-term investment, one with no maturity date. How else to explain, then, all the short-term trading except by a consuming interest in trivia? Or as one market professional said, only half in jest, the brokers and analysts get to know everything about a company, except for one detail: that before long it will be in bankruptcy.[6]

There are two explanations, and one can agree with both. The unsophisticated one is that there are tens of thousands of brokers, people of quite ordinary skills, who need to generate commissions if they are to keep up with the payments on their cars. The "simple-minded" investor who bought Capital Cities twenty years ago and put it away in a safe deposit box may be rich and happy today, but his stock broker is poor. The more sophisticated explanation is the one from John Maynard Keynes.[7] Given, he observed, the overwhelming uncertainties affecting any long-term estimates of business and competition, given the lack of a sufficient basis for calculated mathematical projections, as business people (and stock pickers too) we take the next best course. We simply and conveniently do two things. First, we assume that the current state of the world—the economy, politics, war, climate, and so on—represents a state of equilibrium and that the existing pattern or trend will continue indefinitely into the future until something happens to disturb it. Second, we assume that the stock market's valuations (and other markets' as well) reflect everything there is to know about business realities and prospects and that *they will change only as new information appears*. These assumptions are reflected in such bits of Wall Street dogma as, "Don't argue with the tape."

Keynes's insight has important implications that range far beyond stock picking. Corporate financial managers fall victim to this very human but dangerous tendency to assume that the world is in a steady state until *Women's Wear Daily*, or some other paper, brings fresh news. In the 1980s, for example, Drexel Burnham Lambert, the investment bank that was the patron saint of junk bonds, created a new market in short-term, low-quality commercial paper, about $5 billion in all. Now, "junk commercial paper" is almost a contradiction in terms. Highly leveraged companies should not depend on thirty-day notes as a continuing source of capital. There is a basic tenet of finance that says, "Never, never borrow short (term) to invest long." It is especially true for weak companies. But corporate financial officers accepted the idea that since this new market had existed for several years, since 1983, it would continue to exist. Even if the rate changed, the window would still be open. Think of it as mental inertia. Just as Keynes had observed, companies assumed that the commercial paper they sold today could be refinanced with equally short-term commercial paper sold tomorrow. And for a time it worked, at least until one of the issuers, Integrated Resources, defaulted in 1989, exposing the fallacy.[8] Whatever the lesson for investors, and it was painful, there was a lesson in nonsense for corporate managers too.

The other nonsense in modern financial economics also has a central theme. Economists like to assume that Wall Street, even more than most markets, is utterly and consistently rational. In the way that economists use the term, *rational* means that the players—at least the professionals who dominate the market—are in fact thinking long term and that their guesses are on average sound. Some of the theories—efficient market theory, the dividend-irrelevance proposition, and others based on this assumption of extraordinarily widespread rationality—are quite elegant in the intended sense of providing a unifying frame of reference that ties together the whole scheme of finance in a consistent fashion that can be mathematically and rigorously applied. (Note the emphasis on mathematics.) My view is that the theories may be elegant, but like many another single-minded approach to financial or economic policy, they can be quite mischievous, because too often the issues that matter most have been assumed away.

Take dividends, for example. Economists tell us that a company's dividend policy will have no effect on its stock price. How can that be? If it is a mature company, shareholders rightly expect it to pay out a high percentage of its earnings and not to go off on a (probably) wasteful diversification spree. Keeping the money, or paying it out to shareholders, should be a major concern for management, as we will see in chapter 7. But the dividend-irrelevance theory so favored among academics never reaches that issue. It conveniently assumes that the investment policy of the company is known and fixed, as if the fact that excess earnings are sloshing around in the company's treasury might not tempt a CEO to buy a jet or expand a corporate empire. No matter how talented or foolish the CEO may be, we are asked to believe that (taxes aside) a dollar left inside the company, with little or no control over how it is utilized, is as valuable to investors as one outside.

Scholars have been straining to make of finance a hard science that can be reduced to algebraic compositions and tested by quantifiable data. They sluff off history and social insights that do not fit the algebra. The price of this mathematical elegance is that it obscures hard, practical questions that executives should be asking, even one as basic as whether to pay a dividend or keep the money for internal growth. I will not devote a great deal of space to these scholarly doctrines, but since several of them have become commonplace in business and financial analysis, some attention to them is necessary.

1

Corporate Finance

A MODESTLY USEFUL DISCIPLINE

Money and finance have become front page news: INTEREST RATES UP. THE DOLLAR UP. A few years ago, these were arcane topics. Now the evening network news follows them closely, reminding us that if those numbers keep moving up, we may soon see business, housing starts, and employment moving down. We also know that companies with household names—RJR Nabisco, Kraft, Bloomingdale's, Duracell—have been bought and sold, and sometimes bought and sold again, at prices that would have excited Croesus. Most of us know something, too, about greenmail, golden parachutes, poison pills, and junk bonds. It was not just the glamor and excitement that captured our attention. Finance was the visible scalpel that forced wrenching changes on American society. For better or worse, new owners have come on the scene, factories have closed or moved, and once-secure middle management jobs have disappeared.

A lot more people have become involved in finance. For a time, more than half the graduates of the major law and business schools were going off to work on mergers and other financial matters. It would be surprising if they hadn't; the market was sending very strong messages. For bankers, and lawyers working with bankers, large six-figure incomes became routine. Kids were earning more in a year than their fathers had in a lifetime. True, on an hourly basis the pay still fell short of Darryl Strawberry's, but if those new graduates had decided instead to manufacture and market something at Middle American, our fictitious drug company, they would have gotten their hands dirty, eaten cold sandwiches for lunch, and lived in places like Toledo. That's how O'Rourke started out at Middle American.

As a society, we have spent heavily on financial services and advice. How valuable are they, and how much can they contribute to the success of a company?

Corporate finance provides a series of tools and an analytic framework: when to raise money, when to pay it out, how to invest and spend it. We need to know what finance can do, but because in recent years some quite extravagant claims have been made for finance, we also need to look at its limitations.

THE USES OF CORPORATE FINANCE

CAPITAL STRUCTURES AND NEW SECURITIES ISSUES

Corporate finance concerns almost anything having to do with business corporations and the flow of funds beyond the routine production or movement of goods. Originally it referred only to the financing of the corporation—literally the raising of capital needed to build a railroad, launch a bank, and so on. Corporate finance meant dealing with commercial and investment bankers. It therefore involved the analysis of a company's capital structure, the choice and design of the securities to issue, and the process of underwriting or marketing them.

Good investment bankers and their corporate counterparts still play a very creative role, constructing different securities, with different maturities, marketed to different types of investors, so as to produce the needed funds at the lowest possible cost. That is corporate finance at its core and often at its best.

Many of the leveraged buyouts of the 1970s, before the excesses set in, showed these skills to advantage. Bankers looked for public companies with stable cash flows, meaning businesses that might not be growing and so did not require steady infusions of new capital. They were stable and almost boring. Being perceived as dull, the stock market often valued them at low multiples of earnings, and because the cash flows seemed to be steady, they could apparently support a larger amount of relatively low-cost debt than was then considered appropriate for a publicly owned company. Still, to keep the interest cost within reasonable limits, some ingenuity was called for. Typically there was senior debt secured by tangible assets, such as real estate or inventory. Just below the secured debt was bank debt, which was unsecured but scheduled to be paid off before any other debt, including the secured debt. Still further below was subordinated debt with one or more maturities, usually sold in so-called strips with some sort of equity participation. The net effect was to finance the company on a highly leveraged basis, with a debt-to-equity ratio as high as 6:1 but with sufficient cash flow from operations to cover interest charges and capital expenditures and—note this—provide even for retirement of the debt. (Success would bring imitators, and in time the margin of safety would disappear, but that was later on.) No one investor would have bought the entire package of securities, but with a wide range of institutions each could find something attractive somewhere on the menu.

There is nothing new about these creative aspects of corporate finance. Bankers have been exercising financial ingenuity for a long time. In the 1870s and 1880s, when they were building the nation's railroads, they created a capital structure for the Erie Railroad as complex as any leveraged buyout a hundred years later. And while there was no Eurobond market in London in the nineteenth century, Europeans supplied much of the capital.

One can talk a good deal about the principles of corporate finance, but seen from this perspective it is an intensely practical subject. Bankers earn their pay because they know what is happening in the market—what can be done and what can't. If they don't know, the deal will quickly look shopworn, and then it will not be saleable at all. To be sure, the principles of corporate finance can be taught and discussed, but the best way to understand them is to get your hands dirty, looking at a lot of companies and reading bond indentures. Finance is not a good business for those who want to skate by on generalizations and abstractions.

The old books on corporate finance, such as Arthur Stone Dewing's *The Financial Policy of Corporations*, recognized that finance is an intensely practical discipline. In the 1926 edition, Dewing devoted over 150 pages to a description of bonds. In the section on secured bonds alone, he cited no fewer than thirty different companies and fifty different securities, often quoting from the indentures, to explain the form, and sometimes the very different reality.

If you think that 150 pages about bonds would necessarily be boring, then you underestimate the ingenuity that companies and their financiers have shown in manipulating markets and tiptoeing on the brink of fraud. Dewing cared about the integrity of corporate finance, and no doubt he was intrigued at the prospect of unmasking some (otherwise) respectable manipulators. Mortgage bonds, for example, were much sought after in the 1920s because of the security they promised. But very few people read bond indentures (then or now), and mortgage bonds soon appeared that had a lien on nothing of substance. This sort of triumph of form over substance was the case with the Chicago and Alton Railroad 3½ percent bonds. They were called "first lien," but the property of the rail*road* consists almost entirely of the equity in the Chicago and Alton Rail*way*, which had its own bonds outstanding. "The first lien of the railroad," Dewing concluded, was "therefore not on physical property, but merely on a leasehold of physical property covered, quite fully, by another mortgage."[1]

Mortgage bonds are rarely issued publicly today. But guaranteed bonds, which had fallen out of favor, have recently come back. As Dewing recognized, a guaranteed bond is something of an anomaly. A strong issuer does not need a guarantee to market its bonds, and if it is a weak one, the added endorsement may not add much, in which case the arrangement signals financial risk, not safety. In 1989, for example, Kohlberg Kravis & Roberts financed the $25 billion purchase of RJR Nabisco by setting up four tiers of RJR companies. All the operating earnings were in the company at the bottom of the pyramid, but much of the financing was done at levels above it.[2] Most of the purchase price was raised by the issuance of over $20 billion of debt by the first-tier holding company, parent C, which owned the operating company. A portion of that debt consisted of bonds issued to the public that were guaranteed by parent B (which owned parent C) and by parent A (which owned parent B) and was at the top of the ladder. Were the bonds intrinsically weak? You bet. Parent C showed a pro forma loss for 1988 of over $500 million (without including the amortization of goodwill). What did the guarantees add? Nothing. Parent A, for example, had no source of income not already available to parent C, and (directly or through parent B) it had large additional obligations to boot.

As the Chicago and Alton Railroad and RJR Nabisco bonds indicate, the contracts written by issuers and bondholders are an endless game of cat and mouse, with corporate issuers playing the cat. It was true in Dewing's day, and it remains true today. The rules of the game have always been that any protections for bondholders must be spelled out precisely. What's not there, the mice don't get.[3] If bondholders are fooled by so-called first mortgage bonds, guaranteed bonds, or any other ingenious contrivance, courts will rarely intervene. And a corporation that can find a loophole in a covenant is generally free to exploit it.

This book is an unapologetic throwback to another era, the era of finance books like Dewing's, which were rich with anecdotes and stressed the importance of accounting. Current books on corporate finance talk about clean mathematical models, not about messy companies.[4] One widely used textbook contains over a thousand references to other scholars and no more than a handful of passing references to specific companies.[5] There was no need to do more because under the "certain conditions" assumed by the textbook models, stocks become interchangeable. That book's section on capital structures is all algebra; there's not a company in it. The discussion of leveraged buyouts is so theoretical that it fails to mention junk bonds. For those caught up in it, this is a bright new era in finance, described time and time again by the single word *elegance*. For those of us who are not believers, the word *elegance* is anathema, a sure signal that we are on treacherous ground.

As a discipline, corporate finance is more art than science. Management needs only a range of answers, a range that provides for contingencies pleasant and unpleasant, rather than anything algebraic or precise. Precision is a helpful selling tool for academic consultants who have developed elaborate software for anxious clients. It's a comfort for those who are troubled by uncertainty; but in grappling with an uncertain future, financial precision is at worst a snare and at best an illusion.

OTHER USES OF CORPORATE FINANCE

While the core meaning of corporate finance is the issuance of stocks and debt to finance a company, it encompasses much more that is useful. Finance helps companies to decide such wide-ranging problems as how to allocate funds to specific divisions and projects, the formulation of a dividend policy, the merits of an employee stock ownership plan, and the timing of a bankruptcy declaration. The menu is long and broad. It is no wonder that at times corporate finance—and the people in it—threatens to swallow the world of money and business, leaving little that is not theirs.

One part of the menu that has never been as well understood as it should be is dividend policy and its cousin, share repurchase programs. How much of a company's earnings should it keep, how much should it pay out to shareholders, and what form should the payout take? It is the rare company that has formulated a coherent dividend policy. Some companies have maintained and even increased their dividends only at the expense of issuing new shares or debt, or often both. At the beginning of the 1980s, Ford continued to pay large dividends, maintaining an illusion of liquidity while it was hemorrhaging cash. Public utilities have done much the same thing, paying to shareholders dividends that were taxable and then asking them (or others like them) to buy new shares with whatever dollars were left from those dividends after taxes. It was money out, money back— except for the tax collector.

Corporate finance provides a helpful framework for thinking about when companies *should* pay dividends, as well as when they should *not*. The annals of American finance are replete with corporate diversification programs that were eagerly and ambitiously conceived but, with some few exceptions, destined to fail. Companies that were generating large cash flows from good existing businesses, larger than they could reinvest there, wandered off into the dark forest of conglomeration, buying businesses about which they knew little but for which they happily paid premium prices. Properly understood, dividend policy is the issue that forces the exacting, and humbling, realization that there are not all that many good businesses in which to invest and that an enthusiastic argument can be made for distributing the excess cash flows as cash dividends or, often better, as part of a share repurchase program. As we will see in the discussion of share buybacks in chapter 8, companies as large as Exxon and as small as Audio/Video practice this form of financial humility. It works.

THE LIMITATIONS OF CORPORATE FINANCE

Although corporate finance is a useful discipline, it is only modestly so. It is not nearly as powerful, as all-encompassing, as we sometimes hear. Companies, consultants, and business school academicians increasingly act as if the tools of corporate finance somehow provide a disciplined, scientific, and perhaps even foolproof, approach to capital investments. "In the middle 1950s," according to a popular finance text, "new methods and techniques for selecting capital investment projects led to a framework for *efficient allocation of capital* within the firm. . . . *Powerful analytical tools* could be applied to [these] financial problems."[6]

Sounds marvelous. I'm glad I bought a copy of the book.

The Quaker Oats annual report for 1988 held out similar promises. For Quaker Oats a primary tool is discounted cash flow (DCF), which lets the company "assess the relative desirability of future investment and do it in terms of today's dollars. . . . After we weigh the strategic business issues, we use the discipline of DCF analysis to choose investments producing a profitable return, equal to or better than our minimum required rate of return, which is also known as our 'cost of capital.' That way we keep improving our profitability for shareholders."

Sounds as easy as oatmeal.

Discounted cash flow, the concept underlying both those statements, is straightforward and sound. It is a way of comparing the cash that goes into a project with the estimated cash that will come out, adjusted by a discount rate to reflect the difference between a dollar today and one tomorrow. That is a simple, direct way to define the value of an investment. What's missing from these glowing descriptions, of course, is that the process of estimating future cash flows is not at all simple or direct. And if the cash flows cannot be estimated with any degree of confidence, then where is the vaunted "discipline" in a "powerful analytical tool" for discounting those cash flows to a present value?

A few years ago I ran a simple test, one that had been used by Ben Graham and David Dodd, the fathers of security analysis, to demonstrate how treacherous it is to forecast business earnings. Wall Street analysts and money managers study the thirty big-name, visible companies in the Dow Jones Industrial Average with great intensity. The stock market then puts a price on the earnings of each company, the price-earnings (P/E) ratio. The glamorous growth stocks are those with high P/E ratios—as much as twenty times earnings—and the older, smokestack industries usually get low ones—six times earnings or so. Whether it's worth paying so much more for a dollar of earnings of a growth stock is hotly debated. But even if the *stock price* of IBM or Exxon won't grow as quickly as its earnings, the P/E ratios should at least tell which companies are more likely than others to show significantly improved *earnings* over the next few years. Otherwise why pay so much? The results of this test, however, were quite revealing, tracking those of Graham and Dodd years before. As the table in the appendix to this chapter shows, the consensus predictions by Wall Street—the P/E ratios—failed even at the relatively modest task of forecasting changes in corporate profits. The numbers are almost random.

A better way to think about these "powerful analytic tools" is that they leave all the genuinely difficult problems unanswered. How likely are cost overruns? How much cash will this new project throw off? As a French philosopher is supposed to have said, everything is hard to predict, especially the future. The future depends on the competition here and in Japan, inflation, OPEC, German interest rates, and a host of other unknowables. Even after estimating cash flows, there still remains the hazardous problem of selecting the best rate at which to discount those cash flows to a present value.[7] The rest of that high-tech formula is just low-tech arithmetic.

An almost mystical faith in discounted cash flow and similar tools grew up in the 1960s when companies established stand-alone planning units filled with computers and specialists fresh from business schools. The specialists rarely talked with people in the field but nevertheless produced reams of plans and forecasts. They were firmly ensconced at corporate headquarters, close to the executive suite, where the senior managers were looking for just such tools that would give them confidence in their ability to manage diverse and far-flung operations. Large companies, in particular, adopted formal and sophisticated approaches, set out in written investment procedures and manuals. For any project above some threshold amount, they now required a written presentation with a description and justification of the proposal and a financial analysis of the investment and cash flow projections.

All well and good, or so it seemed. But as one irreverent but insightful group of researchers in England concluded after looking at companies here and there, these strategic planning techniques seem to conceive of each investment as if it were a single act of top management. What they overlook is that it is the operating people in places like Toledo or San José who propose a project, provide the supporting data, and eventually carry it out.[8] The information needed to evaluate the proposal usually lies with people many layers down from where the investment decision is ultimately made. At companies the size of Quaker Oats, no one at the top may have had any direct experience with, say, Fisher-Price, the toy business whose capital budget was under review. By the time a proposal arrives at that level, all the alternatives may have been scrubbed out, leaving only the one that the operating people want. For the toy people, now is a time for selling, not for balancing, and that is what they do. There is nothing conniving or insidious about that. Having worked hard to shape and reshape a project, divisional managers believe that it is in the interests of the company to adopt it, leaving senior management with very few choices. Whether they realize it or not, senior management is largely bound by the prior performance and judgment of those in the field. Powerful analytical tools won't help much.

Investment decisions may work out well in practice, in the sense that good projects tend to win approval and bad ones lose, but the process is vulnerable to all sorts of errors. Consider, for example, the cost of capital, which, as Quaker Oats noted, is a necessary aspect of capital budgeting, one that says in effect, "Money is never free." Almost every company uses the concept in one way or another.[9] But they use it very differently because so many of the elements are indeterminate. No one really knows what the inflation rate will be or how to calculate the true cost of equity capital. Coca-Cola, for example, rarely changed its target rates of return, despite changes in market conditions. Others, like Quaker Oats, Philip Morris, and NCR, reviewed theirs annually. In theory, the cost of capital should reflect not just market rates but also the risks of the project in question. Outside investors expect a higher return if the outcome is speculative, and the company should be no less demanding with its own internal capital. The problem is that, when all is said and done, no one knows how to calculate the degree of risk.

The solution at Quaker Oats was to adopt as a measure of risk a model, the capital asset pricing model, based on the volatility of stock market prices.[10] The minimum return, or "hurdle rate," in the Quaker Oats formula was a blended cost of all capital, 11 to 12 percent after income taxes.[11] The number itself was reasonable, but as we will see in chapter 10, it was only coincidentally reasonable. The mathematical model on which it was based had been shaped by the need of consultants and scholars to find a measurable proxy for risks that are inherently immeasurable. What they chose were not any criteria or data generated directly by that business or even that industry but instead the fluctuations in the company's stock relative to the price movements of the stock market as a whole. Those inside the business were told to look to the outside, to Wall Street, for instructions on how best to determine the predictability of investments in their own markets and products.

CONCLUSION

Even if conceptually sound, these intricate financial techniques would be difficult to implement. At some companies the discounted cash flow analysis errs by taking inflation into account in one part of the formula, the calculation of the discount rate, but fails to do so in calculating the cash flows that are to be discounted.[12] At other companies, the system collapses, or at least bends, under the weight of corporate politics. People simply produce the numbers that are needed to justify the desired result. Tell them how high the hurdle is—12 percent after taxes?—and they will produce a steady stream of 12 percent hurdlers.

Like some other aspects of corporate finance, the appeal of a discounted cash flow analysis is that it seems to think broadly and reduce to a common denominator any type of proposal, large or small, in any industry. A corporate staff sitting at headquarters can contemplate a new food product one day, a new electronics factory another, and a major business acquisition the next. All of them fit neatly within the discounted cash flow "discipline." Most business diversification decisions were subjected to just this sort of analysis. Alas, as Michael Porter found in a 1987 study, the results have been awful.[13] Thirty-three large, prestigious companies had made over 2,000 acquisitions in new fields (or industries) between 1950 and 1986, an average of 61 per company. Included were some of the best managed companies such as General Electric, and some of the worst, such as Wickes. The number of acquisitions retained (and divested) were used as a rough but reasonable measure of success. Of the businesses acquired by 1980, 53.4 percent had been divested or shut down by January 1987. And the results were conservatively calculated, because a good number of the failures had been buried privately.

Quaker Oats, a profitable company, said that it is trying to maintain a return on equity of 20 percent, far above what American industry as a whole has been able to achieve.[14] But neither "scientific" financial tools nor any other off-the-shelf formula will get it there. In fiscal 1989, the same year the company distributed the annual report that exulted in these tools, the company's Fisher-Price toy division stumbled badly, as did the pet food division. The following year, having absorbed substantial losses at Fisher-Price, management decided to spin it off while it grappled with declining sales elsewhere. The company may once again achieve those high overall returns, but only rare ideas and rare good people, rather than scientific finance, will enable it to do so.

Admittedly there is a seductive aspect to finance: the possibility of making money in the purest form, by dealing directly *with money*— selling parts of the business, raising a war chest for hostile acquisitions, and framing ingenious new capital structures. All the world becomes an oversized chessboard, and people, factories, and products figure only as bit players in ambitious strategies. Finance is a modestly useful discipline, and only that. It is a mistake to let it get out front, as we did during the 1980s, in the process attracting to it much of the nation's young talent who should instead have gone to a no-nonsense city, such as Toledo, and gotten their hands dirty. One purpose of this book is to reinforce that message.

Appendix 1A

Dow Jones Industrial Average: Comparison
of Average 1976–1978 Price-Earnings
Ratios and Percentage Increases in Per–
Share Earnings 1976–1978 to 1979–1981

Company	Average Price-Earnings Ratio, 1976–1978	Percentage Increase (Decrease) in Average Earnings per Share, 1976–1978 to 1979–1981
Inco	28.5	34
U.S. Steel	26.2	133
Eastman Kodak	16.6	48
Merck	16.3	41
Minn. Min. & Mfg.	14.4	42
IBM	14.3	21
Procter & Gamble	13.9	34
Sears	13.0	(35)
International Paper	11.6	17
General Electric	10.7	38
Du Pont	10.6	25
AT&T	8.6	17
General Foods	8.3	27
Goodyear	8.2	4
Exxon	8.2	101
Allied Corp.	8.2	55
Texaco	7.9	137
Union Carbide	7.9	41
Alcoa	7.9	49
Owens-Illinois	7.7	46
Manville	7.4	(46)
Bethlehem Steel	7.3	(41)
American Brands	7.3	108
American Can	6.9	(16)
Standard Oil (Calif.)	6.8	119

Appendix 1A

Continued

Company	Average Price-Earnings Ratio, 1976–1978	Percentage Increase (Decrease) in Average Earnings per Share, 1976–1978 to 1979–1981
United Technologies	6.7	30
Woolworth	6.3	22
Westinghouse	5.9	46
General Motors	5.7	(73)
International Harvester	4.9	89
AVERAGE	10.5	37

2

The Road to Junk Heaven

A TALE OF THREE COMPANIES

Let's do some comparison shopping at Bloomingdale's, Macy's, and Lord & Taylor, all of which were embroiled in the debt binge of the 1980s. Their respective owners—Federated Department Stores, R. H. Macy, and May Department Stores—had once looked very much alike: strong department store franchises, each earning about the same profit on a dollar of sales, and all having conservative balance sheets. Sooner than they could have guessed, however, the resemblances would all but disappear.

After having been acquired by Robert Campeau in 1988, Federated was utterly awash in debt. Cash shortages and other financial distractions took management's eye off customers and the stores, and the company soon foundered. Macy, in many respects the best run of the three, did a leveraged buyout (LBO), which before long robbed management of financial flexibility and ruptured the pattern of success. May Department Stores, the only one still soundly financed, was the only one able to keep its attention where it belonged. Better yet, the turmoil in the industry created unusual opportunities for May to seize market share from now-troubled competitors and to make opportunistic acquisitions.

Campeau put Federated Department Stores into play in January 1988. At one point May was to be the white knight, rescuing Federated from the hostile bidder, Campeau. But the bidding had already pushed the price way up. May's CEO, David C. Farrell, who was about to make a formal offer, had second thoughts and dropped out. Macy promptly took May's place, and the bidding continued. When the bruising contest was over, the Federated shareholders, who only a few weeks before had owned a stock that traded at $33 a share, received over $73 a share from Campeau. For the shareholders, it was a triumph. They received $6.5 billion, or over twenty times the company's $313 million of net earnings in its most recent year.

But Campeau had borrowed virtually the entire purchase price and now was forced to sell off large pieces of the Federated business. He sold to Macy two West Coast divisions, Bullock's and I. Magnin, as part of the settlement of the bidding contest. Then he sold to May two others, Filene's and Foley's. Following the same script he had used with some initial success at Allied Stores in 1987, he then sold off or transferred elsewhere a few other divisions. Even so, the new LBO enterprise, Federated/Campeau, ended up with a highly attractive group of stores: Abraham & Straus, Bloomingdale's, Burdines, Lazarus, and Rich's/Goldsmith's. These divisions accounted for about 41 percent of the sales of the old company in the year ended January 30, 1988 (fiscal 1987), and 56 percent of total divisional profits. If the company had been financially viable, Campeau would have bought a good business.

The bidding for Federated climaxed a period of intense LBO and takeover activity in the department store industry. It's hard to say what attracted so much money because doubts had been widely expressed about the prospects for the traditional department store. Skeptics warned that department stores would be nibbled to death by specialty chains, such as The Limited, which could focus on a well-defined niche, and by other, even lower-cost retailers, such as Wal-Mart and the growing number of off-price outlet stores. Nevertheless, the customers were still coming, although at times it was difficult to separate them from the crowd of bankers milling around, trying to buy the whole store. Marshall Field, Dayton Hudson, Saks Fifth Avenue, Carter Hawley Hale, and other department stores were the object of takeover bids, friendly or otherwise. In 1986, May acquired Associated Dry Goods, including Lord & Taylor, for about $2.4 billion. That same year, Campeau acquired Allied Stores for $3.6 billion. In the midst of this feeding frenzy, having decided that it was better to eat oneself than to be eaten by others, Macy did its LBO.

Wall Street had several stories to explain this bizarre financial caper: (1) department stores were not cyclical; (2) being mature businesses, they were not capital-intensive, so that cash flow, not just earnings, would be available to service high levels of debt; (3) despite the bloated acquisition cost of an LBO, the debt could be reduced to manageable levels by selling off pieces of the business at even better prices; and (4) for developers, such as Campeau, department stores offered a big play in real estate. All of the stories were wrong, way wide of the mark, or, in the case of the high break-up values, dependent on the continued willingness of the world to suspend disbelief about the proper measure of price and value. At the time, though, almost everyone on Wall Street was going along with the stories. As the head of the merchant banking group at First Boston, which had helped to engineer the Federated deal, later said (while wiping the egg off his face), "In the market of the time, it seemed perfectly plausible."[1]

THE SUMMER OF 1985—BEFORE THE FALL

Federated, May, and Macy historically operated in the same, traditional, full-service segment of the department store business. They competed in many of the same markets, with roughly similar merchandise and expense structures. Table 2–1 contains some comparative numbers for the three companies for the years ended February 1, 1986, for May and Federated and August 3, 1985, for Macy, the last full year before the Macy management buyout. Because May and Federated also operated discount stores, supermarkets, or other noncore businesses, some data are for the department store operations only. This core business is especially important, because both Federated/Campeau and May would soon shed all or almost all of their other operations.

The similarities of the three companies were striking, particularly in their core business, department stores. Operating profit margins—the ratio of department store profits (before interest, taxes, and corporate overhead) to sales—ranged from 9.3 percent for Federated to 10.4 percent for both May and Macy. Sales per square foot at Federated were better than at May but less than at Macy. Because Federated had been doing poorly in other lines of business, however, its overall return on total capital was only 8.5 percent, compared to 11.8 percent for May and 13.2 percent for Macy. At all three companies, the ratio of long-term debt to total capital was in line with the conservative tradition of the industry. Federated and May enjoyed an excellent AA credit rating, and Macy (Credit Corp.) was rated AA−.

Contrary to the doomsayers, the department store business was very much alive in 1985. (Or as Mark Twain had once said of himself, the reports of its death were greatly exaggerated.) Specialty

Table 2–1
Before Campeau—May, Macy,
and Federated (Millions
of Dollars)

Financial data	May (year ended Feb. 1, 1986)	Macy (year ended Aug. 3, 1985)	Federated (year ended Feb. 1, 1986)
Department stores only			
Sales	$3,327	$4,368	$6,685
Divisional operating profit	$345	$455[a]	$622
Divisional profit margin	10.4%	10.4%	9.3%
Sales per square foot	$121	$179	$152
Companywide Totals			
Earnings before interest and taxes (EBIT)	$485	$474	$655
Interest expense	$51	$102	$86
Ratio of EBIT to interest expense	9.5 X	4.6 X	7.6 X
Interest expense as % of total sales	1.0%	2.3%	0.9%
Capital expenditures	$225	$266	$364
Bond rating[b]	AA	AA−	AA
Return on assets	8.1%	10.7%	6.3%
Return on total capital	11.8%	13.2%	8.5%
Long-term debt as % of total capital	30%	13%	22%

[a]Assumes elimination of corporate overhead equal to 0.9 percent of sales, the same rate as at May.
[b]S&P ratings. Macy's rating is for Macy Credit Corp.
Note: Sales per square foot are in dollars.

stores had seized market share, partly because department stores had been slow to react, but the department store format has many advantages, including an enormous ability to reallocate merchandising emphasis and resources to meet the changing and unpredictable preferences of consumers. In addition to the May and Macy groups, Dillard, Mercantile, and Nordstrom had been doing very well, showing excellent returns on capital. A veteran retailer, Robert M. Warner, explained that what had changed was the gap between winners and losers. There was less room than before for the also-rans to muddle through. Or as James M. Zimmerman, chairman of the Rich's division of Federated in the mid-1980s and later president of the parent company, said to me, since department stores are a mature business and there are no tail winds to help, success depends almost entirely on execution and implementation. Mature, yes, but a dinosaur, no.

Still, behind the statistical similarities, there lay some striking differences. While May and Macy had been moving up in the 1980s, Federated was slipping down. May and Macy were led by two brilliant retailers who had headed their respective companies for years, Farrell at May and Edward S. Finkelstein at Macy. They had different styles, and they had molded different companies. Farrell had seen early on that regional differences in retailing were disappearing; his customers in one part of the country had tastes similar to those in the others. At May he created a truly national company—centrally managed, tightly managed, and well managed. A high degree of central buying, for example, gave the company bargaining power with suppliers over terms and deliveries, as well as the ability to hire better buyers and to reduce operating costs. Perhaps for a group of high-fashion stores, the strategy would not have worked, but May was the premier middle-of-the-road store. Even competitors gave Farrell an A+ rating.

Finkelstein was also a strong executive. He had transformed a once-dowdy Macy's—one that could have been left by the wayside, as were B. Altman and others—into an industry leader with big stores in big cities, with more fashion and higher-price merchandise. He spent heavily on store presentation and created an exciting image. Finkelstein and Farrell had both succeeded admirably but each by different roads. Put each in a store, give him some money to spend, and Finkelstein would have emerged as the more creative merchant of the two.

By 1988, when Campeau launched his bid, Federated, created in 1929 as a federation of regional department stores, was still loosely run. At the store level, there were some first-rate merchants, such as Marvin S. Traub at Bloomingdale's, but the company's CEO, Howard Goldfeder, had neither the strong managerial skills of a Farrell nor the merchandising genius of a Finkelstein. Inside the company he was known as someone who, fearing mistakes, would study a problem endlessly—"analysis/paralysis," a colleague would later describe it.

Too respectful of the culture of autonomy that he had inherited, cowed by Traub and other divisional chiefs, Goldfeder was slow to centralize operations. Once the dominant department store group in the country, Federated had stumbled even in its core business. Same-store sales increases—a key figure in retailing—were a skimpy 2.5 percent in 1987. Over time, the impact of such slow growth is chilling.

Even if Goldfeder had been Farrell and Finkelstein wrapped up as one, however, it is doubtful that anything would have saved Federated from a takeover once Campeau set his eyes on Bloomingdale's and those other great retailing names. And when Campeau did strike, by all accounts Goldfeder was superb: he tried to engineer a management buyout until the bidding escalated beyond $58 a share, the highest price that seemed sensible. Thereafter he never wavered from the goal of obtaining top dollar for shareholders, from whichever bidder was foolish enough to pay it.

AFTER THE FALL

By 1988 Federated was ripe for a shake-up. There had been only slow progress in adopting a program similar to the one unfolding at May: spinning off the unrelated operations, buying back a major amount of stock, refocusing and centralizing operations, and improving returns to shareholders. Given a more decisive CEO and a less lethargic board, it would have happened. Surely the surgery Farrell had performed on May was far less costly and less disruptive than an LBO. Thus, one could have rightly said in 1988 that Federated was a candidate for an LBO—at least an LBO of the more prudent kind that had been done earlier in the decade.

But Federated was an abominable choice for an LBO of the high-leverage sort in vogue in 1988. As we will see, even Macy would soon strain the limits, but in Federated's case, the foolishness was palpable from the outset. Strong companies will stagger under a heavy debt load, but those that are already slipping, need to change or realign management, need to make quick asset sales, must reinvest in the business the cash flow from depreciation simply to maintain market position, must soon refinance a large amount of short-term debt, and, for good measure, do not have owners with deep pockets standing on the sideline, will almost certainly collapse. That was Federated. It collapsed.

Managers, particularly newly arrived ones, need time to make changes in an orderly and efficient way and with scalpels, not meat cleavers. They need time to make some mistakes. In short, they need a margin of safety, and in a thinly capitalized LBO, such as Federated, with a ten-to-one or even higher debt-to-equity ratio, there is only a margin of peril. Instead of producing success, a push-to-the-limit LBO is likely to produce trauma, unnecessary costs, and, far too often, failure.

How else can we explain why Federated, which had consistently earned over $600 million before interest and taxes before the LBO, was bankrupt within eighteen months after? The popular explanation was that Campeau was a loon, but as every retailer and creditor in and around Federated with whom I talked agreed, this mountain of debt would have buried almost anyone. It just would have taken a little longer.

By 1990, when Federated filed for bankruptcy and Macy was limping, a retailer who studied their financial statements would have been unable to identify them as belonging to the same companies as those presented in table 2–1. The numbers would have drawn a blank stare, not simply because the two companies had assumed so much debt but because the operations had been so badly shaken. Table 2–2 summarizes the changes at all three companies, May, Macy, and Federated.

MAY DEPARTMENT STORES—RIGHT ON COURSE

May Department Stores had also changed considerably during the four years since fiscal 1985 (the year reflected in table 2–1). Like Macy, it had been the subject of takeover rumors, and the ubiquitous Haft family, which had shaken down so many other retailers, had accumulated shares of May and was making threatening noises. Later, in 1990, Thomas A. Hays, the president of May, said laughingly that someone up above must have been watching over the company. The more probable explanation is that May did not own a group of stores as prestigious and highly visible as Federated that could be sold quickly to pay down acquisition debt. In any event, no hostile bid emerged, and although the company took steps to defend itself, it did not resort to anything so drastic as the Macy LBO.

May bought the poorly performing Associated Dry Goods in 1986 believing that its management would improve the stores, which it soon did. Point-of-sale equipment was installed, and much of the buying was centralized. Management knew very well, too, Hays later said, that the acquisition, which was done for $2.4 billion in May

Table 2–2
The Sequel to Campeau (Millions
of Dollars)

Financial Data	May (year ended Feb. 3, 1990)	R. H. Macy (year ended July 28, 1990)	Federated/Campeau (year ended Feb. 3, 1990)
Sales per square foot[a]	$159	$221	$162
Earnings before interest and taxes (EBIT)	$1,032	$423	$151
Interest expense	$233	$717	$516
Ratio of EBIT to interest expense	4.4 X	0.6 X	0.3 X
Interest as % of total sales	2.4	9.9	10.6
Capital expenditures	$427	$161	$111
Bond rating[b]	A+	CCC+	D
Return on assets[c]	8.1%	4.8%	0.9%
Return on total capital[c]	9.2%	−4.9%	−10.8%
Long-term debt as % of total capital	56%	103%	134%

[a]Department stores only. In dollars.
[b]S&P ratings. The Macy rating is for its subordinated debt.
[c]Excludes bankruptcy-related charges at Federated. For Federated and Macy, return on assets is a positive number even though return on capital is negative, because return on assets is calculated by adding back to net income the after-tax cost of interest expense, then dividing by average assets.

common stock, would make the company harder (though not, of course, impossible) to swallow. Then in 1988 it acquired the two Federated divisions, Filene's and Foley's, for $1.5 billion in cash and notes. May also sold off several noncore businesses for over $600 million, and it reduced its ownership in much of its real estate, whose value had not been reflected in the stock price. In 1989 the company bought back almost 20 percent of its outstanding stock. In all, the company's long-term debt jumped by $2.4 billion, and its credit rating slipped from AA to A+.

Chart 2–1

May Company: Capital Expenditures, Interest
Expense, and Operating Profit (as a Percentage
of Sales)

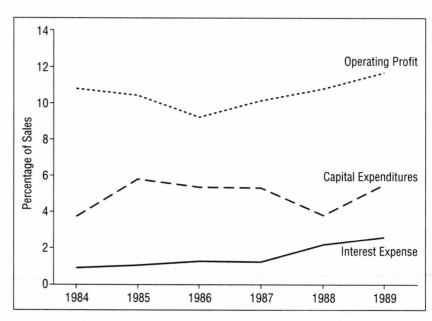

Note: Interest expense is company total while operating profit and capital expenditures are
department stores only; operating profit is calculated before deducting interest and corporate
expense.

Remarkably, however, four years later, after all these changes, it
was still pretty much business as usual at May. The company was
operating on a far larger scale but at the same high level of performance. Return on assets was precisely the same 8.1 percent it had
been in 1985. While return on equity in fiscal 1989 had increased,
from 16.7 to an even better 18.5 percent, that was largely a reflection of the additional leverage. Return on total capital declined, from
11.8 to 9.2 percent.

May is a marvelous yardstick for measuring the dramatic changes
at Federated and Macy. What was the impact of the general economy
on the department store business during the second half of the
1980s? What would Macy and Federated have looked like if they had
not been so distracted by financial concerns? Chart 2–1 tracks three

revealing ratios, year by year, for May from fiscal 1984 to fiscal 1989: capital expenditures, interest expense, and earnings before interest and taxes (EBIT), each as a percentage of sales. (By looking at earnings before interest charges rather than after, we can see more readily how the underlying business was doing, apart from changes in financial structure.) The results are clear. Business was good, and there were no great surprises over the six years. Interest expense moved up as a percentage of sales, but not greatly. Capital expenditures and pretax profits as a percentage of sales increased over time, but also only moderately. More important, profits, as they should be, were always far greater than interest expense. The company had the financial flexibility "to do opportunistic things," as Hays put it, and with so many struggling competitors, May still expected to see more department stores up for sale. Sure enough, soon afterward, in December 1990, May was able to buy the Thalhimer group of stores in the Southeast for $317 million from a financially terminal Carter Hawley Hale.

FEDERATED—DEBT IS DESTINY

The story on Federated is painfully simple (as well as simply painful). In a mere eighteen months between the buyout and bankruptcy, there were 8,000 layoffs in the five divisions of Federated/Campeau—more than half of them in the first few weeks. Robert Campeau visited each of the divisional chiefs and, depending on the size of the operation, told them that he wanted $40 million, $50 million, a year in savings, with none of it from the sales force—and no discussion, please. He got them. Some of the cuts were appropriate, but many were not. And for what? Given the company's Humpty Dumpty financial structure, the odds that Federated/Campeau would have a great fall were close to 100 percent. The company began life with interest charges that would, on a pro forma basis, consume 11.9 percent of every dollar of sales. No retailer can do that and expect to survive without divine intervention. Everything has to go just right, and that's not the way retailing is.

The numbers at Federated/Campeau were so, so simple. Wall Street was saying that retailers were "cash cows." An LBO entrepreneur, they said, could rely on the celebrated EBIT-DA—earnings before interest and taxes *and before depreciation and amortization*— to pay interest charges. But, alas, this cow had already been milked. The pro forma EBIT-DA at the time of the LBO was about $700 million. One senior official at Federated said that the annual level of capital expenditures required just to maintain market position, without growth, was about $200 million and that an additional $75 million to $90 million a year was required to fund the additional working capital for same-store growth in accounts receivable and inventories. Even EBIT-DA would not be enough to cover those outlays and also $600 million of interest charges. The Wall Street "story" was smoke and mirrors.[2]

Much of the real story for Federated/Campeau is captured by chart 2–2, but this one tells a very different tale from the one for May. Beginning in 1988, interest charges as a percentage of sales soared at Federated. And with that both capital expenditures and earnings—even earnings *before* interest and taxes—plummeted. The drop in capital expenditures was predictable. A company that is overtaxed by interest payments has little money left for investments.[3] Even if the will is there, developers begin to look for other retailers to anchor their malls.

The explanation for the other drop-off, the one in earnings, is only slightly more complicated. As the chart shows, Federated/Campeau's interest charges exceeded its earnings by a wide margin from the day of the takeover. Such a company will survive only if it runs swifter than the rest of us and with no time for a warmup. Like firebugs, there was already a crowd waiting for the Campeau groups of stores, Allied and Federated, to self-destruct. According to Frank DeRita, a senior officer of Congress Talcott, a major commercial factor for a number of Federated's suppliers, the factors gave the company the "usual" six-months-to-a-year grace period that was considered safe after an LBO. By late spring 1989, however, about ten months after the LBO, Federated/Campeau lost its financial credibility. For DeRita, the event that crystallized his worst fears was the realization that in the first quarter of 1989 the company's bullish projections had not been met and, ominously, Federated's working capital was being diverted to pay down some of the bankers' bridge loans. With that, things began to unravel. Factors represented only 20 percent of Federated's 80,000 suppliers, but factors talk to each other, and they are a catalyst for worry throughout the marketplace.

Retailers like to talk about having momentum; although they mean momentum on the upside, it works in both directions, and for Federated it was all downhill. Federated's suppliers became discouraged, many of them reluctant to make goods, say, in the Far East, where

Chart 2–2

Federated Department Stores: Capital
Expenditures, Interest Expense, and Operating
Profit (as a Percentage of Sales)

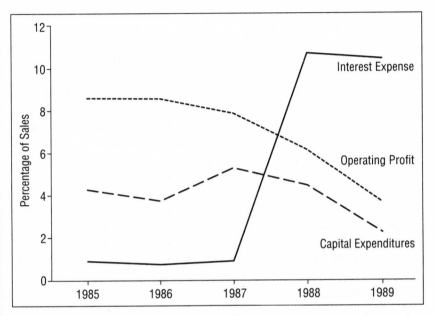

Note: Interest expense is company total, while operating profit and capital expenditures reflect only those divisions retained after the 1988 acquisition; operating profit is calculated before deducting interest expense and unusual items.

lead times are long. Worse, once the initial group of stores had been sold to May and Macy, the asset sales on which Campeau had been relying to pay down debt began to draw lower prices and fewer bids, reflecting the less buoyant retail climate and the poor experience of those who had overpaid for divisions of Allied/Campeau. And as the buyout lost credibility, lenders kept interest charges at levels that were higher than had been initially projected by the bankers. (The poor always pay more.)

By the fall of 1989, Bloomingdale's and its sister stores were being run for cash, not profit. Discounting was heavy. The traditional Thanksgiving sales were extended right through Christmas.

The Federated management was distracted. Financial issues took time from business issues. A veritable army of suppliers and lenders were increasingly nervous and would have to be stroked. There were also errors of execution, reflecting the pressures of the LBO itself, the excessive leverage and, to a lesser degree, Campeau's destabilizing personality. Underlying many of the errors, said Zimmerman, was the simple fact of too much change all at once. In an industry with no tail wind, one where execution and implementation were everything, management's attention was continually diverted.

Zimmerman, who became president of Federated at the time of the LBO, would later say, wistfully, that a lot of good things were done in the year and a half between the buyout and the Chapter 11 filing, but the darkening clouds of bankruptcy obscured them. The company had regained its focus, eliminated layers of management, and, with the merger of Goldsmith's into Rich's, slimmed down to five department store divisions. There were new programs, long overdue, for centralized data processing, buying, and credit. On the "dumb" side, he said, the most costly error, for which he accepted responsibility, was a so-called inventory intensification program, much like the one at Macy, which was intended to push more sales through the stores, even at lower margins, in order to close the gap between earnings and interest charges. But management had overlooked that carrying the additional merchandise, together with the other strains, would put an intolerable burden on the company's cash position.

Stepping back from the details, there is no mystery at all about why Federated collapsed. *In an industry that runs on credit, a company that has no financial credibility is soon out of business.*

Yes, it was true that Robert Campeau, the "crazy optimist," as someone called him, should not have reached for an exotic, variable-rate $2 billion financing instead of the $1.1 billion mortgage financing that was still available to Federated as late as the summer of 1989 and would have relieved the company's immediate financial strains. That was an error. But the mortgage financing would not have changed the fact that 11 percent of sales were being drained off by interest charges. Nor would it have changed the fact that Campeau had exhausted his financial resources and then some. (He had also drained Allied of credit.) And people close to the company, including creditors, all seem to agree that even had the mortgage financing been consummated, the company would nonetheless have ended up in Chapter 11. The train would have arrived there a bit later.

Why "Prudent Bankers" Is an Oxymoron

Where did it all go wrong? Fingers were pointed first at the bankers who structured the deal, particularly First Boston, which was eager to show that it still had financial muscle, if not brains, after Bruce Wasserstein and Joseph Perella, who had headed First Boston's mergers and acquisitions department, left to form their own firm. And, of course, they were pointed at Wasserstein too. In preparing their projections, the bankers had stitched together the best year ever from each of the divisions and then married them to optimistic assumptions about interest costs, gross margins, expense reductions, and the rest. No one assumption may have been off by much, but the end result were spreadsheet projections—EBIT-DA for 1989 of $1.1 billion—that were pure pie in the sky.

And fingers would be pointed at Citibank and other commercial bankers too.

The bankers did the Federated LBO because, foolish as it seems today, it was no more foolish than those being done elsewhere. Did Federated's pro forma EBIT fall far short of its interest charges? Of course, but so did many others.[4] Had Campeau overpaid? Of course. He had paid $7.8 billion (including assumed debt) for a company that in its previous fiscal year had earnings before interest and taxes of $634 million—12.3 times EBIT. At that price, he would be earning, on a pro forma basis, about 8 percent on capital while the capital was costing him as much as 16 and 17 percent. But data for all of the corporate mergers in 1988 of $500 million or more (in 1989 dollars) show that the average price was an even more boisterous 15.3 times EBIT. And in the 1989 mergers, prices were higher still. The Federated LBO was foolish but no more so than others.

Remarkably, Federated's financial disclosures and SEC filings were of high quality. The numbers were all there. It was the refusal to read and heed them that was the problem.

That is not to say that Campeau was blameless. His disruptive personality was notorious. Federated's senior management tried to keep him away from the operating people, on the whole successfully, but it was yet another drain on their time. The essential damage, however, was that Federated/Campeau had been launched on a keel of financial myths and nonsense, and for that the fault lay primarily at the feet of the financial community. Dazzled by the gargantuan fees that they received in LBOs, fees paid at the closing, bankers soon lost sight of the fact that today's myths would return as operating nightmares.

They lost sight even of their own self-interest. Where once they had been content to sell junk to others, now they began to make the same bad investments—the so-called bridge loans—themselves, without asking why it was that no one else was willing to step forward. The ultimate failure, of course, was the abdication of social and financial responsibility. Campeau was a real estate developer, and like his breed, he would borrow as much as bankers would lend. If bankers would not set standards, then who would?

The Inevitability of Bankruptcy

At a company that is troubled financially but sound at the business level, the CEO knows that it would be foolish to allow it to slide into bankruptcy. The direct costs alone are enormous. According to an informed estimate, the out-of-pocket fees and similar expenses for the Allied Stores/Federated bankruptcy proceedings were going to average $60 million *annually.* That included the lawyers, bankers, experts, and the like, hired not just by the debtor companies but by all the committees whose expenses would ultimately be paid by the two debtors when they emerged from bankruptcy. Congress could support a decent Central American army at those prices. (Their generals are less costly than our lawyers.) And those were only the direct expenses. Beyond them, the costs were more difficult to quantify but also significant. Management would have to be segmented so that the Chapter 11 process and the development of a plan of reorganization did not intrude (too much) into the day-to-day running of the business. And, of course, bankruptcy proceedings often damage a business permanently, some more than others.

Logic would also tell our CEO that he or she should, as a resourceful executive, be able to negotiate an informal, out-of-bankruptcy reorganization with the creditors, who, after all, also know how costly and disruptive bankruptcy can be. During the 1980s, while the great LBO bubble was still building, it was repeatedly said by Michael Milken and his numerous, sometimes subsidized, and often sycophantic followers that bankruptcy would be the exceptional case rather than the usual one. Reorganizations would now be accomplished speedily and informally.[5] The basis for this happy turn of events was the concept of an LBO as based on so-called strip financing, in which the investors would own a "strip," or portion, of each level of financing, from senior debt on through the subordinated debt and preferred stock ("mezzanine") level and on down to the equity.

Compared to the typical public corporation with publicly held debt, an LBO would thus have many fewer but more sophisticated investors. And with everyone owning a piece of almost everything, the conflict among different classes of investors would be muted, and most of the players might even fit around a single conference table.

The theory didn't hold up at Federated, but not for want of trying. Working with Merrill Lynch, the company tried diligently to put together a package that would avoid a filing. But the issues, the capital structure, and the personalities were too complex for a plan to be worked out in a few months. Vince Lombardi used to say that his Green Bay Packers never lost a game; it was just that the clock ran out. The clock, said Zimmerman, also ran out on Federated.

This may have been an LBO, but the capital structure of Federated was anything but simple. Claims against the subsidiary operating companies were effectively senior to parent company obligations. The bank debt was secured. There were "temporary" bridge loans in three different flavors, with different security protections. The long-term debt of the pre-LBO company had not been paid off and was held by quite different interests from the newly issued junk debt. In short, with 80,000 vendors, 150 or so banks, and other creditors as well, their representatives alone would require 450 chairs in a meeting hall. Where the boosters had spoken of LBOs as if the investors and lenders were a choir group singing in harmony, this crowd would sound more like the Tower of Babel.

While trying to work out an informal plan, Federated/Campeau could not even talk to the trade creditors. After all, the very purpose of the discussions was to reassure the trade that they could keep shipping goods on normal terms. And, said Nathan Thorne of Merrill Lynch, the banks were in no mood to make any concessions.

In the end, it was the holders of junk bonds who would be asked to bear the brunt of the reorganization by exchanging their bonds for common stock. The textbook reality was that these Federated bondholders were institutional investors, such as Prudential Insurance, and so would not insist on a Chapter 11 filing that would hurt everyone. That was one reality, and it was no doubt heard. There were other realities, however. One was that First Boston had allegedly kept selling junk bonds out of its unsold inventory well into the summer of 1989, when the dark handwriting on the wall, spelling "bankruptcy," was becoming visible to First Boston. Some of the bondholders were unwilling to let First Boston off with the relatively modest concessions that, as a holder of Federated's exchange notes, it was to have made. Another reality was that the holders of junk bonds were being asked to give up roughly 70 cents on the dollar, while the holders of other, pre-LBO bonds, for example, were not asked to give up anything. One of the participants recalled, too, that the "hate" for Campeau was so deep that some of the creditors were intent that he get what was coming to him. That was a reality too. Finally, it was a reality that even if the informal plan had been worked through and approved, it would have been only a temporary fix, not much better than outpatient surgery, so to speak.[6]

R. H. MACY—LEVERAGE IN THE HANDS OF A GOOD MERCHANT

Of the three companies in this profile, Macy is the most interesting because it's the most puzzling. It's not that the LBO as such was a mistake. As one insider told me, the sharks were circling the company, and so were bankers offering to help "in any way," meaning to sell the business. An LBO would eliminate the threats to this well-run company, and by including over 300 executives in the buyout, it would also put golden handcuffs on the management group. But to preempt the bidding and to placate some directors who were cool to Finkelstein, he would have to offer top dollar—$3.7 billion (including assumed debt)—which he did. At the time, it was the largest management-led LBO ever, and Finkelstein himself emerged with 4.7 percent of the equity.

The Macy LBO was always quite risky. Federated/Campeau began its short-lived LBO career with 11.9 percent of every sales dollar committed to interest payments, but Macy, at 10 percent, was not far behind. Ten percent is a daunting number for any company, and certainly for a retailer. Still, for a year and a half, it worked well. In fiscal 1987 the company was in the black, earning $60 million before income taxes, and it seemed to be one of the LBO success stories. The press began to calculate just how rich—very!—Finkelstein and his associates would soon be, when the expected public offering enabled them to cash in. True, there were some whispers that the company was pushing too hard to show good short-term numbers and that it was betting too much on its ability to achieve higher margins by substituting private-label merchandise for well-known brands, but mostly what was heard were cheers.

Macy was far better situated than Federated. As table 2–1 indicates, Macy had achieved superior sales per square foot and returns on capital. It had a first-rate group of senior managers, people who knew their company. Except for some real estate holdings and a few stores in the Midwest, it was not relying on quick asset sales. It did not have substantial short-term debt that would have to be refinanced. And in the group that owned a majority of its shares—General Electric Capital, Loews (Laurence Tisch and family), Goldman Sachs, Mutual Shares, and Equitable Life—Macy had investors who were not only knowledgeable but had exceptional credibility in financial markets.

Then the roof fell in.

By the spring of 1990, only a year after *Forbes* had been adding up the management group's potentially awesome wealth, Macy had become one of the more suspect credits on Seventh Avenue.[7] (Federated, then operating under the protection of the bankruptcy court, had plenty of cash and was not a risk.) The same vicious cycle that had brought down Federated was now hovering suspiciously over Macy. The company had a CCC+ bond rating, barely more than a step short of insolvency, and soon Standard & Poor's would threaten to lower the rating further. Factors put the company on restricted lists, and while factored vendors accounted for only 15 percent of sales to Macy, there was a question whether the company would get the merchandise it needed for fall and Christmas. (It did, but not without the promise of a capital infusion from those oh-so-credible shareholders.)

Just how far and how quickly Macy had fallen is clear from chart 2–3. As a percentage of sales, interest charges rose to 10 percent in 1987, the year after the Macy LBO, and they remained at a perilously high 9.9 percent in fiscal 1990. Much like Federated's, Macy's burden was too great. Shortly after the LBO, Finkelstein had boasted that he would open four or five big stores a year.[8] Instead, capital expenditures were slashed. And for a variety of reasons, EBIT, that is, earnings even *before* interest and taxes, plummeted—not as badly as at Federated but badly enough.

Only a few years earlier, May and Macy had looked, financially at least, like peas in a pod, each with EBIT that exceeded interest charges by roughly $400 million. (See table 2–1.) Now, in the year ended February 3, 1990, May's EBIT exceeded interest expense by $800 million. By comparison, in the year ended July 28, 1990, Macy's EBIT *fell short* of interest charges by $290 million. Compared to May, Macy's operating results had deteriorated by over $1 billion in just a few years' time. No wonder the factors fretted.

Chart 2–3

R. H. Macy & Company: Capital Expenditures,
Interest Expense, and Operating Profit (as a
Percentage of Sales)

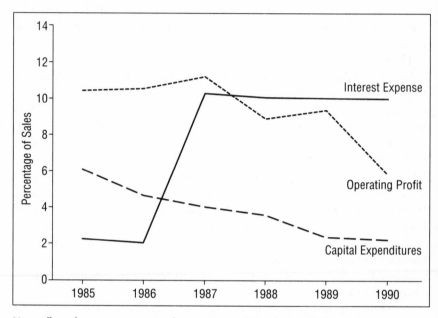

Note: All numbers are company totals; operating profit is calculated before deducting interest or adding income from nonmerchandising sources.

To be sure, some of Macy's problems in 1990 were not of its own making. Federated's promotional selling, forcing Macy and others to follow suit, had hurt 1989's Christmas season profits. (For geographic and other reasons, May was affected far less.) Then the bankruptcies at Federated, Allied, and Ames Department Stores aggravated the already considerable skittishness of Macy's own suppliers. Finally, in the spring of 1990, the retail climate turned down, particularly in the Northeast, which accounted for over 40 percent of Macy's sales.

While Macy publicly attributed much of the blame to Federated, more of the problems began at home than Finkelstein was ready to concede. His strategy had been to overcome the high but fixed level of interest charges by pushing more private-label and other merchandise through the stores. But private-label is a risky strategy because of the large commitments and long lead times. In the fall of 1989 the company owned far too much inventory and was forced to move it out at promotional prices, even in markets where Federated did not compete, such as California. And with so much of its merchandise—up to 80 percent according to one source—being sold at off-price, customers soon caught on, and Macy lost credibility as a regular-price retailer. There were other problems too. Some divisions, such as those in the Northeast, were consolidated too hastily, with attendant confusion and unnecessary costs. According to people in and around the company, Finkelstein's ego, never small, had, like Pinocchio's nose, grown and grown. And although he was a creative merchant, his style was not well suited to a defensive game.

In the larger scheme, the predicament was that for Macy, much like Federated, everything had to go just right. Finkelstein's merchandising skills were undimmed, but he had left no financial margin for uninvited problems, whatever the source. Yes, an LBO was probably appropriate, and it was probably right also to bid high enough to preempt the bidding. The puzzle is why the new Macy decided to issue so much debt—and so little equity—that, even in fiscal 1989, well before the Federated collapse, the company's EBIT would fail to cover its interest charges. As of 1990, the vendors were still betting that the company would survive, and there were still some "excess assets" that could be liquidated. But no well-run, responsible company should be the subject of such bets.

The enigma inside that puzzle is why investors as sophisticated as General Electric Capital, Goldman Sachs, Laurence Tisch, and Mutual Shares had not built a stronger capital base for their new company. True, the company's projections circulated in 1986 by Goldman Sachs, banker for the LBO, showed that it would soon grow its way out of the debt problem. But the projections suffered from the same spreadsheet disease as did Federated's two years later. Macy told itself and the rest of the world that sales would grow at a compounded 11 percent annual rate for the foreseeable future. In fact, by the spring of 1990, after adjusting for the purchase of the Federated West Coast divisions, Macy had achieved a compounded growth rate of only about 6 percent, just what it had been doing in the years immediately before the buyout.

By 1990 it was already late for a major restructuring. The business was fundamentally sound, but Macy needed a substantial infusion of new equity—more debt was certainly not the answer—and the world was now shying away from junk bond casualties. The days when a financially weak company could raise capital simply by offering a higher interest rate were over. Capital was being rationed by quality, not by price. In December 1990, after considerable effort, the company succeeded in raising up to $187 million in new equity, most of it from existing shareholders. The new money would not make a large dent in $5.5 billion of debt, but Macy did retire some of its junk bonds, which were selling at huge discounts. In the first half of fiscal 1991, the company lost an additional $73 million from operations, and the retail climate generally was poor.

Macy, the (Unnecessary) Failure

As 1990 ended, management took pains to reassure the trade, but despite the recent injection of new capital, there was continued speculation that the company would eventually file for bankruptcy. For the moment, it seemed unlikely. An unusually large management group at Macy had bought almost 20 percent of the common stock (on a fully diluted basis) in the initial buyout, and they would bend every effort to avoid bankruptcy. There were no major debt repayments scheduled before 1993, giving them some room to maneuver.

In a broader sense, whether Macy slides into bankruptcy is the wrong question. Even if it does squeak by, the damage will have been serious. Its development will be permanently stunted, much like a tree that has suffered through years of drought. May Department Stores, the company that had not turned itself inside out, opened in 1990 twenty-one new department stores, a total of 2.6 million square feet of new retail space, and remodeled or expanded thirty-two others. The emphasis at May has shifted to higher-price merchandise, which competes more directly with Macy (and Federated too). It projects fifteen additional new stores for 1991. As recently as 1985, Macy had been of equal size and profitability, but now its roots were parched for money. In 1990 it did not open a single new department store, and for 1991 only one was planned. There was little that Macy could do to cheer its impoverished troops who watched those bright new May stores compete for market share with Macy in New York, Washington, and elsewhere. Those numbers for 1990— twenty-one new department stores versus zero—tell an eloquent story. In football, three touchdowns to none, it would be called a shutout. And the raw score only hints at the debilitating impact on employee morale and motivation.

CONCLUSION

In a mature but competitive business, such as department stores, a business with no strategic tail wind to help, execution and implementation are everything, as Zimmerman said. Management needs to devote its energies to merchandising and to stores and people. May Department Stores could do that, and indeed the chaos at Allied, Federated, and elsewhere gave it openings to move into new markets and to seize additional market share in existing ones.

Meanwhile, at Federated and Macy, finance had moved from the back of the store, where it belongs, to the front. It was not just that the financial arithmetic was bad, although it surely was that, but financial pressures seriously distracted management from its normal, day-to-day operations. The stability and the strength that are essential for a company to work effectively with people, and for people to respect the leadership, were damaged or destroyed. Both companies stand as object lessons of the evil effects of excessive leverage—Federated for the speed of its arrival at Chapter 11 and Macy because there is every reason to believe that it would have continued on a vigorous course had it not been engulfed by debt and by problems and stresses induced by debt.

Ben Franklin said that it is difficult for an empty sack to stand upright. In a competitive environment, half empty is not much better.

3

Capital Structures

A LARGER VIEW

In 1990 Middle American, our mythical drug company, acquired a biotechnology company, Bitech, for $800 million. Charles E. O'Rourke, Middle American's chairman and CEO, worried about the acquisition, but the technology was promising. He was also reassured by the fact that the two companies had been collaborating successfully in a joint venture.

Like other major companies, Middle American does almost all its borrowing through the bond market or by selling commercial paper. This acquisition, however, was too large to be financed by commercial paper, and Middle American preferred to do its permanent financing on a less hurried timetable. In the first instance, the funds were obtained from banks, which were only too happy to oblige.

At a board meeting a month after the deal closed, one of the outside directors, Sam Slugge, himself a retired CEO elsewhere, asked how the acquisition was going to be permanently financed. Sam was a big man, with a shock of silver hair, who could have been elected to almost anything on appearance and graciousness alone. He was also a director of four other companies.

O'Rourke turned to the company's chief financial officer, Phineas Nance, for a summary of what the credit markets looked like and what debt or other possibilities were being considered.

"I've put on the projector," Nance began, "several charts that describe the profound changes that have recently taken place in the capital structures of American industry. What happens elsewhere doesn't dictate what we do, but it's important to understand the climate.

"Looking at chart 1[3–1], which shows the amounts of capital

Chart 3–1

Net Corporate Bond and Equity Proceeds,
Financial and Nonfinancial Corporations
(Billions of Dollars)

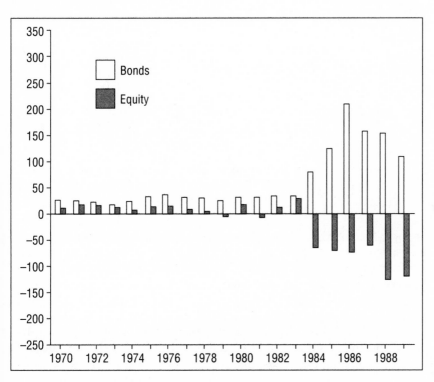

Source: Federal Reserve Board

raised in the bond and equity markets, we can see that in the 1970s
and early 1980s, American industry was still borrowing in moderation. While corporations were consistently raising more debt than
equity during the 1970s and early 1980s, remember that corporations were retaining over half their earnings.[1] Balance sheets looked
pretty good. In December 1983, the median industrial bond issue
was still rated an investment-grade single-A by Standard & Poor's.

"I'll come back to chart 1[3–1], but if we now look at chart 2[3–2],
we see pretty much the same picture. During the recession of the
early 1970s, net interest costs rose to historically high levels of

Chart 3–2

Interest Cost–to–Cash Flow Ratio for
Nonfinancial Corporations° (End of Quarter)

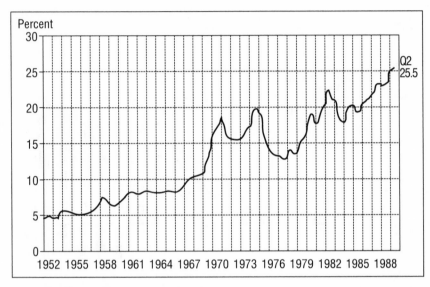

°Interest payments and before-tax cash flow.
Source: Federal Reserve Bank of New York

corporate cash flow. The Federal Reserve was trying to curb inflation, and the combination of high interest rates and sharply reduced
profits produced the spikes that we see in the chart. Otherwise, however, the interest burden, as a fixed charge on pre-tax cash flow, was
quite tolerable in the 1970s.

"Obviously something changed in the mid-1980s. In a word, we
began to strip the equity out of much of American industry. The effects can be seen from chart 2, but just how we went about it can be
seen more directly from chart 3[3–3] which shows the amount of
cash distributed by corporations in one fashion or another. Historically, when corporate America distributed cash, it did so almost entirely by paying dividends. Investors who wanted money could always sell shares in the open market, but if the company was to be the
source, dividends were the usual medium. Beginning in the late
1970s, as chart 3 clearly shows, the pattern began to change, and in
the mid-1980s, it changed dramatically. First, there was a wave of

Chart 3–3

Cash Distributions to Holders of U.S. Corporate
Equity (Billions of 1986 U.S. Dollars)

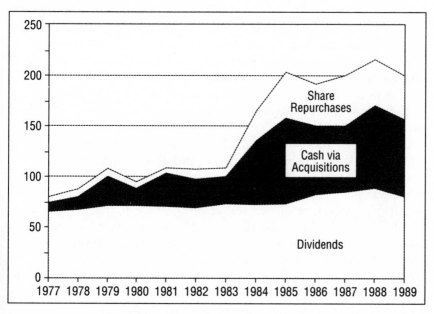

Source: Compustat and Federal Reserve Bank of New York

takeovers. In the merger wave of the 1960s, companies had been
bought for stock, but in the 1980s it was for cash. The competition
for target companies unleashed by hostile takeovers made speed essential—bankers learned to sleep standing up—and cash was the
currency that greased the wheels. Second, in the mid-1980s, share
repurchases soared to unprecedented levels. We know that many
share repurchases were no more than a defensive response to the
same takeover phenomenon, but whatever the reason, the $78 bil-
lion of buybacks in 1987 was more than thirty times the level only
five years earlier.[2] No wonder there was a hemorrhaging of equity.

"The combined effect of these essentially new factors, takeovers
and share repurchases, produced a result unprecedented in American financial history. In order to fund its growth, industry had tradi-
tionally raised in the capital markets more money by issuing new
shares than it lost by retiring 'old' shares. That is clear back in

chart 1[3–1]. True, the net amount of these new issues was never very large. In the three decades beginning in 1950, they added on average only about 1 percent to the float of stocks already outstanding. But from positive, if modest, amounts of new equity, the pattern became mixed in the late 1970s and then turned sharply and increasingly negative in the 1980s. In 1988, in particular, although $40 billion of new stocks were sold, *on balance* $118 billion of equity was drained from the system, an amount that was more than two times the net amount of new equity capital raised in the entire decade of the 1970s."[3]

One of the directors asked if Nance was saying that the aggregate net worth of American companies had in fact shrunk in 1988. "Yes, but not by $118 billion," Nance replied. "With corporate profits at record levels, there were substantial retained earnings—roughly $60 billion[4]—to cushion the drain. But the profits coming in the front of the corporate store were often absorbed in the business, and what was going out the back door was almost entirely cash. It was inevitable, therefore, as we see again in chart 1, that corporations would rely on debt to fill the gap. The money had to come from somewhere. It was also inevitable that even with strong earnings, corporate credit would deteriorate. Going back to chart 2, we see that despite a prolonged period of prosperity, interest costs began to chew up more of corporate cash flows in the late 1980s—25 percent in 1989—than at any other time since World War II.

"Bond ratings tell a similar story. In December 1983, of industrial companies with bonds rated by Standard & Poor's, only 32 percent were rated BB or lower. Just three and a half years later, in May 1987, however, 57 percent were rated BB or lower. The median industrial bond was junk.

"Incidentally," Nance continued, "that trend was unique to the United States. Chart 4[3–4] uses 1982, a recession year worldwide, as a jumping-off point, and it measures changes in the ratio of interest expense to cash flow.[5] In the United States, the ratio rose. Everywhere else, even in Australia, not generally a model of financial discipline, the ratio of interest expense to cash flow declined after 1982, as it should during better times. In most industrialized countries the ratio declined by a third or more. German and Italian corporations, in particular, historically noted for their reliance on debt, cut their interest expense (relative to cash flow) by about half.[6] In the United States, on the other hand, looking at chart 4[3–4], one would think that we had just come through seven rather lean years, not fat."

Chart 3–4

Gross Interest Expenses as a Share of Cash Flow

1982 = 100

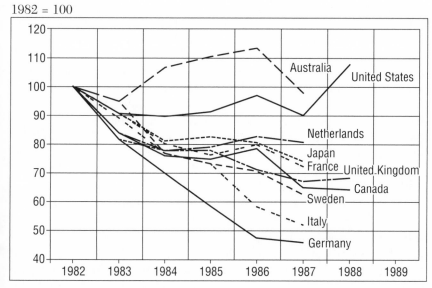

Source: Federal Reserve Bank of New York

Nance looked around to see if he was losing his audience, but the board was all ears. One of the directors was making extensive notes to review with *his* chief financial officer.

"I should add," Nance said, "if we were to look at ratios of debt to corporate net worth, or debt to market value of equities, we would see a somewhat more benign picture. For financial planning purposes, however, we put much more emphasis on income streams than on balance sheets and volatile stock prices. We pay the 'grocer' and other fixed charges out of current income and cash flows. I don't mean to suggest that assets and stock prices are irrelevant, but the values usually depend on earnings, and if the earnings are not there, the values soon evaporate. Fixed assets, in particular, are not a source of cash in the ordinary course of business."

Why, one of the directors asked, did the leveraging become so much more dramatic in the 1980s, and what were its implications for Middle American? "Surely," Nance replied, "the reasons were many. Takeovers played a major role, both directly and indirectly. Second, even with lower corporate income tax rates, taxes were an important inducement because value could be created by substituting debt for equity, thereby eliminating much or all of the government's slice of corporate profits.* At times it seemed as if Wall Street and corporate America were only just discovering that interest is deductible. It was not a truly new idea, but it was newly fashionable, and Wall Street is as trendy as Seventh Avenue.

"The one entirely new element was the junk bond market, which began slowly but mushroomed later in the decade. As the volume grew, the quality deteriorated. Again, the reasons are many, but the sustained prosperity of the 1980s appears to have dulled investors' wits. They bought bonds for blind pools, with virtually no protective covenants and with no known source of income. They bought bonds of companies with earnings that even under rosy scenarios failed to cover the interest charges. Chart 5[3–5] shows the growth of the junk bond market in the 1980s.

"My favorite story from that era is Simplicity Pattern, a once-upon-a-time glamor stock," Nance said. "The company was bought and sold three times in a period of a few years, each time at a more inflated price. It was Russian roulette, financial style. By 1988, when the third sale was completed and the financing had been done, the company was in a *declining* industry. Women had joined the workforce and no longer had the time to sew. For 1988, Simplicity had only $80 million of annual sales, but it had $16 million of annual interest expense, and an accelerating level of losses. The third time, alas, there was a live bullet in the chamber. The 'victim' fell into default within months of its junk bond offering.[7] None of this would have been quite as notable if the revolver had been a Saturday night special in the hands of an amateur gunslinger. But the third-time buyer was a knowledgeable group led by Wesray Capital, a firm headed by Raymond Chambers, an experienced deal maker.

"It was, I am told, Ben Graham who first said that you can get in more trouble with good ideas than bad ones. It is so much easier to push a good idea to excess. For companies that came to market in 1980 with speculative grade debt—rated BB+/Ba1 or lower by Standard & Poor's/Moody's—the coverage of interest charges by earnings averaged 199 percent—not great, but for speculative bonds not

---

* The appendix to this chapter contains the author's proposal to the House Ways and Means Committee in May 1989 for tax reform.

Chart 3–5

High-Yield Bond Market for Nonconvertable
Debt

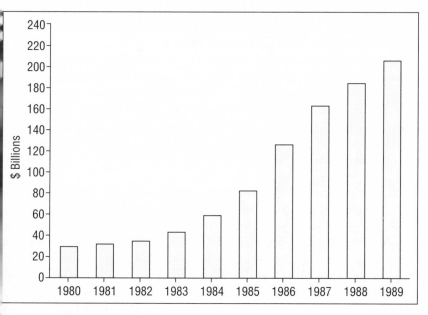

Source: Drexel Burnham Lambert

too bad. By 1988 the coverage had fallen to 71 percent of interest charges.[8] By then, of course, the junk bond game was almost over. In 1989 the window began to close for weak credits, and in 1990 it slammed shut. Suddenly companies were trapped, unable to refinance with cheap loans or even to sell assets to those who, they had thought, would in turn have access to easy credit.

"It's very tempting to tee off on junk bonds. But while they were certainly a factor," Nance concluded, "the problem did not stop there. The erosion of credit standards in the 1980s was pervasive and affected many of the best companies, even those that had not been acquired in an LBO or otherwise taken over. Business was good, there was a general prosperity. Even so, the earnings coverage of interest charges for the S&P 400 Industrial Index fell sharply, from 5.20 times in 1984 to 3.78 in 1988.[9] That's too much to be blamed just on junk."

What does it all mean for Middle American? Here it was O'Rourke who led the discussion, because it touched on concerns close to his heart. "The immediate issue," he said, "is only how to refinance our recent acquisition. We are still reviewing a number of possibilities. Ordinarily, we would suggest that the company issue ten- to twelve-year bonds because we would be confident of our ability to repay them out of normal cash flow. This new Bitech venture, however, is likely to require additional funding for some time to come, and that's the reason for the hesitation. Seeing the dramatic swings in the credit markets over the past few years, from extraordinarily lax to increasingly tight, we decided to take a broader look at our debt policy, one less influenced by the trends of the moment. While there has been a shortage of credit, the much-discussed crunch, none of us see that as a permanent state of affairs. Strong companies like ours can borrow at any time, and even for those in the middle of the pack, the window will be open sooner or later.

"Debt is seductive. Swiss bankers make it a rule never to lend to those who cannot repay out of their ordinary profits, without borrowing again. Very few junk bonds were placed in Zurich. But for a variety of reasons not entirely of their own making, bankers and other lenders in the United States have not shown the same restraint. The lesson, we think, is clear. Financial discipline is not something imposed by the marketplace. It must be acquired here, at home."

O'Rourke paused to be sure he had undivided attention and then spoke in a quite measured tone. "For purposes of this review, we took a larger, longer-term look at our finances. We assumed, for example, the possibility of floating a large new bond issue, one large enough not just to finance the Bitech acquisition but also to retire a significant part of our common stock. Despite the present crunch, the market is still hungry for good corporate debt such as ours. For these purposes, we also assumed that the stock market would applaud, and the price of our stock would jump substantially. What then should we do?

"Our conclusion was to reject any such substantial restructuring as an option, much less an obligation. When all was said and done, we realized that some ways of boosting stock prices are simply repugnant to us. That should not have surprised anyone, but it was not something we had ever made explicit. Any corporate executive is familiar with a range of opportunities in employee relations, accounting practices, and other aspects of the business that can be exploited for a while, for the immediate benefit of shareholders. All are legally permissible; still we would reject them.

"High levels of debt are in that class. One reason is that for the long-run, continuing shareholder, we would not be creating real business values if in the process we jeopardized our financial viability or even flexibility. It was that very flexibility that helped convince the Bitech management that we were the buyer of choice. But the issue is more than one of flexibility. We try very hard never to bet the business in product development and marketing. Why do it in finance?

"There is a place for debt, of course, but it's a question of degree. What bankers forgot in recent years—or just ignored —is the enormous volatility inherent in the capitalist system. Ford lost $3 billion at the beginning of the 1980s, but because of its financial reserves, it weathered the storm and was able to achieve a significant turnaround. Were we to borrow anything like the amount of money that lenders here or abroad would happily lend, the continuity and vitality of our business would, *for reasons entirely of our own making,* increasingly depend on events outside our ability to control or even to predict.

"Where to draw the line is not easy. I do know that you should not have to carry the calculation out to two decimal places. This company, like most others in the drug industry, is very profitable at the moment, but competition is a leveling force. Almost all successful companies, even IBM, have tended to regress toward the mean. I doubt that we are exempt.

"Phin and I are aware of the academic argument that a high debt-to-equity ratio works wonders as a restraint on management. It forces them to sell the fancy jets, and it gives them the courage to face up to some of the cutbacks that otherwise would be left for another day.[10] We all need restraint, and the often-heard argument is partly right. But it is more wrong than right. The question is whether to discipline industry by stripping the shock absorbers out of our capital structure. Cash and reserve borrowing power act as a cushion against the inevitable but unpredictable rainy days and help assure the best practicable long-term growth and efficiency. On average, they upgrade morality. Being corporately poor may make you lean, but it's not viable for the longer pull."

One of the directors, C. Newton Pilgrim, senior partner of a Boston investment banking firm, asked what would happen if the company held a plebiscite on the question of a restructuring. He guessed that shareholders would vote overwhelmingly in favor of a major stock buyback financed by new debt, just as they would probably like to see the company the target of a takeover bid.

Pilgrim had raised a good question. While O'Rourke believed he had answers, everyone needed a chance to call his or her office, and he wanted a few minutes to put his thoughts together. They took a break for coffee and the best Danish in town.

On reconvening, O'Rourke was ready to pounce on the issue—and perhaps the director, too. "Newton," he said, "let's put takeovers and defenses against takeovers aside. They raise separate legal issues, which, so far, Middle American has not had to deal with. Someday our company may be up for sale, no matter what, and then the rules will change.[11] But I'm sure you're right that if we polled shareholders about a radical refinancing in order to boost stock prices, 80 percent of the shares would be voted 'yes,' either by the usual run of shareholders or by arbitrageurs drawn to the event.

"What you've done, however, is raise the second of the two issues I wanted to discuss. And that is this: while the shareholders own the company, I reject the recent wisdom that it is the duty of management to maximize the market value of our shares on any given day. Corporation laws leave the issue unanswered, because the issue didn't exist when they were written. Nor does the recent spate of antitakeover statutes provide a coherent response. But there's more to business than maximizing tomorrow's stock price. This is a social institution—one of some importance, I might add, though not different from many others. An institution organized for profit but a social one nonetheless. How could it be otherwise? All of the ethical drugs in this country are produced by private companies, such as ours, in a complex web of trust. There are suppliers with whom we have enduring relationships, talented researchers and other employees, and, not least, customers and doctors who depend on the integrity of our product. Good, fairly priced drugs are the reason we exist. Shareholders have a role in that scheme. They contribute capital, and they are entitled (by dividends and price appreciation) to the profits. They are entitled to monitor management and to intervene, if necessary, to be sure that management is competent and honest. But stock price appreciation is the consequence, the mere reflection, of a successful enterprise, rather than the overriding objective.

"The rhetoric of private property tends to obscure this basic distinction. That self-styled buccaneer, T. Boone Pickens, said that the stockholders own the company; it's theirs, and they can do whatever they want with it.[12] I have a different view. I keep thinking of all the greed factors—what economists call perverse incentives—that undermine the financial integrity of the system. The government, through the tax structure, promotes leverage. Fees for putting together an LBO were often 5 to 6 percent of the total transaction value, payable immediately, and the way to win those fees, the way to emerge victorious from the general melee, was to push debt to the limit. CEOs walked away with $20, $40, $100 million to stay out of the path of 'progress,' whether the new company was sound or not.[13] And of course shareholders also cheered for more leverage because they did not have to live with the consequences. In these and other ways, we tempt people to become individually richer even though their companies and society are left poor.

"I don't think that the Pickens view meets the needs of a complex industrial society.[14] Companies whose income stream is dedicated to paying bondholders, whose senior management is distracted by a fear of financial crisis; whose divisional managers are under pressure to meet short-term goals or else; whose rank and file feel abandoned by the recklessness and self-aggrandizement of top management, are tempted in a myriad of ways to cheat on their primary responsibilities. Our friend Charlie Munger says that we should think of corporate control as a form of financial engineering. Just as we build into a bridge or airplane a series of redundancies to meet extreme stresses, so too should we construct the financial base of a major corporation with enough resilience to withstand the winds loosed from time to time by competition, recessions, oil shocks, and other storms.[15] Inserting more than a moderate amount of leverage is like building a bridge to meet only the expected load, with no margin for error. 'It is a crime in America,' Charlie said, 'to build a weak bridge. How much nobler is it to build a weak company?'

"The stock market is a perverse institution. It may at times be more profitable for shareholders to build a bridge with no (financial) margin of safety, but we think the argument for that, if not the bridge itself, falls of its own weight.

"When Ben Graham said long ago that the stock market is perverse, he meant that an intelligent investor can generally find companies that are selling at significant discounts from their real, business values. Investors, far from being dismayed by the perversity, would find in it both opportunities and ultimate profit.[16] But with occasional exceptions, that perversity did not affect anything except the stock market itself and those who speculated or invested there. Corporate America could, and often did, pay very little attention (at times, of course, too little). I don't for a moment think that Graham, or anyone else in the 1950s, intended that these discrepancies between business values and stock market values be corrected by the sale of companies as a whole, except for mismanagement. For a well-run, socially useful company, the socially appropriate investor action, the one Graham contemplated, was simply to buy up shares and wait the few years that would typically suffice for true value to emerge.[17]

"In the 1980s, however, Pickens, Coniston Partners, and others argued that shareholders are entitled—*and managers are obligated*—to maximize stock values immediately, even by putting the business as social institution at risk. In 1988 Coniston initiated a proxy contest at Gillette designed to force a sale of the business. They had no complaint whatever with the progress of the business, which was excellent.[18] Their dispute was essentially with the stock market, not the company: the company could be sold for more than its then trading price.

"Investment bankers were crisscrossing the country, using buzzwords like *pro-active, preemptive restructurings,* and *management of leverage,* to frighten companies into action before the Coniston lightning struck.[19] In order to maximize shareholder values, they admonished, we need to manage leverage as between good times and bad times, as if we could predict when those would be."[20]

"Charlie," said Sam Slugge, "obviously I agree with almost everything you've said. But why put it on social grounds? It seems to me all you've said is that industry should be managed for the long-, not the short-term, shareholder. Many of the mistakes—the low rate of capital investment, the high leverage—would be corrected if we were less concerned with quarter-to-quarter results."

"No doubt," O'Rourke answered, "that would resolve much of the conflict. What's good for shareholders is usually—no, almost always—a good proxy for what's good for the nation. A lot of tricks that look smart in the short run become just plain dumb if you look further out. Every once in a while, however, an issue arises that goes directly to the core of the business, and still we see that the shareholders' bottom line, no matter how patient, is not bottom enough. The barely aborted takeover of UAL (the parent company of United Airlines) in 1989 would by all accounts have left United Airlines losing money, burdened with debt, at a time when earnings were already slipping and huge capital expenditures were scheduled. This was not the kind of airline the country needs. But even a patient UAL shareholder would have been foolish to turn down $300 a share, *payable in cash*, for a stock that had sold only shortly before for $120.

"Takeovers are something of a special case, of course, but they are not the only one. Sometimes an investment or a new technology may in fact be quite rewarding, but the crystal ball is just too cloudy to justify, with the usual degree of arithmetic assurance, the expenditure of shareholder capital. In effect, the capital drifts off into something more predictable. It was partly on this basis that the United States retreated from consumer electronics, facsimile equipment, and other businesses. Those businesses moved overseas, lock, stock, and barrel, taking with them the R&D and other supports that, without domestic manufacturing applications, are like coaches without a team.[21] From a shareholder point of view, there was probably no realistic cash flow analysis that would have justified ploughing money into public utilities in the inflationary and regulatory climate of the 1970s. Should we have closed down Con Edison? Conversely, we have private hospitals that operate the primary general care facility in cities and towns across the country. Working from a shareholder-entrepreneurial perspective, some of them have shut clinics, turned away patients, and tried to operate on a financial shoestring.[22] A Norwegian friend of mine was shocked at the notion of a (deliberately) leveraged hospital. We all should be.

"I have no off-the-shelf solution; the problem is complex. If we want to keep a Con Ed on stream, with whose money are we to do it? But I am suggesting that a single-minded pursuit of shareholder interests, no matter how long term, leaves something seriously missing from the social equation.[23]

"I also want to be careful using a phrase like *social responsibility*, which suggests peripheral issues, such as divestment in South Africa. Those concerns are genuine, but they are not what Phin and I have in mind when we speak of excessive leverage as being a social or moral dilemma. In this day and age, we shy away from moral imperatives, but that's a mistake. Even economists use the language of morality in this context. When almost all the capital consists of borrowed money, when almost none of the risk but a lion's share of the potential profit belongs to the shareholders, economists call it a moral hazard. What they mean is the risk that shareholders will play fast and loose with other people's money.

"Sometimes, too, social responsibility acts as a catchword for insulating slack managements from the consequences of their ineptness, as if to say that while the company is not very profitable, it does employ lots of nice managers and contributes to the Little League.[24] We don't mean that either, although if the earnings drop off, we'll give it some further thought."

The meeting adjourned, and amid a buzz of conversation, the usual preluncheon sherry was served. Jake Winthrop, the company's corporate counsel, still sat at the table, wondering how to write the minutes. He was mindful that the company might someday be faced with an unsolicited tender offer. The time might come when the company's defense would rest on its insistence that a bidder, despite a premium offer, had failed to maximize shareholder values. With the wisdom handed down from generation to generation at his distinguished firm, Winthrop knew that detailed minutes never help anyone except dissident shareholders and raiders. And that is why those who look for a summary of the remarks by O'Rourke and Nance will find only the following: "There was an extended discussion of current developments in the credit markets. The company's plans for replacing its short-term bank debt are still under review."

Appendix 3A

Following is an edited excerpt of my testimony before the House Ways and Means Committee in May 1989 proposing changes in the tax law to eliminate the tilt toward corporate debt. As I feared at the time, the outcome has been lots of hearings, lots of bills, lots of inertia.

In thinking about how to chill excessive corporate debt, let me suggest several guidelines:

1. The problem is not just an LBO problem, or a takeover poblem, or a junk bond problem. By that I mean that we should be concerned about the loss of corporate financial flexibility and the risk that we will end up socializing the losses, just as we are doing in the banking system, whether or not the debt is incurred to finance an LBO or to restructure. In short, legislation should focus not just on takeover-related debt but on debt generally, not just because the problem is broader but because earlier efforts to legislate on the basis of a borrower's purpose proved to be unworkable. Money is marvelously fungible, and tracing the proceeds of a loan is a mare's nest. It didn't work for Section 279 of the Internal Revenue code [intended to curb takeover-related debt twenty years earlier], and I doubt that it would work here.

2. The double-tax system, by which we tax income at the corporate level and again at the shareholder level, should be retained, with only minor exceptions. The debt dilemma is a function of how we tax business, how we measure corporate income, and can be solved well enough within the present two-tier framework.

3. What is important is to level the playing field between debt and equity so that the corporate tax structure is neutral as between the two. My suggestion is the quite simple idea that the amount of corporate income tax should not be affected by a corporation's capital structure, by whether there is more (or less) debt. *Dividends and interest should be treated alike.* The form of the investment should matter to lenders and shareholders, but not to the Treasury.

There are two basic choices that meet this goal of tax neutrality. First, we could make both dividends and interest payments equally deductible from corporate income. There would, of course, be a loss of corporate tax revenue, if that were the only change. To avoid a loss of revenue, Congress could either increase the tax rate, which I don't suggest, or it could limit both the interest and dividend deduction, for example, to 80 percent of the amount of the payment (or whatever other proportion would be revenue-neutral). This eighty-twenty proposal is sometimes called the hybrid solution. In addition to being revenue-neutral, it would also be essentially neutral as between debt and equity. But not perfectly so. Interest is deductible as it accrues, regardless of when it is in fact paid out, whereas the earnings that accrue on common stock would be deductible only when paid. There would be pressure, therefore, for payouts, which may be a good thing or bad, but the arrangement is not wholly neutral.

The second choice is to make neither interest nor dividends deductible *at all*. Relying on data in a January 1989 study prepared by the staff of the Joint Committee on Taxation, it appears that eliminating the interest deduction would roughly double the amount of taxable corporate income. The tax rate therefore could be cut in half, to about 16 to 18 percent, thus making this proposal also neutral as to the amount of revenue collected. This second proposal may well be more attractive as a conceptual matter. The corporate business would be taxed, but the tax would not be affected by purely financial decisions. The tax would be the same regardless of the choice between debt and equity and regardless of the payout ratio on the common stock.

I regard both proposals as attractive, with a mild preference for the second one. Under that proposal, the corporate income tax would be measured solely by operating income. We would not be able to use debt/equity choices to jiggle the result. In addition, the no-deduction proposal also solves the problem that at present some U.S.-source income escapes taxation here altogether, that is, in those cases where the debt is held by foreign investors. On the other hand, I recognize that the loss of any tax incentive to pay out income would be regarded by some as a disadvantage.

In either case, it would be necessary to phase in the changes over a period of several years. The second choice, in particular, would otherwise prejudice companies that are capital-intensive, such as finance companies and public utilities. Those problems are not insuperable, but they do need to be dealt with. (For utilities, the phase-in period might be stretched out. The finance company problem could be solved by a rule of general application that would tax interest income on a "net" basis, that is, tax it only to the extent that it exceeds interest expense.) A rule would be needed to deal with leases and other debt alternatives. Similarly, we might elect to exempt small companies entirely from the double tax, much as if they had all elected to be taxed as partnerships, as many of them now do.

In conclusion, let me urge you not to fall into the trap of so many other committees that have addressed these issues: lots of hearings, lots of bills, lots of inertia.

4

Leveraged Buyouts

WHAT'S NEXT?

The Basic Materials division of our mythical Middle American was a source of both pride and frustration to the company's CEO, Charles Edward O'Rourke. The division ran almost letter perfect in terms of quality of production, pricing, delivery times, research, and leadership. O'Rourke and Middle American's chief financial officer, Phineas Nance, had just completed a semiannual review with the management of the division, and as usual they had done little more than sit back and listen with respect for the group's thorough knowledge and good judgment.

The frustration was that the division, although it had very cost-effective plants, had never been able to break out of its historic pattern and become more than just a captive supplier to Middle American. Within the company, everyone knew that Basic Materials produced good products at good prices. But there was a chicken-and-egg problem: the group had a very small sales force calling on other potential customers, but since they had very few outside customers, it seemed foolish to spend much on a sales force. The heart of the problem, O'Rourke had long suspected, was that those other customers were loath to buy from a competitor, Middle American, no matter how good the product or the price. It was no different from asking Chrysler to buy radios from General Motors.

Basic Materials had always been profitable, but its potential was not being fulfilled. The risk was that a top-notch management group would begin to disperse, and while O'Rourke would be able to find opportunities for some of them elsewhere in the company, that would be no better than a partial solution. As they talked on the way back to headquarters, Nance told O'Rourke that he would think some more about the problem. He seemed to have something in mind, but as usual he preferred to give O'Rourke the package all at once, not bit by bit. Today was the day for those further discussions.

"Boss," began Nance, "my assumption has been that as long as we own Basic, it will be a good business but not the very good one that it could be. Moreover, for a variety of reasons, this is not a business we would sell to another company. It would be seen as a breach of faith with Basic's management. They have done everything and more that we've asked, and a sale of the division would give the wrong message there and elsewhere in the company. We would also lose some of the special relationship that has been valuable to both Basic and ourselves."

While not aware of the pattern, Nance tended to call O'Rourke "boss" when he thought he would be sledding uphill. And what he was about to suggest would seem at first blush to be in conflict with some principles that O'Rourke (and Nance too) held dear—indeed, some principles on which O'Rourke had expounded at length with the company's board of directors only recently. (See chapter 3.)

"One solution," Nance continued, "might be to sell Basic to a management-led group in a leveraged buyout. LBOs are in disrepute these days and credit is very tight, but the stronger LBO banking firms are still in business. For the right business, and with more emphasis on the buyout and less on the leverage, credit is still available. I think a deal is possible. The question is whether it is desirable.

"An LBO is attractive for both Basic and for us because it solves some problems in a way that nothing else can quite do. The key is that Basic would be an independent enterprise. By contract and otherwise, we could maintain the special relationship, the sharing of research and product development, at least for a period of time. Nothing is forever, and ten years from now, an independent Basic will probably see us as no different from any other customer. But that may not be a loss because if we continue, willy-nilly, down the present path, Basic will not grow and develop as it should and then where will we be? Yes, we might still feel comfortable with each other, but the special quality of the business will probably have been lost. We will end up owning a mediocre business instead of creating a potential star.

"By making Basic a separate company now," Nance went on, "one in which Middle American has no significant equity participation, we can create the credibility it needs to build a sales force and to reach the large potential market that you believe is out there. It's usually sales that drive research, not the other way round, as some people believe. Without a larger market, it would be difficult for Basic to justify R&D expenditures on the scale that is increasingly required. But if we are willing to set Basic free, not just in the United States but abroad as well, and with adequate capital, I think that Williams (the CEO) and the rest of the Basic management people would jump at the opportunity, and my guess is they would make a go of it."

Nance had slipped in the phrase *adequate capital* because he knew full well that O'Rourke was bug-eyed on the subject of LBOs and the junk debt that had proliferated a few years earlier. The press was writing almost daily about companies skirting the edge of Chapter 11 or falling into it, just as the press had been singing the praises of those same companies just a few years before. Nance also knew O'Rourke well enough not to answer every question before O'Rourke had a chance to raise it.

"Listen, Phin," began O'Rourke, somewhat peevishly, "why would I want to do a thing like that? If we sell Basic to the management group at a modest price, we would not be getting full value for it, the price that some established other company might pay. How could the board do that? And if we do get full value, then the LBO investment banks would almost certainly press for more leverage than Williams at Basic could accept. Those LBO guys still have target returns for their clients of 40 percent or so compounded annually, and the only way to get that is either to pay a low price or to leverage the business up to the hilt. Even if Williams did go along, given our continuing dependence on Basic, we would not. It's a trap. Tell me where I'm wrong, but I didn't like LBOs in the eighties, and I don't much now either."

"There are several answers," Nance responded slowly, as he tried to moderate the tone of the discussion. "The first is that you're right—there is no assurance that a sensible deal can be structured. And I certainly don't want to set things in motion and build up expectations, only to see them fizzle. But if we are willing to accept as a price a reasonable multiple of Basic's earnings and free cash flow— not the top dollar from an auction but not a bad price either—the legal obstacles are not all that great. If this were a stand-alone business, the lawyers tell me, it would be difficult to accept anything much below the full market value, but it is a business with which we have extensive ongoing dealings. In a situation like this, the business judgment rule provides for directors an enormous amount of protection, as it should. With the right backup, counsel is optimistic about its ability to give the necessary opinions.

"More to the point, perhaps," Nance went on, "the LBO market is much closer to where it was before the insanity set in. The commercial banks are lending less, as they should, but the interest rates are more reasonable. Once again the banks want to see sufficient free cash flow to retire the bank debt in five years. That would be acceptable to us because it ensures that the buyout is on a firm financial footing. The better LBO investment banks still have substantial pools of equity money. A couple of them even have committed pools of subordinated debt money. If the numbers are right and the business is right, as this one is, bank credit will be there. What's important is that the two companies take an active role in structuring the buyout and not let the investment bankers run the show. This proposal is not your everyday LBO, where the seller cares only about the price.

"There are a lot of question marks," Nance concluded, "and at this point I know of only one other company that has done an LBO of this type. In financial terms, the key is to increase the proportion of equity money, so that we take some of the L-word, leverage, out of the deal. The trick would be to achieve that while still leaving adequate incentives for the LBO investment bank and sufficient cheap stock or options for whomever Williams wants to bring into the group. There are no guarantees, but I think it can be done. The immediate question at the moment is only whether you want me to explore the possibilities further and whether to do so with Williams and Conley (Basic's chief financial officer) as part of the discussion. There's a risk of premature disclosure, but I think it's worth it. If you agree, we'll come back in a month with a feasibility report."

Seeing that he was not being pushed too hard at the moment, O'Rourke's humor improved, and he gave his OK. He also asked Nance to explore an initial public offering or a spin-off of the shares of Basic as an alternative to an LBO. But O'Rourke recognized that much of the potential value of Basic had yet to be realized and that, for a time at least, private ownership might be the way to go.

As a result of the excesses of the 1980s, leveraged buyouts got a deservedly bad name. In some circles, they are being written off as just another phenomenon that has (mercifully) passed into oblivion. That is characteristic of Wall Street: bury your dead and move on. But it overlooks the fact that there had always been LBOs that made sense, particularly in the early years before the market overheated, and that for some problems they still offer a viable and attractive solution. What is needed is to separate the proper use of LBOs from the abuse. One way to begin is by looking briefly at what was one of the great bubbles in American financial history, both for its own sake and as an object lesson. By culling out the chaff, we can then focus on what remains as useful.

THE GREAT LBO BUBBLE

The 1980s were one of those rare periods when we could see, even while it was happening, that the financial markets were rushing, lemminglike, toward a precipice. A number of people, notably Jim Grant of *Grant's Interest Rate Observer*, tried to call attention to the fact that buyouts and takeovers were causing companies to issue tens of billions of dollars of junk debt that they could never hope to repay, short of a miracle. None of the warnings accomplished much. For anyone with an eye to history, in fact anyone who could read a financial statement, the eventual outcome of this sorry episode had been painfully predictable. This was, however, one of the great bubbles in financial history, and it is an inexorable law of finance that no amount of wisdom from the pulpit will arrest a bubble before it has run its course.[1]

An intense mysticism had sprung up around LBOs. Like snake oil or some other nineteenth-century patent medicine—good for gout, arthritis, toothache, and whatever else ails you—this new remedy was being touted as a financial cure-all. LBOs, it was claimed, enable managers to think as owners, and the "power of leverage" would contribute to increased value, especially in mature businesses.[2] Where the boards of directors of public companies have failed, said an article in the *Harvard Business Review*, "sophisticated outside parties [will now fix] an unyielding debt repayment schedule that provides precise and unforgiving targets."[3] Seldom has the gap between sense and nonsense been more palpable—or more dangerous.

The junk bond market collapsed in late 1989 and 1990 with a vengeance—not just for a few companies but across the board. When it broke, the LBO market did too. What broke the bubble? In an immediate sense, it was the bankruptcies of Integrated Resources and the two Campeau groups of stores, Allied and Federated, plus the sudden collapse of the financing for the $300 a share buyout of UAL and the failure of Drexel Burnham Lambert. The public's faith in the ability of bankers to do new deals or even to patch up the old ones was broken. And since a bubble is, in substance, an act of collective faith, that was enough.

When the market broke, it plunged. The higher-quality junk was soon dumped because it at least could still be sold. The poorer-quality stuff was driven into the ground, selling at 10 or 15 cents on the dollar. And with a huge overhang of bonds selling at yields of 20 percent or more, it became impossible to issue new junk bonds. Even for companies for which public financing should perhaps have been available, the market dried up.

In the summer of 1990, after the market had broken, there were $210 billion face value of public-issue junk bonds outstanding. (In addition, according to Salomon Brothers, there was an estimated $150–$200 billion of low-grade debt that had been issued privately to banks, insurance companies, and others.) That was about one-fifth of all corporate bonds. About $190 billion had been rated as junk when first issued—that is, rated BB+ or lower or not rated at all— while the balance consisted of bonds that had been downgraded from investment grade, the so-called fallen angels. (The distinction is subtle, however. Many of the angels had fallen not because of business setbacks but because they were victims of the very takeovers and restructurings that were producing most other junk bonds.) Most of the debt was takeover-related, so that the market's treatment of junk tells us a good deal about the outcome of the underlying mergers and buyouts. According to Salomon Brothers, over 75 percent of all these bond issues were selling at distress prices; at current market prices they would yield 20 percent or more to maturity, or they were already in default. Many of them did not trade at all. And all this had happened in the first half of 1990, before the general business downturn.

In 1934 Graham and Dodd had explained that when speculative-grade bonds break, they are likely to sink like a stone because they will then be shunned by a large portion of the investment community.[4] This is precisely what took place.

DEALS, DEALS, DEALS

During the 1980s, we bought and sold much of American industry— about $1.4 trillion worth, or the equivalent of two-thirds of the average value during that time of all publicly traded stocks.[5] Some businesses were not sold even once, but others, such as Playtex, Budget Rent-A-Car, and Dr. Pepper, were sold several times over.

Some of these takeovers made good sense, particularly the divi-

sional buyouts in which the managers of a subsidiary of a large conglomerate bought their freedom, so to speak. Although these
buyouts were only a small piece—less than 5 percent in dollar
value—of the picture, there were other success stories too.[6] But as
almost anyone in the investment banking business was ready to say,
along with the good deals (usually the ones they were doing) there
were lots of bad ones. Some studies were run during the 1980s, but
the meaning of them was ambiguous. Companies that had gone private were showing higher operating profits (before interest charges)
in the short run, but at the same time they were generally reinvesting
less in new plant and equipment.[7] What did it all mean for the long
run? There was no way to know.

While it may have been difficult for economists to see whether
LBOs and other takeovers were improving or hurting the long-run
efficiency of American industry, anyone looking at the more purely
financial aspects would have been alarmed. Financial accounting is
like the thermometer of business. It doesn't give a complete diagno-
sis, but it does tell us a good deal about the general well-being of the
patient. The finance thermometer told us that the merger-takeover
patient was running a fever. The prices being paid for companies
were so high that the buyer was frequently losing money from the
beginning.

The buyers eventually paid absurd prices. In earlier merger waves,
a bidder might pay a premium of 20 percent or so over market for a
target company, but in the contested takeovers of the 1980s, the
premiums consistently averaged 80 percent. In some of the largest
acquisitions, such as RJR Nabisco and Kraft, the premiums were almost 100 percent. A study by a knowledgeable analyst of all acquisitions of $500 million or more by American corporations during the
1980s showed that while the mean prices (including assumed debt)
paid in 1980 were a reasonable 8.5 times the acquired company's
earnings before interest and taxes (EBIT), by 1985 they had risen to
a quite unreasonable 13.2 times EBIT, and by 1989 they had risen to
a perfectly absurd 16.6 times. And remember: this was 16 times
earnings in a peak period, not at the bottom of the business cycle.

A premium of 80 percent has far-flung implications. Take a "simple" company, worth a billion dollars or so, and in no time at all you
had "created" $800 million of additional wealth. The theoretical im-
plications of those high premiums may have puzzled scholars, but
the practical implications were crystal clear to bankers and lawyers.
Wall Street, working around the clock to mine new deals, had be-

come a real-life El Dorado, paved with stretch limousines. If deals could be made at 80 percent premiums, those who assisted the process, including the target-company CEOs who obliged by getting out of the way, would be able to take more gold out of the enterprise, with more finely tuned excuses, than had ever been dreamed of by a Spanish conquistador. Fees totaling 6 percent of the deal became commonplace—not just for small deals but for large ones; there was no discount for volume. With, say, $12 billion of new "value" created out of an RJR Nabisco that a few weeks before had been worth only $13 billion, it was not long before the fees exceeded $1.5 billion. And no one cared about the level of fees because everyone at the conference table was getting their share. The fees were coming out of new-found wealth—out of the "deal," whatever that meant.

The pressure for results, for fees, was enormous. One young banker at First Boston commented that it was "like driving a car at 100 miles per hour with a blindfold on." Retaining some vestiges of prudence, he found that his bids were not high enough to win the bidding. But with fewer fees to show for his efforts, his stock within the firm was soon sinking.[8]

THE FUNNY MONEY SYNDROME

At some point in each merger boom, two things happen. The first is that a number of apologists insist that everything is fine—the market is working its inevitable magic, even if it's not visible—and we should relax and enjoy the ride. The second is the invention of funny money. As prices escalate and buyers begin to pay thirteen to sixteen times EBIT for a company, there isn't enough "serious" money—cash or investment-grade securities—to keep the game going. The newly acquired business is producing a 6 to $7^{1}/_{2}$ percent return, plus whatever improvements can be generated, while the money invested in it may cost as much as twice that, or more.

The funny money syndrome is inescapable. In the 1960s it was common stock in one form or another. Conglomerate corporations, such as Gulf & Western, were the darlings of Wall Street, and their stocks were selling at inflated prices. Using their high-priced stocks as currency, Gulf & Western, ITT, and other conglomerates could pay $800 for an ordinary cat by selling, in effect, a $900 dog. In the 1920s, Samuel Insull and others had used pyramided holding companies to accomplish the same thing.

For the empire builders of the 1980s, people like Campeau, William Farley, Frank Lorenzo, and Kohlberg Kravis & Roberts, Wall Street created an updated version of funny money, the junk bond. Over $200 billion of these low-grade bonds were issued. And since banks also lent aggressively to the same borrowers, the aggregate LBO-type debt was about $350 billion to $400 billion.

There is an inexorable logic in the creation of funny money. An LBO company cannot seriously promise to pay $1.40 of interest for each dollar of available income without resorting to smoke and mirrors. To solve the cash shortfall, the bankers ingeniously created some wholly new securities: zero-coupon, discount, pay-in-kind, and reset debentures. The nomenclature is confusing—my preferred term is *superjunk*—but the underlying concept is simple enough. The issuers, whether they were Ann Taylor, Fort Howard, or Turner Broadcasting, had assumed so much more debt than they could service that they needed an immediate moratorium on part of the interest payments. Fort Howard, for example, issued zero-coupon debentures that carried an interest rate of 14⅛ percent a year. The company made all the usual entries on its books. But until 1994 the coupons on the debentures all said "zero." *Fort Howard kept the cash.*

Zero-coupon bonds were symptomatic of how far we had strained the usual bounds of prudence. Were there not enough earnings or even cash flow to pay the interest? Zero-coupons neatly dodged the problem. You simply could not default on a zero obligation.

Zero-coupons are a modern-day version of the old U.S. savings bond, which, bought for, say, $18.75, would pay no interest but would turn into $25 a few years later. They first appeared in commercial life as a form of U.S. Treasury bond and served several useful purposes. As Treasury bonds they were appropriate because there was no question about the government's ability to pay. Under the pressure to bid ever higher prices for takeover targets, however, investment bankers adapted the zero-coupon to loans that stood at the *bottom* of the credit heap instead of the top.

The essentially similar pay-in-kind debentures also paid no cash currently. Instead of being issued at a deep discount from par, they were sold at or near par, but the company had the privilege, invariably exercised, of paying the interest by issuing new bonds of the same class. These pay-in-kind bonds typically carried very high interest rates. If the interest was not payable currently, the rate did not seem to matter.

The ultimate piece of superjunk was the reset bond or note. Companies, including Chicago and North Western, Western Union and RJR Nabisco, issued in all about $16 billion of reset notes. The Western Union senior secured notes, for example, issued in 1987, carried an interest coupon of $16\frac{1}{2}$ percent. To reassure the bondholders that all would be well no matter what, the company agreed that in June 1989 it would, if necessary, increase or "reset" the interest rate so that the notes would once again sell at or above par. With the company's business deteriorating, the notes were soon selling at a large discount, raising the interesting question of how much higher the interest rate would have to go for the noteholders to be made whole—or, to put it differently, if the earnings were insufficient to pay $16\frac{1}{2}$ percent, how much help could the bondholders receive from a "promise" to pay a bigger share of an already denuded larder?[9] The answer was that the coupon was reset at $19\frac{1}{4}$ percent, but the notes were soon again trading at a deep discount.

At this point the obvious question is, Who bought this junk? The answer, surprisingly enough, was that over 90 percent of all junk bonds were bought by institutional investors, primarily mutual funds and insurance companies—not the small investor. A person investing his or her own money would never have bought a Fort Howard zero-coupon bond because it paid no interest for five years and was so junior a security that it earned none. Worse, the federal government would tax you as if you had received the money. In short, it would have meant buying a bond that paid no interest and in substance earned none but was taxed as if it did both. At the end of five years, you would have paid out an extra 35 cents or so in taxes for each dollar originally invested, with not a nickel in return. You don't have to work on Wall Street to know the difference between paying and receiving.

The junk bond business was driven by the appearance of earnings rather than the substance. Mutual funds were one of the hottest part of the junk bond market, accounting for about 30 percent of the total. What sold these so-called high-yield mutual funds was the bonds' advertised yield. And as in other periods of excess, such as the 1960s, accountants and the SEC were letting operators hide behind last year's rules—adequate for the period for which they were written— to conceal this year's tricks.

The accounting problem grew out of the fact that until the 1980s, an investor in a bond fund could safely assume that the bonds in the portfolio represented securities that were senior to some significant shareholder net worth. For many junk bonds, however, the equity existed in name only. To understand what then happened, assume that you owned all of Fort Howard, with no debt at all. You would have been earning almost $262 million a year before taxes and amortization of goodwill. That's not bad, but it was all you earned. But when the new LBO company promised to pay interest at the rate of $469 million a year, the accountants allowed mutual funds and other institutional investors to tell the world that they were earning *from Fort Howard 79 percent more than Fort Howard itself was earning.* A dollar there was turned into almost two dollars here.

Worse, junk bonds were typically at the bottom of the credit heap, subordinated to the prior claims of banks and other senior lenders. If an issuer had, say, 70 cents to cover a dollar's worth of interest, the average coverage for all of the debt was deceptive. It was only the more senior debt that was covered. No income at all was left to pay interest on the newly issued junk bonds. The so-called interest was, in substance, a payment not out of corporate income but out of bondholders' capital.

Speculative bonds were not really new. Almost nothing in finance is new. Graham and Dodd used an analysis much like this in the original edition of *Security Analysis* in 1934. If Fort Howard had earnings of $262 million and if the senior lenders had claims that equaled or exceeded that amount, then what the junior bondholders as a group had bought was in substance a common stock—or perhaps only a warrant to buy stock. As common stock, there would have been little confusion about the lack of earnings. (Common stock would, in fact, have been the superior security because the investors would have had voting control and would also have owned the claim to all the earnings in excess of $262 million, not just the next slice of it.) But when a clearly paupered common stock was dressed up to look like a princely bond, there was an opportunity for deception. You could put a 12 percent coupon on that bond. You could put a 14^{1}/8 percent coupon on it, as Fort Howard did. But if there were no earnings for that bond, the more likely it was that investors would be misled by the form of the instrument.

There were high-yield mutual funds reporting to their investors that they were earning an attractive 13 percent or so. Reading the sales literature, one saw a list of fine old companies and a message that almost insisted that prudent investors could capture these unusually high returns with low risk. Consider the following statement in a report—no worse than those issued by many others—issued by the T. Rowe Price High Yield fund, which focused on the income earned by its portfolio companies while studiously ignoring their massive debts: "We continue to focus on stable, well-managed businesses with strong cash flows. . . . We have favored categories which tend to be recession resistant, such as Hotels & Gaming and Entertainment & Leisure."[10] The fund seemed to be saying, Sit back and enjoy it; casinos are somehow bulletproof. In fact, by the end of 1990, of the total junk debt issued by casino companies and rated by Moody's, 46 percent was in default.[11]

THE STRENGTHS OF LBOs

Just as it was junk debt that drove the market for LBOs up in the 1980s, it was the collapse of junk at the end of the decade that virtually closed it down. In a sense, that is an event to be profoundly applauded because it reopens the possibility of allowing rational buyers once again to do buyouts at rational prices. At twenty times net earnings, LBOs were nonsense. At six to eight times earnings, depending on the business, we can once again think about why or when an LBO makes sense.

There's nothing intrinsically wrong with LBOs. (In fact, there's rarely anything intrinsically good or bad about any financial technique, and this one can be quite useful.) One company that successfully used an internalized LBO, or leveraged recapitalization as they are called, was FMC Corporation. Assuming that a good management group is already in place, the only significant difference between the usual LBO and a leveraged recapitalization is that the latter does not force out the public shareholders and is therefore inherently fairer.

FMC owned several quite diverse businesses—industrial and other chemicals, defense systems, machinery and equipment, and precious metals. In 1986, fearing a potential raider, it underwent a financial restructuring. The company borrowed $1.8 billion, which it used to pay an $80-a-share dividend, taxable at capital gains rates. The transaction had various elements, but when the dust had settled, total debt had risen to $2.2 billion, shareholders' net worth had dropped to a *negative* $591 million, and the employees of FMC had increased their ownership of the company to 35 percent. Public investors continued to hold the rest.

Four years later, it was clear that the recapitalization had succeeded. The company's operating earnings before interest charges had grown modestly. Capital expenditures had been slashed, though never below the $125 million level necessary to maintain existing facilities, and by 1989 they had been restored to earlier levels. More tellingly, by 1990 FMC's total debt had been reduced by about $700 million, and the company's future was no longer in doubt.

There were several reasons for this success. One was a management that got consistently rave notices from financial analysts. Another was the generally strong economy. Despite FMC's huge borrowings, EBIT never fell below 1.4 times the company's interest charges—hardly a great coverage ratio but far better than the average junk-bonded company of the period. The company did not have to conduct a fire sale of assets, but it did enjoy some one-time gains, totaling almost $400 million (net of marginal taxes), from liquidating an overfunded pension plan and selling a minority interest in the gold mining subsidiary.

The critical plus factor, however, according to William H. Schumann III, the treasurer, was the diversified nature of the company's operations. In the aggregate, earnings continued to meet the 1986 projections, but the defense and machinery businesses underperformed, and gold did better than expected. If the company had been solely in defense, for example, the outcome would have been very different.

The most appealing LBOs, however, are the divisional buyouts rather than those of whole companies. Divisional LBOs come about for a variety of reasons, most often because the parent company has decided that a division no longer fits. Sometimes the fit is truly poor, suggesting that the business should not have been acquired in the first place. At other times *fit* is merely a euphemism for the fact that the parent company needs money, or for its belief that the division's prospects are poor and this is the time to bail out.

Opportunities for the local management to buy out their subsidiary or division often arise as a new CEO is installed at the parent company. Eager to clear the decks of a predecessor's mistakes, he or she looks to sell off the dullards or anything else that no longer fits with his or her own, new "strategic plan." The new broom is often eager to sweep clean, and price may not much matter. After all, they were someone else's mistakes. Bargain prices become a real possibility. The central-office management may not know a division's business very well because it is so small a part of the overall picture or perhaps because it was not meeting the targets set for it and the corporate management has lost interest. Knowing so little, the parent company may even have starved it for capital, thus depreciating it further. Now being eager to divest, the parent company may accept a modest offer, encouraged by the tax write-off that can compensate for as much as 40 percent of any losses.

O. M. Scott, the lawn-care company, was a division of ITT until the Scott managers, together with the buyout sponsors, Clayton & Dubilier, bought the business in December 1986. Sales and operating income leaped ahead, reflecting a reorganization and decentralization of decision making, increased capital spending, a strong incentive compensation plan, and monitoring by the sponsors, plus a carefully selected group of outside directors. As Martin Dubilier would later say, where ITT challenged managers to make budget and not to rock the boat, the new owners saw their challenge as trying to improve the business.[12]

A buyout may speed the process of changing managements or at least the management culture, just as attentive therapy helps psychiatric patients. As happened at O. M. Scott, it is particularly helpful at the divisional level of a conglomerate, where the local managers might use it as a device for freeing themselves from the dead hand of corporate headquarters. Where, too often, a publicly owned company has neither owners, directors, nor bankers who are willing to dig in and play a constructive role, an LBO might have all three. It is this aspect, rather than an aggressive debt-to-equity ratio, that makes a divisional buyout potentially so attractive.

The Scott business was a stand-alone business, and ITT probably looked at divestiture as little more than a financial transaction. Contrast the buyout by an LBO banking firm of the so-called information products business of IBM in the spring of 1991. The products, principally typewriters, printers, and keyboards, had been sold by the same IBM sales force that sold, and paid more attention to, computer systems. The decision to sell the information products business, whose sales were about $2 billion annually, reflected a number of considerations, among them the expectation that with an independent sales force and management group, the new company, Lexmark, would be able to wring more value out of the line. What was new and different about the buyout was that even after the closing, the two companies would cooperate closely for years to come. They would be developing and selling products that would for a time bear the same name, IBM, on the outside and integrated technology on the inside. From the consumer's point of view, these products would constitute integral parts of a single system. Apart from loan agreements, seventy contracts in all would survive the closing, dealing with such problems as the exchange of information and patents, supply, transitional arrangements, and ongoing product development. From initial handshake on the buyout to the closing, the transaction took a year, twice the usual period. The price was slightly over $1.7 billion.

The time when LBO firms could stitch together deals with no ready dollars of their own is probably over. In the 1990s only LBO bankers with established pools of money, those who can supply at least the equity portion of the purchase price (and preferably at least part of the mezzanine as well) from already committed resources, will be able to fulfill their promises. But it would not be surprising if this IBM transaction were the forerunner of others like it.

Still, some cautionary notes are in order. Let's sound a few.

LBOs: TURNING BAD MANAGERS INTO GOOD?

LBOs can still be done, but it's important to think about what they can do well and what they cannot. It is still sometimes said, for example, that LBOs are a broad-spectrum antibiotic for what ails American industry. Corporate managements, the argument goes, are in need of much greater external discipline than the board of a public company can usually provide, and an LBO meets that need.

This is a superficially appealing thesis, but it is remarkably incomplete. It assumes that the problem with American industry is almost entirely managerial. Twenty or so years ago, American business was the envy of the rest of the world, and since then the process by which managers move into the executive suite has not changed much. Which is the group that has done so much better? Surely not the run of commercial or investment bankers, to whom so much power passes under an LBO regime. It would be hard to find any group with as successful a record of finding a range of holes down which to stuff money as commercial bankers. They have squandered money in loans to Third World countries, speculative oil drilling operations, real estate, and, most recently, takeovers. Eager to grow, willing to accept brokered money at devilishly high interest rates, they were then "forced" to find high-rate places to put that money. Always willing to match the competition, no matter how reckless, commercial banks are hardly the paradigm of discipline. Investment banks have been no better. There are exceptions, but of those that existed just a few years ago, most have disappeared, and many of the survivors have needed massive infusions of capital.

LBOs AS A LONG-TERM FIX

LBOs have been advertised as a good fix for the admittedly short-term focus of the stock market. In an LBO, the top management receives large financial incentives, and it is monitored by a board that usually has experience and, just as important, itself has a large stake in the company. But to say that an LBO management will be more responsive to the interests of its shareholders begs the question, What are those interests?

LBOs have tended to be at best a short-term fix. The various banks that put together LBOs are very transaction- and finance-oriented. They are not at all like the German merchant banks that never sell. They are not at all like J. P. Morgan, the Doctor of Wall Street, who time and again put his own resources on the line to rescue banks, railroads, and even the credit of the U.S. government. Morgan was hardly averse to a profit, and he adored power, but he saw himself as a long-term builder of companies, like U.S. Steel, and he never doubted that with power came commensurate responsibility.

In the 1870s, for example, the Morgans and a Baltimore financial house came to the rescue of the Baltimore & Ohio, a railroad with which they had worked closely for years, supplying not only most of the railroad's banking needs but also a good deal of advice.[13] When the B&O now found itself overextended, the bankers placed some bonds with customers, but eventually they bought the major part of a new issue for their own accounts, *knowing that the railroad's immediate prospects were poor.* It was a decade before all the bonds could be resold. For a variety of reasons, this kind of intimate, relationship lending, based on reciprocity of trust and obligation, has almost entirely disappeared in the U.S. Kohlberg Kravis & Roberts recently invested in RJR Nabisco an additional $1.7 billion from their clients' pool of funds in order to help that company through a difficult period, but it was an exception that (even for Kohlberg Kravis) proves the rule. Ironically, it was Morgan Stanley, the successor to J. P. Morgan, that invested $46 million in 1987 to buy control of Burlington Industries in a highly leveraged LBO. As Burlington stumbled, Morgan Stanley took out fees and dividends totaling $176 million. In 1990, with the company now reporting significantly larger losses, Morgan Stanley turned in its voting common stock, taking a senior, more protected position.[14]

LBO banks have a horizon of five years or so, often less, and then they want out. A senior partner at one of the major LBO firms, when asked why they were not content to own a good business, one they already knew, rather than selling it off and looking for another, forthrightly answered, "That's not the banking business." What he meant is the perceived need for a so-called exit strategy that will enable the LBO firm to liquidate its clients' investment in fairly short order. Indirectly he meant the fee structure of the investment banking business, which is transaction driven. Commercial bankers, hungry for the chimera of immediately visible earnings of their own are not very different. Much of the attraction of LBOs was the banks' ability to report some of the large closing fees as earnings today rather than as income over the life of the loan.

The corporate executives who will be on the firing line in an LBO are in this respect not much different. They typically share in a rich pool of stock incentives, but what happens after the contractual handcuffs expire and, assuming all has gone well, they are millionaires? What can the company do for them as an encore? It's the same problem we saw in the so-called earnout deals of the 1960s, when conglomerates bought smaller companies on terms that required the selling shareholders to earn out large contingent payments over five years or so. If they succeeded, well, fine, but it was impossible to give them the same lucrative incentives over and over again, and anyway many of them would then be rich enough not to be interested any longer in working a sixty-hour week.

Studies have been run about whether LBOs improve productivity, but they are inconclusive. LBOs sometimes produce some good financial results in the short run, but when the message is clear and pressing, almost anyone can do that by cutting expenses, reducing capital expenditures, trimming pension costs, and rearranging some accounting practices—for a while. Macy, for one, added about $40 million to its 1989 earnings by changing some assumptions and accounting rules. After an LBO, companies generally cut back on capital expenditures. Is it fair to assume that the cuts were sensible efforts to reduce waste, as LBO enthusiasts argued?[15] Or given the fact that FMC and Macy, say, already had good managements, is there reason to believe that we were seeing a stop-and-go pattern of expenditures, which, longer term, is a hindrance, not a help?

Too many transactions spoil the broth. (Many economists, believing that transactions are inherently beneficial, would disagree with the statement that there can be such a thing as too many transactions.) It's important not to make a virtue of stagnation, but there *is* virtue in a sense of stability—not just for the managers and investors on whom the LBO fans have focused so much attention but for the customers who depend on continuity for parts and upgrades, for suppliers called upon to invest in the company's future products, and, of course, for employees. These relationships are subtle and complex and cannot be measured. Contracts rarely capture them, and they fall through the spreadsheets prepared by bankers and the empirical tests run by economists. (As has been said, it's better to be roughly right than precisely wrong.[16]) But for a well-run business, they are enduring, and in the long run they are the source of much corporate wealth.

An LBO management group should be alert to these concerns at the outset, when the buyout and the financing are still being structured. Depending on the size of the business, management is unlikely to emerge from an LBO owning more than 10 or 12 percent of the stock, so control will be in the hands of bankers of one type or another. While the LBO is being negotiated, the bankers may talk about patient, long-term investing, but their definition is not the same as management's. Once the transaction closes, bankers are subject to very different sorts of pressures and constraints, particularly if the projections are not met. It is not possible, of course, to get a commitment for additional capital beforehand. Even on the assumption that the business will do well, however, the management group should be very concerned that it will someday be forced into an inappropriate exit strategy. Ideally, management would like assurances that control of the company will not change hands without their approval, except by a public offering. But the market for new issues is often weak, and LBO bankers are unlikely to give up the opportunity to cash out their investment. For management, therefore, while the resale of their company may be quite profitable, the dream of continuing independence may be short-lived. At the least, they should be able to negotiate with the LBO bank, *as part of the initial buyout,* for a choice of buyers on the list of candidates or a right of first refusal. Anything beyond that will depend on their ability to exercise a more than ordinary amount of bargaining power.

QUALITY IS LIQUIDITY

Some amount of debt in an LBO is inevitable. But how much? The amount depends on the industry, the competitive pressures, the discretionary cash flow of the business, and other factors. There is no generic answer. It was easy to see that the LBOs of a few years ago violated all norms of prudence, but it is not easy to say where the boundary of prudence lies.

In the right circumstances, a moderate amount of debt enables investors to take advantage of a stable earnings stream to maximize returns. If a business can earn a steady 15 percent on total capital before interest and taxes—a very big "if"—it will produce for its owners an arguably acceptable, but hardly outstanding, after-tax return of about 10 percent if there is no debt at all. If, on the other hand, the owners elect to raise 50 percent of the capital by borrowing at an interest rate of, say, 9 percent, the return on shareholders' equity will be a far better 14 percent.

Unfortunately, the LBO banker will probably try to keep the equity investment by its clients to a minimum so as to achieve far greater rates of return. Those should not be management's priorities, however. In these as in other matters, the suggestion is that management should rely primarily on its own judgment and not allow the banker to fashion the deal singlehandedly. True, the market might accept additional leverage, but that is not a sufficient test.

An LBO strangled by interest charges leaves management no room to respond to a changing and unpredictable environment. Who thought that the Russians would turn from grizzly bears to teddy bears, thus hurting the defense business (Tracor)? Who thought that the Iraqis would drive up the price of jet fuel and discourage foreign travel (TWA)? Who thought that gas stations would decide to compete with 7-Eleven's convenience stores (Southland)?

The liquidity that matters is not the liquidity of the financial markets, about which there has been so much public discussion in recent years. For corporate managers, market or trading liquidity is secondary to corporate or financial liquidity, meaning the ability to raise new money when needed. It's the strength of a company's balance sheet and income statement that counts. *Quality is liquidity*, meaning that for good companies, A-rated or even better, the window is almost always open, no matter what the market. The money will be there.

In circles where markets and their presumed discipline command so much respect, this belief that one should not borrow all that markets are willing to lend will seem curious. It grows out of a profound preference for a defensive posture and a margin of safety. It is also realistic. In a world of securitized markets, where there are few relationships that remotely resemble that of the elder Morgan, companies have almost no choice but to rely on their own inherent strengths as the source of financial liquidity. Markets have no loyalty.[17] Bankers? At best, the record is spotty.

This often means that the LBO management should have due regard for its balance sheet, and not just for the earnings statement and cash flow projections. The usual emphasis in an LBO is on the ability of the business to generate sufficient earnings and cash flow to cover interest charges and other disbursements. While earning power is important, there is much to be said on behalf of adequate capital, as measured by the balance sheet. Capital is something that is already in hand, it is less subject to optimistic inflation than earnings estimates, and it is less vulnerable to rapid and radical change.

Does that mean that LBO debt of less than investment grade should never be issued? "Never" is a long time, and while the division's executive group wants to be prudent, it also wants very much to come to closure and to escape from the bondage of its conglomerate parent. One is reminded of Ben Graham's counsel in such matters, which was Phoebus Apollo's three words of advice to his son: *Medius tutissimus ibis* ("You will go safest in the middle course").[18] Graham's principle, intended primarily for investors, holds true also in corporate finance. In fact Graham was quite explicit about the fact that the appropriate amount of debt that a "company can safely borrow . . . is no more and very little less than investors may safely lend to it."[19] The buyout of IBM's information products business was structured with 28 percent equity, not up to Graham's standards but still a considerable improvement over the 10 percent equity-to–total capital ratio that was common in the second half of the 1980s. For the management group, perhaps the best way to leave the matter is to suggest that they know their own business better than the spreadsheet crunchers at the LBO bank. The burden of proof should be on those who are arguing for more debt.

THE OFTEN SECRET INGREDIENT IN A WHOLE-COMPANY BUYOUT: FRAUD

Divisional buyouts can be very attractive. Now that hostile bids have fallen off dramatically, however, it will be the rare case that a whole company, not just a segment of it, should consider a leveraged buyout in order to go private. Some arguments have been made on behalf of these whole-company buyouts. They offer, it is said, new and better compensation incentives for management and a cure for a too-low stock price. The arguments are not convincing. With executive compensation in the United States already at levels far, far above those elsewhere, it is difficult to see why that is the problem. As for depressed stock prices, patience and perhaps a stock repurchase program are a better cure. Stock prices correct themselves over time.

What is disturbing about a whole-company buyout are the profound conflicts of interest. In a divisional buyout, the parent company management is on one side of the table, able to protect its shareholders from overreaching by the buyer of the division being sold. Not so when a whole company goes private. At a time and a price of its choosing, armed with information that it alone possesses, management decides to buy the company from the very shareholders for whom it has ostensibly been working. Management names its own price. The shareholders are left to the tender care of outside directors, most of whom have usually been selected by management and who may receive special fees—awarded by management, of course—for the extra "work" entailed. Sometimes the outside directors acquit themselves extremely well, as happened at RJR Nabisco. Often, however, management is able to tilt the process in its favor, even if there is an auction and certainly if there is not.

For a management intent on an LBO and ready to short-change the shareholders, the preparations might include such tactics as these: speed up expenditures on advertising and repairs so as to reduce reported earnings, discourage security analysts for a while so that they stop recommending the stock, refuse to raise the dividend, jiggle the accounting a bit, and, then, after taking a few other such "creative" measures to depress the price of the stock, announce a bid that offers a premium over "fair" market value. After that, purchase from any of a number of cooperative bankers an "expert" opinion or two for which the fee will be much larger if management's bid wins. It's done all the time.[20] If the buyout goes ahead, the senior executives will probably take more money out of the old company than they reinvest in the new one. No risk there. And if perchance the bid fails, then, to be sure that management will not be out of pocket, they may, as happened at UAL (the parent company of United Airlines), allow the company to reimburse them for their expenses.[21]

CONCLUSION

Despite the criticisms of LBOs and the now-greater difficulty of financing them, there is still a good deal to be said for private ownership and the ability to manage a business for its own rewards rather than with what is often an obsessive eye for the stock market. The value of a business is the present value of its future income stream, large or small, sooner or later, certain or uncertain. Soundly financed long-term private ownership offers freedom from the distractions that beset publicly owned companies. It may also supply the support and oversight that is often missing from the board of directors of a public company. That is particularly true of a divisional buyout, which may liberate a management that has been hampered by the disinterest of a conglomerate management or by a shortage of capital.

The next advance would be to encourage LBO banking firms to see themselves more as owners of companies rather than as jobbers who hold the "merchandise" for a few years, spruce it up, and then peddle it—a change of attitude not yet visible.

5

Financial Accounting

DON'T LEAVE HOME WITHOUT IT

It was Wednesday morning, and Charles E. O'Rourke, the chairman and CEO of Middle American, our drug company, was reading the annual report of another drug company. Wednesday mornings were a prized interlude for him. The natural culmination of many a review or decisional process in the company was to obtain the blessings of the boss, to shine in the spotlight if he approved, and to displace some of the responsibility if things later went wrong—commonplace functions for a CEO. O'Rourke recognized that he contributed not just by the specific decisions he helped to shape but, more intangibly, by how he coped with pressure and by the standards he set. Still, he also knew that if he were not careful, he could easily attend a half-dozen meetings a day, participating actively in this decision, blessing that one, and at times playing only a limited, ceremonial role. No time would be left for stepping back from day-to-day responsibilities to read something other than internal memoranda and reflect about whatever he cared to reflect on.

O'Rourke's solution was to guard jealously Wednesday mornings as an unscheduled period. He liked to call it "my time," and he believed that he earned his keep best during those few hours.

SuperRx, the company O'Rourke was studying, was a pharmaceutical drug manufacturer that a few years earlier had acquired a specialty chemical company, Finchem, which had a historically excellent market share in a variety of products. While SuperRx had also paid an "excellent," that is, very high, price for the acquisition, its management claimed that there would be considerable savings in production and administrative costs, as well as other synergies.

92

O'Rourke was skeptical. Had SuperRx, never in the top tier of drug companies, done anything very good for its shareholders by going so far afield and by issuing so much stock to buy Finchem? He had asked Phineas Nance, Middle American's chief financial officer, to take a look, and Nance, who had just entered the room, was now ready. Listening to Nance make some company's financial statements talk, hearing him extract from the cold numbers a lively story, was not a bad way to spend a Wednesday morning.

"As a result of the merger three years ago," Nance began, "we have only a consolidated, unitary report for two quite different operations, drugs and chemicals. Except for the limited information provided by the line-of-business reporting, we no longer get a detailed look at either one of them. But even so, we can learn a lot. Measured as a return on shareholders' equity, the company's overall profitability was 18 percent before the merger and since then has slipped moderately to 16 percent, which is still not bad. At the divisional level, however, there are some troublesome signs, particularly in chemicals."

Working solely from the publicly available data, Nance proceeded to paint a picture of two stagnating businesses. Finchem's operating income was about what it had been when it was acquired by SuperRx, but the assets and capital committed to it were much greater than before. Finchem had added several new products plus the plants to produce them, but the new capacity was not being fully utilized. Although the division's sales had risen and its overall income was being maintained, profit margins were slipping. The division's return on total assets had declined. Turning to the drug business, Nance said that for different reasons, it, too, seemed to be making little progress. Research and development expense continued at a high level, but for several years there had been no major new products. Unlike the new chemical division plants, which are carried as assets, the investment in drug research is charged to each year's earnings and not capitalized. The drug division's balance sheet therefore did not show the same degree of underperforming assets as did Finchem, but the substance was the same: large, new investments and not much to show for them.

SuperRx seemed, according to Nance, to be one of those companies with a business—in this case, two businesses—that are doing reasonably well by the usual yardsticks but are living largely off the successes of earlier years without being able to replenish them. He believed the merger had hurt the quality of earnings from the drug business. "The financial statements make it quite clear," he said, "that the new chemical business is much more capital intensive than drugs and also more cyclical."

Quality of earnings is a concept that Nance and O'Rourke used a great deal. For them, it was the true bottom line, and while their analysis would vary with the company, the underlying concept was crystal clear. In their financial lexicon, quality of earnings refers to the ability of an enterprise to create substantial returns on capital and excess cash flows over a sustained period on the basis of conservative and consistent financial reporting. Sometimes called free or available cash flow, these excess cash flows are the cash flows (net earnings plus depreciation and other noncash charges) left after taxes and after making whatever capital expenditures or other investments are necessary to maintain the competitive position of the existing business. (In an inflationary environment, for example, almost any business will have to put more dollars into inventory and accounts receivable simply to sell the same number of units as the year before. See the discussion of Federated Department Stores in chapter 2.) Beyond that, quality of earnings refers to the stability of earnings, whether they are highly cyclical, as is certainly true of many chemical products, and whether a company has some distinctive geographic or brand-name identity that enables it to compete on a basis other than mere price. Businesses with a unique proprietary position—*The Wall Street Journal*, Marlboro cigarettes, the American Express Traveler's Check, or more prosaically the established, low-cost producer of a specialty product—have enjoyed a high quality of earnings. Their success is likely to continue, and the cash flow they generate beyond their immediate needs provides the financial muscle to innovate, expand, seize market share, or simply pay dividends. On the other hand, companies that compete primarily on price without any built-in cost advantage, as most must do, usually work on razor-thin margins, and by definition the quality of whatever earnings they do generate is likely to be poor to middling.

"As a result of the merger, it was difficult to trace the quality of earnings, division by division, year by year," Nance noted. "Looking at several years as a whole, however, I think that the still substantial free cash flow of the SuperRx drug business is being drained off by the needs of a thirsty, capital-intensive chemical business, and without much to show for it. The quality of earnings has deteriorated."

O'Rourke was intrigued. He had always insisted on not diluting Middle American's business mission, and he doubted that many others, no matter how talented, could successfully do so. "Anything else?" he asked.

As usual, Nance had saved something for a second course. "Now that you mention it," he said casually, "the earnings at SuperRx we have been discussing until now—the earnings as reported—are not quite all that they seem to be. There's nothing technically wrong with SuperRx's accounting, but it looks very much as if they've worked hard to make the Finchem acquisition look better than it was—a little too hard, perhaps."

Nance looked up to see if O'Rourke was still with him, which of course he was. Referring to a columnar table that he handed to O'Rourke, Nance proceeded to reel off a handful of accounting changes or practices that SuperRx had adopted, with the effect of bolstering the company's reported earnings either immediately or in the years following the change. Just before the merger, for example, Finchem took a large, extraordinary write-down in connection with certain of its plants and products. The write-down was curious. On the one hand, SuperRx was paying a high price for Finchem and congratulating itself on having acquired such a wonderful business, and on the other hand the Finchem management was writing off assets— and taking a charge against earnings—that raised questions about the inherent profitability of the business. With the merger in the offing, no one had paid a great deal of attention, but the effect for years to come was to increase the earnings of the merged enterprise by reducing depreciation and other expenses. (The Finchem acquisition was accounted for as a pooling of interests. Had it been on a purchase basis, the assets of the acquired company would have been written up to their fair market value, notwithstanding the write-down.) A second adjustment grew out of changed assumptions with respect to the SuperRx pension plans: the assumed rate of return on plan assets was increased, and the life expectancy of retirees was reduced. Both changes reduced the company's pension costs.

A third change grew out of the fact that SuperRx valued its inventories on the last-in, first-out (LIFO) method—the method used by most other companies in the industry. Assuming even a moderate degree of inflation, it produces a conservative result because the more recently acquired (last in), higher-cost inventory is assumed to have been sold first, thus increasing the cost of the goods sold. The effect is to eliminate most of the inflation factor from profits. But the corollary is that, having sold off the "new," higher-priced inventory, the company's books show as remaining on hand the low-cost, "old" inventory that may have been purchased years or even decades earlier. Physically, of course, the units on hand are new, but the accounting cost is old and low. Nance had found that toward the end of each of the last two years, SuperRx had sharply reduced its year-end stock of certain categories of these "old" inventories. Having liquidated or sold these very low-cost inventories, SuperRx had increased its profit margins and given its profits a nonrecurring boost.

"There were several other adjustments as well," said Nance, "all of them also in accordance with accepted accounting principles. All of them were disclosed, although in some cases the disclosure was in the footnotes and nothing was said in the letter to shareholders. But it was all there and, with some digging, not too hard to find."

They talked some more. All in all, Nance had given O'Rourke a remarkably complete picture both of how SuperRx wanted to be perceived and of its somewhat more tarnished look to a practiced eye. By then it was 10:45, and while he didn't know what else O'Rourke had planned for that Wednesday morning, Nance knew that the boss would not want to devote all of it to SuperRx.

As that brief episode illustrates, there is a rich lode of information and insights to be gathered just from the routine financial reports of any public company and others in its industry. Nance had been able to construct a wide-ranging review using only those primary sources.

Over the years the range and quality of information in the reports required by the SEC have been greatly enriched. Working largely with a little-noticed part of the proxy rules, the SEC has gradually required that annual reports contain more and more of the information needed for a thorough analysis: income and cash statements for three, not just two, years and selected financial data for five; separate data for each significant segment of the business; and more specific disclosure about pension costs. Beyond these and other quantitative changes lie a variety of useful qualitative ones. The most important of these is the so-called management discussion and analysis, which calls for an explanation of any liquidity concerns and of any events, trends, or uncertainties that would make the reported earnings less than a complete picture of where the company is headed.

Nance's analysis of SuperRx did not require any inside information or special tools. SuperRx may have been less than forthright, but most of the necessary data were somewhere in the annual report, even if only in the footnotes. The quality of financial disclosures in the United States, imposed partly by the accounting profession and partly by the SEC directly, is unparalleled.

Hostile bidders have been willing to bet billions of dollars, and banks have been willing to lend them billions of dollars, relying largely on annual reports and supplemental filings at the SEC. That is not to say that the published data are complete or that there is never fraud, but in no other country would the confidence level be so high.

This is a book on finance, not accounting, but it's important to recognize that you can't work at one without the other. Indeed, if it were possible to have a thorough grounding in just one of the two, accounting would certainly be my choice. In many respects, accounting is much more basic; after all, financial analysis must build on the work of accountants.

It is also true that financial accounting cannot be covered adequately in a single chapter, but the importance of the subject and some of its significant limitations can be addressed. For those who are expert, the illustrations at least may be of interest. But my experience is that there are not many experts. (It would be interesting, and probably dismaying, to poll the corporate directors of America on a few key accounting issues.)

Reading financial statements to search for hidden nuggets and expose booby traps is tedious work, and not very glamorous either, but it pays. The reports from security analysts and the lively stories in *Barron's*, and *Forbes*, can be helpful, but there is no substitute for reading an annual report, *beginning with the footnotes*. One airline depreciates its 727s over a fifteen-year period, another over twenty-five. If you don't start with the footnotes, how else will you know what accounting language the company has used to write its income statement? Some of the most egregious errors could have been saved by that one step.

All this may sound simple and straightforward, but in practice it is not. A survey found that fewer than half the institutional investors described annual reports as being particularly important.[1]

At one insurance company, annual reports are casually thrown away, unread.

LIMITATIONS OF FINANCIAL REPORTING

Financial statements provide a general-purpose report on the performance of the enterprise and its management and its prospects. As such, they are the single best publicly available tool for evaluating the business. As the Financial Accounting Standards Board (FASB), the standard setter for most new rules, has said, however, they are only a general-purpose report, the product of a number of necessary choices and compromises. They are like a general-purpose map of a region, which while useful, certainly does not include all the information—military, climatic, or geological—that a more specialized map would provide.[2] Because, for example, they lump together all the divisions and subsidiaries in a single statement, there is not nearly enough information, or the right kind of information, to evaluate or manage individual operating units or other specific aspects of the business. The dilemma is more basic, however. Even as a general-purpose report, financial statements have serious shortcomings.

THE ANNUAL REPORTING DILEMMA

A yearly report to investors and creditors is so customary that it is easy to overlook the fact that, depending on the business, the twelve-month cycle forces management and its auditors to make a series of difficult estimates about the eventual outcome of some very uncertain long-term projects and liabilities. Management must make, and its accountants bless, what are little more than guesstimates on some very fuzzy issues and then determine the impact of those estimates on the profit or loss of each particular year.

Some of those guesses are almost arbitrary. On the liability side of the balance sheet, for example, consider the typical pension plan, which provides benefits that will be funded by company contributions and will be based on employees' salaries in the last years of their employment. The amount to be contributed to the plan for any given year, and to be charged against that year's earnings, necessarily reflects crystal-ball guesses about how inflation or layoffs will affect the size of future benefits and about the rate at which the funds in the plan will grow. The impact of these pension cost estimates on a company's net income can be enormous, particularly at old-line manufacturing companies, with their big work forces and commensurately big pension plans.[3] No one pretends to be precise.

The asset side of the balance sheet is also problematic. How long will a computer or machine tool last? We don't know because the rate of technological obsolescence is unknowable. So we make informed guesses, charging against each year's earnings a smaller or greater sum, depending on how optimistic we choose to be. In 1987 General Motors decided to increase the estimated useful lives of its plant and equipment, thus reducing that year's depreciation and amortization charges—and increasing pretax earnings—by over $1.2 billion. The change accounted for $1.28 of the company's $5.03 of net earnings per share that year. At a time of increasing technological obsolescence and competition from Japanese transplants, the change may have seemed questionable. (With the benefit of hindsight, we know that three years later, in October 1990, GM took a large write-off and announced the closing of nine U.S. plants.) But back in 1987, who could say with certainty that GM was wrong? Where was the line to be drawn? On valuation issues such as this, there is no truth; our knowledge is no better than probabilistic. Perhaps auto plants would have a life of forty-five years, the estimate then also in use by Ford, instead of the thirty-five years GM had previously used.[4]

Implicit in these examples is the fact that because we keep books on an annual cycle, they are almost necessarily kept on an accrual or matching basis. Accrual basis accounting means that we try to match expenses, no matter when they are actually paid, against the revenues of the particular year to which they contributed. The accounting picture of a complex business or one changing in size would be very misleading if we looked primarily to the cash disbursements and receipts, counting as "revenue and expense" in, say, 1991 only those items that were received or paid in cash in that year. The matching process usually provides a more realistic picture of the year's profit or loss, but the process is subtle and ripe with choices and, as in GM's case, opportunities to shift expenses from year to year.

Although accrual basis accounting has obvious limitations, it is difficult to see how they could be avoided. To a very large extent, they are simply a reflection of the inherent difficulty of reducing a complex, long-term reality to what is often only a single present-day number.

THE MORE FUNDAMENTAL DILEMMA: MANAGEMENT CANNOT REPORT OBJECTIVELY ON ITSELF

Now that they are being sued so often, accountants continually remind us that financial statements are management's statements; accountants opine on those statements but do not write them. They are right, of course. But when management in effect reports on *itself*, the report would not be worth much without some restrictions on their freedom to write only A+ report cards. (In the 1920s, before the federal securities laws were adopted, too often the reports were good even when the results were bad.) We need rules—in this case, the celebrated GAAP (generally accepted accounting principles)—if the accountants are to have some objective standard on which to base their opinions. But GAAP is essential, too, as a fence around management's discretion, which otherwise would know no limits.

Alan ("Ace") Greenberg, the chairman of Bear Stearns, captured the problem in one of his so-called teachings that are disseminated among employees and then elsewhere: "Thou will do well in commerce as long as thou [dost] not believe thine own odor is perfume."[5] Many managers either believe that they are perfumed, or at least would like to have the world believe so.

Unfortunately, like annualized reporting, GAAP has some adverse side effects. One of the most basic of all GAAP precepts is that, with minor exceptions, a profit or gain in the value of an asset will not be recognized in financial reports until there has been a sale or other meaningful transfer. (The rules for reporting losses are not quite so rigid.) The owner of a shopping center must carry the property on its books at no more than its historical cost, less "depreciation," even if all the world knows that it has steadily appreciated. Fifteen or twenty years later when the shopping center is sold, all the profit will be booked in one year.

These accounting restrictions on unrealized income or gain owe something to the tax law, which happily does not recognize income as taxable until it has been realized. But beyond that, GAAP insists on staying with historical-cost values—the original purchase price less any depreciation—primarily out of a spirit of conservatism. Everyone may know that a shopping center (or a machine tool) would cost more to replace today, but GAAP does not permit it to be written up. Switching to current, market-based values might be much more informative, but it would make the determination of values and of income highly subjective. The temptation to write up asset values in order to boost income or to achieve other "perfumed" effects would be too great and too difficult to police.

There is no doubt, however, that historical-cost accounting leaves a lot to be desired. For several years, a real estate company, Rouse, found a novel solution, and the result reveals a good deal about the reason for the rule in the first place as well as its shortcomings. Rouse owned a variety of retail centers, some of them acquired as long ago as 1960. The accounting net worth of the company at year end 1988 was $68 million, far less than the company's stock market value, which exceeded $1 billion. The company believed that its real business was to create asset values, not earnings, and it is true that real estate companies are often perceived and valued in that way. Accordingly, Rouse expanded its balance sheet from the usual one column per year to two. In the first column were the values of its properties on a "current-value basis" and in the second column the values on the customary basis of historical cost. The effect of the revaluation was to increase the company's net worth to $1.49 billion. The methodology used to reach that result was theoretically reasonable: capitalize the estimated future cash flows for ten years or so. The question was the validity of the assumptions. In an already overbuilt real estate market, Rouse reportedly assumed continually higher rents, thereby producing "current values" well in excess of the prices then being paid for comparable space.[6] It claimed that these appraisals were the "most realistic indicator" of its value. The next year, 1989, in the face of much softer real estate prices, Rouse's net worth on a current-value basis was again boosted to $1.73 billion. If perhaps these current-value "statements" had appeared elsewhere in the Rouse annual reports, with appropriate disclaimers, there would have been less opportunity for confusion. But they were included in the balance sheet, and in the front of the report management had trumpeted the fact that they had been "audited" by KPMG Peat Marwick. (The auditors were careful to disclaim compliance with GAAP, but that being so, what did the audit contribute?) An unsuspecting investor could have been excused for not realizing that these values were not based on actual transactions, as they normally are when included in financial statements.

The freedom to mark assets to market brings to mind the remark by Mark Twain that a mine is a hole in the ground with a liar on top. Twain could as well have been speaking of land appraisals of all types.

Still, complaints are frequently heard that accounting is unrealistic and that financial reports should not "look backward," as they inevitably do, when what the world needs is more disclosure of current values and future cash flows.[7] Without suggesting that GAAP has reached a state of perfection, I believe that much of the criticism reflects a failure to appreciate the enormous difficulty of the task. If we ask too much of accountants, we will in fact get less, not more. It is true that investors, directors, and managers care primarily about where a company is going, but they also care about how well management has done up to now. And even if they were thinking only about the future, a detailed look at where the company has been, calculated so as to facilitate comparisons with other companies, is a wonderful place to begin.

One recurring problem is that it is hard to get a grip on the individual segments of a company's business. Here the financial disclosures required by the SEC are much more helpful than they once were, but they still leave something to be desired. Looking back over several years' reports can lead to some insight. (Reading the last three to five years' reports is a good way to expose the frequent lack of candor about disappointing results.) But for a good, comparative analysis, investors will still have to look elsewhere—to other companies' reports and to the research done by financial analysts, trade journals, and the like. A company's audited financial reports are not by any means the sole source of useful information.

In short, it is not that financial reporting is so complete and accurate, because it clearly is not. But a substantial part of the burden falls (properly) on the users of the reports, not just on those who prepare them. The users of financial data are trying to estimate future profits and cash flows and to put a value on the business. Who knows, even roughly, what many businesses are really worth? We could change the form of the inquiry but not the inherent difficulty of it.

Unfortunately, some companies will try to circumvent the spirit of financial reporting, no matter what rules are in force. Consider a well-known incident at American Express.[8] In 1981, when American Express's earnings growth was lagging, its Fireman's Fund subsidiary traded essentially identical pension liabilities with another insurance company. The trade, technically a reinsurance treaty, did not significantly affect the two companies' respective risks. For both insurance companies, however, the accounting effect was to accelerate to 1981 and 1982 income that would otherwise not have been realized, and under GAAP could not be booked, for a number of years. A senior officer at Fireman's Fund conceded that the purpose of the transaction, which was not disclosed to the American Express board of directors until the story broke in the press, was to circumvent the rule against recognizing unrealized income. The eventual disclosure made a shambles of Fireman's Fund's boast of record earnings. For its parent, American Express, the liability swap accounted for 45 percent of the "increase" in profits for 1982. Because the transaction accelerated taxes along with earnings, the shareholders of American Express were in fact left poorer, not richer.

A THIRD DILEMMA: CHOOSING BETWEEN FLEXIBILITY AND CONSISTENCY

The broad problem is that it is extremely difficult to write a set of rules that will provide comparable numbers for companies that in fact are not comparable. The basic historical-cost rule has a very different meaning for companies engaged in oil exploration than for banks or for computer software companies, and one set of rules for all of them is bound to be an awkward fit. Even within an industry, companies have different histories and tend to seek different accounting techniques to meet their needs.

In the best of worlds, financial statements would produce numbers that are truly comparable, both across companies and for the same company across time. Did General Motors' earnings increase from 1985 to 1989? According to the company, they did, rising slightly, even though GM sold only 7.9 million cars and trucks in 1989 compared to 9.3 million in 1985. There were a number of reasons, including a turnaround in GM's European operations, but an important reason was that in the interim, the company had rearranged some of the estimates and assumptions on which its financial statements were based. In addition to the already mentioned 1987 change in the estimated life of its auto plants, in 1986 the company raised the expected rate of return on its pension funds, which increased that year's net profit by $195 million. By 1989 the annual report no longer contained sufficiently detailed information from which to calculate precisely the continuing effects of these and other revisions. One estimate is that, in all, they added over $1 billion of after-tax earnings for 1989. Without that $1 billion, there would have been no increase in earnings since 1985. Yes, GM was able to find that $1 billion without breaking any of the rules. The rules are very flexible.

The problem is obviously serious. *The Wall Street Journal* reports daily the price-earnings ratio of each stock, and analysts look to see which companies earn more (or less) on shareholders' equity than others. What earnings? What equity? Do words and numbers mean only what management says they mean, or is there some consistency? It's a problem of credibility in the marketplace, but it also threatens to distort management's own analysis and the internal discipline. In other words, numbers that are no longer comparable from year to year or company to company are a problem not just for investors trying to make portfolio decisions but for creditors and for management itself.

When I first became involved in the supermarket industry in the

1960s, it was commonplace for the smaller public companies in the industry—typically those that were growing rapidly but had weak balance sheets—not to buy anything larger than a cash register if it meant putting debt on the balance sheet. Instead of borrowing money to build and own, say, a store, these companies would lease the finished store from the developer or pursuant to a so-called financial lease from a lender, such as an insurance company. These lease financings were always more expensive than borrowing the money to own the store outright, but neither the companies nor the financial community seemed to care, so long as the company could keep the obligation off the face of the balance sheet, disclosing it only in the footnotes. This is the kind of seemingly pointless paper shuffling that economists find incredible. But that was how the world was.[9] It's easy to say that this was foolishness, but it was conventional foolishness.

In the 1970s the FASB adopted an accounting standard that succeeded in pushing a large part of this off-balance-sheet financing back onto the balance sheet, but it did not succeed entirely. Many companies still arranged their leases to avoid capitalizing them. They were even willing to give away renewal options and other significant economic values to do so. To paraphrase Kurt Vonnegut, these companies had adopted the philosophy that you are what you pretend to be.

The FASB was right in seeking to treat all debt in accordance with the substance of the transaction, not the form. But each time it tried to nail down the problem, companies and their accountants greeted the action simply as a new challenge to be overcome. Each evasive action taken by the companies was met by a regulatory response, which in turn produced a slightly new form of evasive action. The result is an accounting standard for capitalized leases, FASB No. 13, which is almost fifty pages long and has been amended by nine additional standards and ten technical bulletins.[10]

Consider also the problem where one company invests in the stock of another. In this case, it may be that the accounting rules are not sufficiently flexible rather than too much so. The FASB is unwilling to permit companies to record as "their" earnings anything more than the dividends paid by a wholly independent company, unless the holding company owns at least 20 percent of the outstanding shares of the operating company and has a measure of influence on corporate policy. The undistributed earnings of the operating company represent real value, but because the value goes unreported on the books of the holding company, the rule seriously discourages less-than–20 percent investments, no matter how long term.

In chapter 11, we will see the benefits that frequently accrue to a company if it has a knowledgeable shareholder, one that owns a significant block of stock, is willing to hold it indefinitely, and still is content to remain a minority shareholder. At a time of enormous pressure on American companies for reportable earnings, however, GAAP discourages these long-term, minority holdings. Perhaps there is no better rule. Do we really want any company that owns 1,000 shares of another to count the latter's earnings as its own? Hardly, and yet a line has to be drawn somewhere. But it is not difficult to see how an accounting rule designed simply to report on corporate behavior ends up by influencing (and sometimes distorting) it.

CONSERVATISM, CONSISTENCY, AND CONFIDENCE

Credibility is an immensely valuable but fragile asset. Outsiders cannot come in and kick the tires. They have to settle for management's financial reports and other disclosures, plus whatever other information is publicly available. There is no point even in beginning the exercise of evaluating a company if there is a lack of confidence in its financial integrity.

Companies whose numbers are trustworthy usually write financial statements that, in accounting terms, are boring. They rarely have extraordinary charges or gains, and those that do occur are easy to find and to understand. There are a few affirmative signals that a company is keeping careful, conservative books, but only a few. Valuing inventory on a LIFO basis is one such signal. Almost no company worth its salt would pay extra taxes in order to show the higher earnings that can be reported by rejecting LIFO. But mostly it is the absence of negative signals, red flags thrown up by management itself, that enables outsiders to assume that they can use the company's reports with confidence. That is why boring is better.

Here are a few red flags that can be used as tokens of a lack of credibility. No one of them is fatal, and the significance of each depends on the candor with which it is revealed. For some companies, unfortunately, "nonrecurring" red flags do seem to be a recurring part of the picture. In the 1980s, GM was "recalling" its accounting practices with a withering frequency. Cumulatively, what did it all mean? When would it stop? An experienced analyst or investor will rightly be concerned lest the flags that are visible are just the tip of a submerged iceberg.

- Companies are free to change their accounting principles and estimates within the flexible limits set by GAAP. There is nothing technically wrong with doing so, and indeed a change in accounting principles is permissible only if it provides a better matching of income and expenses or will better coincide with industry practice. That is the theory; the reality is that when a company makes such a switch, it usually signals bad news either then or soon to come. It almost never fails.
- The accrual method of accounting, used by almost all companies, provides that when, say, a company pays an annual insurance bill, the unexpired portion of the insurance coverage should be shown on the asset side of the balance sheet as a "prepaid expense." That is appropriate. What is of concern is not so much the amount of prepaid expenses but the trend. A company that is showing significant increases is often making a conscious effort to defer expenses from this year to next—at which time it will repeat the process, and then some. If so, the earnings probably are not what they seem to be.
- Extraordinary or nonrecurring additions to income, as well as extraordinary or nonrecurring charges to income, the proverbial big bath, tend to be harbingers of ill tidings if they occur with some frequency. The really good news is almost always ordinary news. There is nothing wrong with selling land or factories at a profit, but too often these transactions were conceived or timed to produce a reportable profit and to paper over what would otherwise have been a decline in earnings or some other piece of bad news.
- Watch out if a company has earnings but not cash flow. History is replete with companies that ran out of cash even as they continued to show substantial "earnings." Sometimes the earnings are not real, and the company has been booking income, say, from sales where the buyer has made only a token down payment. Some other companies, though genuinely profitable, simply outrun their financial resources and are unable to translate the earnings into cash quickly enough. A comparison of the income statement and cash flow statement will usually point up the growing gap between accounting income and cash receipts.

THE LACK OF MANAGERIAL CANDOR: CLEAN SHIRTS AND NOT-SO-CLEAN HEARTS

However much we rewrite GAAP (and there will always be room for improvement), we will still have to confront the fact that managers will try to give themselves an A, or at least a B, grade for what may have been only a C— performance. CEOs who think of themselves as pillars of society and who are regularly honored at charity dinners and museums seem to think it's socially acceptable to deceive their shareholders.

The annual report of Prime Motor Inns for the year ended June 30, 1989, was completely upbeat. Ever since 1976, the letter to share-holders said, Prime's earnings had grown at a compounded annual rate of 46 percent, reaching $77 million in 1989. Although the hotel industry was suffering from a glut of rooms and low occupancy rates, management told the press that earnings per share would grow 20 percent annually through 1995.[11] At every turn, the 1989 annual report reinforced the consensus on Wall Street that this was a hotel wunderkind. Celebrating "another record year," the company spoke blithely of its "financial strength" and "its ability to grow at a pace faster than the industry."

That cheery annual report was the last one the company would distribute, cheery or otherwise. Much or all of its growth had come from spurious sources. Prime had been selling off various large prop-erties, and, on the arguable theory that these sales were a regular aspect of its business, it was booking the profit as an integral part of its earnings from "continuing operations" (sort of like burning the timbers as part of a "continuing" effort to keep the house warm). Nowhere in the annual report were these facts discussed directly (though readers could piece the picture together from scraps buried in the footnotes). But wait! Many of the buyers of Prime properties had been unable to obtain credit through ordinary channels. By June 30, 1989, $593 million, almost half of the company's total assets, consisted of mortgages and notes receivable largely acquired as the proceeds of these sell-offs or other transactions out of the ordinary course of business. One company, Servico, alone accounted for $138 million of the total. The following year, 1990, although Prime had never reported during these years even a quarter's loss, the string ran out. Servico filed for bankruptcy, and on the same day Prime filed, too.

If we could psychoanalyze the CEOs of America, we would find, I believe, that the most important explanation of the tendency to window-dress the annual report is their own reluctance to recognize bad news. In some profound emotional sense, many CEOs seem to leave no room for disappointment—ever. Part of the answer lies in the way American corporations are structured, with a single, almost omnipotent leader at the top who is subject to very few critical checks from within the organization. This almost feudal degree of power is seductive. With everyone in the organization, directly or more subtly, telling the boss how smart he is, it becomes difficult for him, once a year, to appraise his stewardship candidly. And who in the company will insist on candor? It would require an unusual degree of audacity for subordinates and the company's financial public relations firm, who write the annual report, to intimate that the company has not moved onward and upward under his "peerless" leadership.

Whatever the reason, many of those annual reports require very careful reading. In 1987, as we have seen, General Motors sharply reduced its annual depreciation charge. Even in the year of the change, the chairman made no mention of that major adjustment in his letter to shareholders, although without it he would have had to report a decline in earnings instead of the substantial increase for which he took credit. The change was not revealed until well into the technical portions of the report. And even there the new depreciation schedule was not described, so readers could not determine for themselves whether forty-five years was a reasonable life expectancy for an auto plant. By 1989, although the depreciation and amortization schedule adopted in 1987 was still giving earnings a healthy boost, the only mention of it in the annual report was back at page 47, in very small print. Something similar happened in the first quarter of 1990 when GM disclosed in a footnote to its earnings release that changes in the actuarial assumptions for its pension plans would increase earnings at an annual rate of $.48 per share. The company did not disclose that, to find that $.48 a share, it had increased the assumed life expectancy of its retirees and had raised the assumed rate of return on its pension funds from an already high 10 percent to an untenable 11 percent. Nor did it call attention to the fact that its pension funds were already underfunded by $1 billion.[12]

GM probably illustrates the bad-news syndrome as well any other company. It had undertaken a major restructuring and modernization program, and while the financial community was looking closely for better results, honest-to-goodness improvements in sales and profits were hard to find. Meanwhile, Ford Motor was doing very well, having caught up to GM in profits, although it was still a substantially smaller company. Were GM's accounting changes just a coincidence? It strains one's credulity to believe that, year after year, no "artist" was at work helping to improve the picture.

It was during these years that the chairman of GM, Roger Smith, was leading a fight on behalf of the Business Roundtable to scuttle the FASB because, he argued, its rules were too rigid.[13] It is breathtaking to think what Smith might have accomplished for GM's earnings in a more flexible environment.

THE MD&A SOLUTION

The number of different tricks that can be played with the bottom line are almost infinite. The most direct maneuvers either inflate assets or deflate liabilities; others are more complicated. If, for example, the economy slides into a recession, we can expect to see a number of companies take a "big bath" write-off. The write-off will produce a large, nonrecurring charge to earnings in the year of the bath, which, unlike a decline in current operating earnings, Wall Street is likely to ignore. Investors are thus encouraged to believe that all the bad news is now behind them and to think of the write-off as a positive event. A more forthcoming analysis, one never seen, would be that (1) the earnings were almost surely overstated in earlier years when the company was accumulating the fluff that is now being washed away; (2) by taking an even bigger bath than is necessary, as big as the accountants will permit, the company's earnings in the future may be overstated because depreciation or other charges against income will henceforth be reduced or eliminated; and (3) the one-time charge will also reduce the stated value of the shareholders' invested capital, enabling the company to report seemingly higher returns on a now-reduced level of equity.

No regulator, neither the FASB nor the SEC, can cope with all the tricks one by one. There are more tricksters than cops, and the latter would always be playing catch-up ball. The SEC, however, has come up with an ingenious solution, the management discussion and analysis (MD&A), which is now a required part of the annual report of all public companies. The commission regards the MD&A as the keystone of financial disclosure, and for good reason. It is intended to add a textual analysis of the numbers and footnotes contained in the financial statements, which, however technically correct, may not provide an adequate picture of the quality and sustainability of a company's earnings. The MD&A solution focuses on a company's prospects rather than on whatever trick was used to make the current year look good. At the simplest level, if for example a company has benefited in the past from a major contract, which, however, is about to expire, it must disclose that fact in its MD&A.

In a 1989 release, the SEC restated the purpose of the MD&A in very broad terms:

> MD&A is intended to give the investor an opportunity to look at the company through the eyes of management by providing both a short and long-term analysis of the business of the company. The [MD&A] asks management to discuss the dynamics of the business and to analyze the financials [and] to address those key variables and other qualitative and quantitative factors which are peculiar to and necessary for an understanding and evaluation of the individual company.[14]

That is the good news. The bad news is that compliance with the MD&A requirement has been spotty. One survey by the SEC found that of 359 companies in twenty-four industries, only 14 had prepared it properly. Too many companies had failed to disclose, say, reductions in their product prices or an erosion in market share. More commonly, they listed a number of such factors without any indication of their relative importance. The results were so poor that the commission staff decided to continue the review. Happily, there are some indications that the review process, the publicity it has attracted, and the action taken against the more egregious offenders are having some good effect.

But the accounting game is still respectable. If the accounting change or adjustment is technically correct, it must be disclosed, but the disclosure can usually be relegated to a remote portion of the annual report, where it may be stated in jargon or with insufficient detail to make it meaningful. Sometimes it appears only in the Form 10-K, on file at the SEC. Sometimes there is no disclosure at all, as happens when companies overvalue inventories or accounts receivable. And it's sad but true that unless the stench is overwhelming, almost no one in management will be held personally accountable.

ACCOUNTANTS AND ANALYSTS

In theory, accountants and security analysts keep the system honest, but the practice does not live up to the theory as well as we would like. Accountants are generally conscientious, and their firms try to do the right thing. But they are paid by the clients whose financial statements they certify, and there is enormous pressure on them to keep a client happy, to help a client survive a period of stress, to not put a worse face on reality than the rules absolutely require. There is also much more fee shopping by clients than was once the case. The sometimes skimpy fee should not influence the scope of the audit, but accountants would be more than human if it did not. Worse, the audit work is often the opening wedge for large consulting and other work from clients for whom the audit continues to act as the umbilical cord through which all the other nourishment flows. As *The Economist* wrote recently, "When auditing becomes a loss-leader it is scarcely surprising that it gets done badly or misleadingly."[15]

Like accountants, financial analysts play a major role in the disclosure process. Indeed, when people speak of the stock market as being efficient in the sense that stock prices accurately reflect all available information, they are implicitly giving much of the credit to financial analysts, particularly those on the sell side who work for brokerage or other firms trying to sell services. They are the ones who have the primary, day-to-day contact with the companies in the industries they follow and who are most likely to produce comprehensive, detailed analyses for public view.

The problem for analysts is that Wall Street is geared to emphasize positive news and to soft-pedal the negative. It is geared to the purchase of securities rather than their sale, for a number of reasons. The whole world is a potential buyer of a stock, but except for the relative handful of traders willing to go short on a stock, only those who already own it are potential sellers. Thus the market for a buy recommendation is considerably larger. And if a sell recommendation is wrong by so much as a hair, the analyst, and firm, will often suffer a lot of pain from the company involved.[16] On buy recommendations, the world is more tolerant.

Merrill Lynch is never bearish on America. If customers are encouraged to sell, who knows when they will come back? A brokerage firm may speak of a possible "correction," always to be short-lived, but it will be very reluctant to bad-mouth the direction of the economy or the stock market as a whole.

The extreme case is that of a veteran analyst who was summarily fired in 1990 by his firm, Janney Montgomery Scott, for having made critical remarks about the junk bonds of one of Donald Trump's casinos in Atlantic City. His analysis was sound. That was the trouble with it. The bonds soon sold at much lower prices and never recovered, but months later the analyst was still unemployed.[17] Up and down Wall Street, analysts nodded their heads, agreeing that they had felt the same pressures.[18]

But beyond all that is the bedrock fact that security analysts who truly want to be rich will rarely get there unless they first succeed in cultivating a close relationship with the companies they follow.

Analysts who develop close ties will get almost any information they want and will be able to talk directly with the CEO. Those who don't will be treated like a spy and left out in the cold, allowed to talk only to the designated underling in charge of investor relations. They will not have the same good peek at this year's earnings, the same information about how this or that division is doing, or any of the other tokens of intimacy that help analysts to generate trades by their investor-clients and keep the order flow moving. More important still, many analysts believe, and with reason, that only by avoiding critical comments about a company can they hope to generate the underwritings and other corporate finance work that will produce for them and their firm a large payoff. At a time when brokerage commissions have shrunk almost to the vanishing point, that is the piece of business that many analysts are seeking to win—or at least not to obstruct.

The pressure works. Only about one out of ten recommendations by analysts is to sell a stock.[19] The rest are either buys or holds. If an analyst thinks that a stock is overpriced and vulnerable, the usual way out is to switch to a hold and then, perhaps, stop covering the company—or switch to a "weak hold" or some other euphemism.

In thinking about the completeness and candor of financial data, we should remember that while accountants and analysts would prefer to be more objective or critical, there's not much in it for them except grief.

CONCLUSION

There are no easy solutions to the accounting riddle. All of us need to have a firm grounding in financial accounting if we are to understand what we are doing. There are no short cuts. No one else can do it for us—not the management of the company we are looking at, not the accountants, not the analysts. The earnings per share, as reported, are not always what they seem to be, and given the excessive emphasis on that one line, there is enormous temptation to jiggle it. The rules allow a good deal of leeway for jiggling, and it would be difficult to eliminate the leeway without also making the rules too rigid. On the bright side, there are usually large rewards for doing one's own homework. Some skeletons remain hidden in the closet, with the door locked, but the advances in accounting over the years have made the disclosure system much fuller and more reliable. The presentation is sometimes poor, with critical information buried in footnotes, stated incompletely and misleadingly, and soon lost from view altogether, but the diligent reader is usually able to reconstruct an income statement on some better, more comparable basis, or at least to identify the missing pieces of the puzzle.

Writing the annual report to shareholders requires a knowledge of accounting. Does it also require a high regard for candor? Judging by the results, many companies do not think so. That seems short-sighted. It's hard to bury information, to dress up the numbers, without leaving telltale clues that this is a company that lacks credibility. Investors and the financial press may not discover every buried body, but they will find enough of them to give the company a painful black eye—if not right away, then eventually. More important, it is impossible for a CEO to give to colleagues the message that deceiving the world at large is permissible without also giving an unintended but clear signal about the standards he or she is setting within the organization. Is a company that fools its shareholders likely to make full disclosure to its directors? Not likely, because the directors would then fear personal liability. It is more "considerate" and more pragmatic, therefore, to lie to them too. The CEO may believe that he wants the jiggling of numbers to stop at that point, but his actions convey a very different message.

Managers who fool shareholders and their directors too are soon committed to embellishing their paper "improvements" year to year. Like a bank clerk with sticky fingers, they become skilled at manipulating the truth. Ultimately, however, they become the prisoners of their own artifice.

6

Cash Dividends

HOW THE BUSINESS SCHOOLS GOT IT WRONG

MEMO

To: Board of Directors of Middle American Corp.
From: Charles E. O'Rourke, Chairman, and Phineas Nance, Senior Vice-President, Finance

In each of the last six years, we have increased the common dividend at the May board meeting. In anticipation of the meeting this May, the two of us intend to review our dividend policy or, more accurately, our lack of a policy. As you know, the board has never discussed the issue in any detail beyond saying that the company should pay out a consistent percentage of its earnings to shareholders. Earnings have continued to grow, which seems to commit us to continuing dividend increases. But the pressure to reinvest here and abroad has grown at least as quickly as earnings, thus forcing us to think about cash flow and dividends in a more thorough way.

The central issue can be stated quite simply. It is whether the surplus, freely available earnings of the company will earn more for the shareholders if left in the business or if distributed to them, either as cash dividends or by share repurchases. This statement of the issue, which treats dividends much like any other capital allocation decision, may seem almost banal, but bear with us. What we are saying, in effect, is that *all* the freely available earnings—what we call available cash flow—are potentially available for distribution to shareholders rather than being routinely reinvested to expand old businesses or diversify into new. On average, American industry has been paying out as dividends a little over 40 percent of earnings,

114

and many companies seem to believe that if they follow the crowd or pay out just a bit more than the crowd, they have given shareholders "their due." We are suggesting instead that, depending on the investment opportunities available to management, shareholders have a moral claim—there's no legal one—to something more than that. And it also reflects our conviction that, shareholders aside, it's a more exacting and appropriate way to run the business.

Underlying that central issue are five distinct problems, and some of them are quite troublesome.

1. How does a company choose between paying a dividend and reinvesting earnings back in the business? While the choice between dividends and reinvestment is ultimately one of informed business judgment, there are a number of considerations or principles that help to guide that judgment. At a highly profitable company, for example, one with attractive opportunities for expansion, the dividend pay-out should be low. Even at one without such opportunities, we realize that not all of the earnings or operating cash flow are truly discretionary. Some capital expenditures are necessary simply to maintain the existing business in its present shape and competitive position. To "cheat" on them is tantamount to a partial liquidation. Having said that, however, we all recognize the temptation to build an empire, or at least to gold-plate the existing duchy. (Some of us have even succumbed to it.)

2. For companies like Middle American that do have sufficiently attractive capital projects to absorb their entire cash flows and have demonstrated by performance that their projections are realistic, does it follow that no dividends at all should be paid? Some people believe that companies like ours should retain all their earnings. Why borrow merely to pay dividends? In practice, some very successful companies have answered that question one way and some the other.

3. In framing our dividend policy, how much weight should we give to tax considerations? At first blush, dividends make no sense, and many economists have said as much because of the double tax on dividend income. (Unlike the interest on bonds, dividends are paid by corporations out of their after-tax profits, and most shareholders then pay a second tax.) If Middle American and its shareholders could both invest at the same rate of return, why not

let the company invest 100-cent dollars instead of the 65-cent dollars that would remain for many individual investors? On the other hand, we must be careful not to allow tax considerations to blunt the need for managerial accountability. Taxes are a factor, but they are not the only one and not even the most important one.

4. Investors love dividends, and dividends help to maintain and increase stock prices. To what extent should our dividend decisions be influenced by these shareholder and market considerations?

5. Assuming that the company does have cash available for dividends, should we pay it out as regular cash dividends or instead use the funds from time to time to buy back shares of stock in the open market or by tender offer? All of us have also seen successful companies that do one and some that do the other.

The primary question that O'Rourke and Nance raise—how much should companies pay out as dividends, as against what they keep for investment—has been a continuing puzzle. Just how much do dividends really matter to shareholders? Ben Graham liked to think about the theoretical possibility of a "frozen corporation," one that by its charter was forbidden to pay dividends or even merge or liquidate. If they could never, ever see any cash or other distribution from the company, why would ordinary investors want to own the shares? At what price would the shares trade? Fortunately companies that can pay dividends eventually do. Even for those that seem frozen, the market does put a value on the shares because it believes that sometime, somehow there will be dividends.[1]

Charlie O'Rourke's problem was somewhat different. Middle American was already paying dividends at the quarterly rate of 40 cents a share. The question was whether to pay out still more. Last year earnings were up 12 percent, and this year he expected another increase. On the other hand, the company's ulcer drug was losing market share, and profit margins were being adversely affected by generic drugs. O'Rourke wasn't crying, but the fact is that in the drug business you have to reinvent the product wheel—or at least find new spokes—every few years. Athough the research department was plugging away, some potential winners were only in the early stages of development, and it would be years before the Food and Drug Administration approved them. The hope was that the terminal phase of some existing products would mesh neatly with the arrival of the new ones. But the development of a drug is a very chancy process.

The phone was buzzing again. Ben Focus, the drug analyst at Third Chicago, was on the line. Phin Nance, the chief financial officer, was out of town, so O'Rourke took the call. O'Rourke knew Focus. He was a walking encyclopedia of the drug industry, but his knowledge of details was not always matched by his judgment. Some weeks nothing much happens in the drug industry, and Focus was now fishing for an indication whether Middle American would increase the dividend at the board meeting in May. O'Rourke wasn't about to tell Focus much, partly not to upstage the board and partly not to leak inside information. But even if he had been completely open with Focus, he wouldn't have known what to say because he didn't know yet what he would recommend. Given the company's history of annual dividend increases, it would be easier to suggest an increase than not.

A few days later, after Nance had returned, O'Rourke raised the dividend question. Earnings were good, and it was clear that the market was expecting a higher dividend. But both of them knew that the company was investing money all over the place, not just on R&D but as part of a well-conceived plan for new plants and distribution centers. Net cash flow this year would be just about flat *without* a dividend increase. If they bumped up the quarterly dividend by a nickel a share, as they had last year, they would in effect be borrowing to do so. By itself, that wouldn't be a big deal; the borrowing power was certainly there. The company's debt-to–total capital ratio, typical for the industry, was a conservative 15 percent. But what about next year and the year after that?

What bothered O'Rourke—and he was bothered—was that he felt trapped by the market's expectations that every May the dividend would go up absent overtly bad news.[2] Being imprisoned by someone like Focus was particularly irksome. He was also irked by the fact that he personally had dug the hole he was in. He was the one who had talked so casually, and so often, about annual dividend increases. "In this case," O'Rourke said to Nance, "if we fail to raise the dividend, the news wouldn't really be bad. It would just be complicated." But the market, they knew, hates complicated stories. They agreed that Nance should think about dividend policy in some larger, longer-term sense than they had before. They would pick the issue up again in a week.

Nance went off to consult the experts and came back the following week.

"Boss," said Nance, "you won't believe how much has been written about dividends. One 1987 paper, which asked whether dividends matter, cited over 150 books and papers, and still the list was incomplete.[3] Whether or not dividends matter for business people, they are a great hit with scholars.

"For our purposes," Nance continued, "it all began about thirty years ago, with a paper by Merton Miller and Franco Modigliani so celebrated that the thesis they propounded now goes simply by the acronym MM.[4] Their concept was that the value of the company in the market should not be affected by whether the dividend rate is high or low or even whether dividends are paid at all. Assuming a company's investment program is known, and assuming efficient financial markets, the absence of taxes, and some other factors too, the value of the company has been fixed, and shareholders should be indifferent to whether the current earnings are reinvested at the assumed rate of return or are paid out. If they are paid out, the shareholders are that much richer, but the corporation is that much poorer. According to MM, a company's dividend policy is irrelevant even for shareholders who want a present cash return. If the company does not pay dividends, they are free to do what the shareholders of any "frozen corporation" can do: sell some shares periodically in the open market. Depending on the tax status of the shareholder, these "homemade" dividends may even be the preferred course.

"If dividends are irrelevant for shareholders, they won't pay more for dividend-paying stocks. Thus, dividends are irrelevant for corporate managers, too.

"To understand the debate over dividends," Nance said, "it is necessary to know that Modigliani and Miller had written an earlier paper in which they argued in much the same vein that a company's capital structure is also irrelevant.[5] Even if a company pays out all its earnings, it could recapture whatever funds are needed for the business by a new stock issue or a new debt issue. No matter what the choice or combination of choices, the financial markets would promptly adjust. The shareholders' total wealth would remain unaffected."

Nance said that he was astonished by the intense interest and controversy that Modigliani and Miller had stirred up among economists and finance teachers. While universally accepting the MM thesis in principle, they have disagreed over when and how to modify various assumptions underlying it. The purists, for example, believe that because of the double tax on dividends, which affects all individual and other fully taxed shareholders, companies should pay little or no dividends.[6] Shareholders who want cash could then "create" their own dividends by selling a portion of their shares from time to time.

Despite all that has been written, one popular text calls the dividend controversy one of the ten unsolved problems that are ripe for research.[7] "Still," Nance concluded, "allowing for all the arguments about this aspect or that, the MM thesis is a generally accepted basic tenet of modern financial theory. I think they have it wrong and I think I know why that is. Economists and finance people are thinking almost entirely about the impact of dividend policies on the current *market value* of the company, not the impact on the business itself. Consider the fact that, in analyzing dividend policy, M&M and their followers put to one side the question of how a company reinvests its cash flow.[8] No sensible business manager would make such an assumption. It's as if the head of our European division asked for a blank check without telling us what his capital budget would be, and, more to the point, we were willing to believe that his capital spending would not be affected by our casual attitude. By assuming that they know how the money will be invested, the only question left for scholars is the purely *financial* one of where the money comes from: retained earnings or (if a dividend is paid) the marketplace. And since the source of the money—a company's choice between debt and equity—is said to be irrelevant in market terms, dividend policy is irrelevant too. In other words, the very issue that you and I see as paramount—the choice between putting money back in the business or paying it to shareholders—they break up into two ostensibly unrelated ones."[9]

O'Rourke broke in long enough to say that Modigliani and Miller had never met Ben Focus. "I mean that, Phin," said O'Rourke. "The stock market likes dividends. Investors don't insist on dividends in every company, but there is a strong preference.[10] The preference depends on the company. Our shareholders are content with a low payout ratio because of our high returns on reinvested capital. But at a good many others, shareholders would cheer a full payout of earnings, and the stock price would jump."

Nance agreed. The economists recognize that the real world has a preference for dividends, but it puzzles them. It's an "irrational prejudice," they say.[11] "Remember," Nance said, "economists and economics-oriented finance people are very busy building econometric models, and they are really in love with the MM one. They speak of it as if there were a law of physics, there being a "conservation of value" regardless of how the corporate pie is capitalized or distributed. As one such enamored finance professor-consultant said not long ago, the traditional view—that dividends *are* desirable—'has about it the flavor of phlogiston [the primitive belief in fire as a natural element]. Not only does it seem wrong, it is difficult to believe that sensible folk could have held such beliefs.' "[12]

O'Rourke's ears went up. He was one of those "sensible folk," and he didn't like the patronizing tone of that professor. Nance dug out from his pile of notes an excerpt from still another article. "Boss," he said, knowing this one would also irritate O'Rourke, "if you think that's bad, listen to this one, written by a former chairman of the Council of Economic Advisers: 'The nearly universal policy of paying substantial dividends is the primary puzzle in the economics of corporate finance.' "[13]

"In 1988," said Nance, ruffling through his papers, "1,641 New York Stock Exchange companies paid out estimated cash dividends of $102 billion, up from $76 billion just two years earlier."[14] As Nance noted, $100 billion a year in dividends make dividends a very large puzzle indeed.

"Unfortunately," Nance explained, "economists are continually searching for and testing universal principles, particularly quantifiable ones, that will support the econometric modeling on which they are so keen.[15] It was necessary, therefore, that business decisions about investments should be separated from purely *financial* decisions, such as dividend policy. Otherwise there would have been too many variables—in which case, good-bye model. What trips them up is the fact that financial decisions, like everything else in business, should not ignore the social and institutional context in which they arise. To adapt an aphorism of Justice Oliver Wendell Holmes, the life of business and finance is not logic, it is experience."

7

Cash Dividends

TO KEEP THE MONEY OR
PAY IT OUT, THAT IS THE QUESTION

In chapter 6 we examined the celebrated Modigliani-Miller thesis, that dividend policy is irrelevant, concluding that it is neither an accurate portrayal of how investors behave nor a useful model for how companies should behave. But don't take the thesis lightly. It was blessed by a Nobel prize in 1990, and it is part of the intellectual baggage of an entire generation of business school students, a large number of them now in positions of responsibility at major corporations. By now, too, they have forgotten the unrealistic assumptions underlying the thesis, and their acceptance of it has been reinforced by the business press and by consultants who either never understood its shaky foundations or find it useful to pass over them.

The potential for mischief in the MM thesis is considerable because it tends to reinforce the obvious preference of corporate managers to keep dividends as low as possible. Many managements would rather hold on to the money, expand the X business, buy and try the Y one, or just feel as cozy as one can feel only with plenty of cash in the drawer. Then along comes the MM theory, blessed by virtually everyone, to put a patina of intellectual legitimacy on these self-serving preferences. If dividends are irrelevant and, beyond that, tax foolish, why not let management keep the money?

A PROPER AND SIMPLE POLICY FOR DIVIDENDS

Dividends are irrelevant for economists. They are consistently applauded by shareholders. They are an afterthought for corporate managements, who often allot to dividends only what is convenient. Properly seen, however, dividends are the framework in which business managers are forced to make quite hard decisions about whether the company or its shareholders should have the money. Has the company demonstrated over time an ability to reinvest earnings successfully, or, like all too many others, should it be making significantly larger distributions to the shareholders, where they can be put to better use? While not always easy to apply, no other policy issue could be more basic or analytically uncomplicated.

THE CASE FOR HIGHER DIVIDENDS

Examples of companies that have been unable to put their retained earnings to good use, and should have distributed more to their shareholders long ago, are easy to find. In 1980, for example, National Steel, an integrated steel company that had been quite profitable, began to diversify into a grab bag of unrelated businesses. Renamed National Intergroup, it bought a number of thrift institutions, a wholesale distributor of pharmaceuticals, a franchisor (and supplier) of general merchandise stores, an aluminum foil producer, a hospital supply business, a pipe and tubing producer, an oil gathering and distribution operation, and others, at a total cost of $1 billion. It sold off most of its steel operations, including all of Weirton Steel and a major interest in National Steel. Quickly disillusioned with its new investments, however, the company sold (or planned to sell) everything but FoxMeyer, a lackluster distributor of pharmaceuticals with operating margins well below industry standards.

The cost of this erratic behavior was staggering. After two years of steel profits at the beginning of the 1980s equal to $9 per share, National Intergroup proceeded to lose $42.45 per share over the next seven years. Dividends could have been—they should have been—the issue on which a more rational use of capital was forged, but the opportunity was missed. The annual dividend, which had been at least $2 a share from the mid-1970s through 1981, was slashed to 25 cents in 1983 as the diversification program heated up.

Later still, the dividend was dropped altogether. In 1988, even as the losses continued and the banks were imposing tighter controls, the CEO who had been in charge throughout this so-called restructuring continued to talk casually of building a base for steady growth.[1] But by then the stock of National Intergroup had fallen from an average of $28 a share in 1980 to $16, and book value had plummeted from about $75 a share to $31.

Fortunately for the shareholders, a dissident group of shareholders won a proxy fight in 1990 and forced a decision by the board of directors of National Intergroup to liquidate what little was left.

Like National Intergroup, Nortek, Inc., bought and sold a number of quite different businesses—over thirty—during the years 1980–1988. Ostensibly a defense contractor, Nortek had asked Drexel Burnham Lambert in 1985 to raise $150 million in a junk bond financing; the bankers responded by raising $300 million (and eventually $600 million in all).[2] Nortek used some of the proceeds to buy other Drexel Burnham junk issues, which for a time covered the high cost of capital. But the company was not able to put its capital to a sustained good use.

Table 7–1 contains data for the years 1980–1988 for National Intergroup and Nortek. Despite a rapidly rising stock market and 50 percent overall inflation,[3] the shareholders' total return for the period was nonexistent at National Intergroup and slender at Nortek. (By 1989, it would be nonexistent at Nortek, too.) Huge sums that could have been distributed as dividends or in liquidation were instead squandered on a program of acquiring unrelated businesses that soon turned to ashes. At National Intergroup, dividends were modest by any yardstick. Nortek was reporting earnings but paying out less than 5 percent of its earnings as dividends.

National Intergroup and Nortek followed misconceived and costly diversification programs that were carried on long after the time that even a modestly diligent board of directors would have called a halt. Cases such as these cry out for more generous distributions to shareholders, because, by definition, the money invested in acquisitions was not needed in the core business of the company. Surplus funds and borrowing power were drained while the board slept.

The fact that a management has one set of skills does not mean that it also has others or that it is wise to pay a substantial premium over market, as it must usually do, to acquire a business that, if the same funds were distributed, the shareholders could purchase on their

Table 7–1
Per-Share Data

	National Intergroup	Nortek
Earnings, 1980–1988[a]	−$33.45	$14.58
Less dividends, 1980–1988	$6.91	$0.64
Retained earnings, 1980–1988	−$40.36	$12.48
Capital expenditures plus acquisitions, 1980–1988[b]	$92.40	$75.10
Ratio of capital expenditures to retained earnings	n.a.	6
1980 average stock price	28	5
1988 average stock price	16	8
Shareholders' compounded annual rate of total return	−2.21%	6.27%
Compounded annual rate of total return, S&P 500	15.90%	15.90%

Source: Value Line Investment Survey, except for cost of acquisitions, where company data were used.
Note: Debt-to-equity ratios rose: for National Intergroup, from 57 percent in 1980 to 65 percent in 1988, and for Nortek, from 100 percent in 1980 to 237 percent in 1988.
[a]Includes nonrecurring and extraordinary items.
[b]Both companies made substantial divestitures, which would reduce the net cost of these investments.

own. Don't buy company X stock yourself, these managements are saying to shareholders, when we can buy it "wholesale," at twice the retail price.

THE WISDOM OF "NEGLECTING" A CORE BUSINESS

Diversification programs are suspect. Sometimes, however, the problem goes directly to the core business of a company. Perhaps it should not be liquidated straight off because it is capable of generating a better return alive than dead. But quite often one can see that there is no reason to plough new dollars into it, and then the dilemma is serious. Managements that are wise or timid or prudent enough not to go into unrelated businesses may still be reluctant to wind down the ones they are already in without trying to sustain them in some "productive" fashion. A high payout would be a confession of failure, and who wants to do that?

Mining companies are a classic case in point. Often the profits of one year's digging go right back into the ground, although the company's history is that the average returns on capital have been quite poor. To be sure, there are companies with deep, rich mines that should be developed. Many of the rest, however, earn a decent return only in a few flush years, when copper or silver prices, say, are unusually high. Perhaps they were overexposed as children to the Con Ed signs in New York, "Dig we must." The managements are mining people; that is the business they know and love, and they seem unable to resist the temptation to put the solid (not great) earnings of those few good years into new holes rather than treating them as a windfall and making liberal payments to shareholders. It is true that the dividend alternative is tantamount to a policy of slow liquidation, or at least stagnation. The fact, however, is that only if they are treated like cash cows will most mining companies produce acceptable results.

In the good years, when even poor mines show good profits, the managers seem to suffer from amnesia. Rather than paying dividends, they speak of building a base for long-term growth. Then the cycle turns; the money is back in the ground, and shareholders, and the company too, have nothing to show for the profits. Hecla Mining, for example, was generally paying a nominal dividend of $.05 a share annually in the 1980s while reinvesting on average almost twenty times that much in capital spending. The company boasted in its 1985 annual report that it owned the largest silver-producing mine in the country but also acknowledged that the mine was unprofitable. (When losing money, it would be better if the mine were smaller.) Undaunted by its past failures, the company periodically announced new exploration programs. To what avail? In 1989 it lost money, as it had during much of the rest of the decade. The stock price, which had averaged about $24 in 1980, fell below $7 in 1990.

Denison Mines was no better. In its 1989 annual report, it waxed poetic about mining, saying that "carving a mine out of the wilderness . . . [is] a highly precise science and a finely tuned art." Perhaps, but not from a shareholder point of view. Between 1986 and 1989, the company experienced heavy losses, cutting the book value in half, even while it continued to invest heavily in capital spending and glossy, four-color annual reports.

MAKING THE REINVESTMENT VERSUS DIVIDEND DECISION PATIENTLY

We should be careful not to overgeneralize. Not all companies that reinvest without prospects for an immediate return are necessarily pouring money down a black hole. A clear case for patience could have been made for Caterpillar, the world's leading producer of earth-moving equipment. The company sustained substantial losses in 1982–1984, and only in 1988 did earnings return to the level of 1980, before declining again. On the numbers, the performance was subpar, as evidenced by a compounded annual total return (dividends plus appreciation) for shareholders of only 3.19 percent over the entire decade of the 1980s. Did that make of Caterpillar another self-serving management, one that would rather reinvest at almost any cost? I don't think so. In an era when American industry was being accused of short-sightedness, when the Japanese could steal market share simply by lowering profit margins for a time, Caterpillar was defending a world-class franchise—first in the industry worldwide—that had been highly profitable for many years. The company still was the nation's second largest exporter, second only to Boeing, and an acknowledged leader in quality. Like other American businesses, Caterpillar was facing vigorous price and product competition from Japan, in this case from Komatsu Ltd., but it was fighting back, holding prices steady as long as possible. Dividends were cut, and capital expenditures in 1989 alone were about $1 billion, more than triple the level just a few years earlier, with more reportedly to come. Admittedly it had been slow to react, but now the company was overhauling virtually all its seventeen U.S. plants, installing robots and streamlining its operations, hoping to trim 20 percent from its production costs.[4]

There was no way to know the eventual outcome. With most of its plants in the United States, Caterpillar's exports are sensitive to currency fluctuations, and in the spring of 1990, for example, the dollar rose sharply and unexpectedly against the yen. Demand in some markets turned soft, and the cost-cutting program may have been moving too slowly. But Caterpillar has an enormous amount of what Charlie Munger calls "social momentum," meaning people, relationships with suppliers and customers, and organizational systems and values that have been built up over decades. It should not relinquish that momentum lightly.

THE DANGERS OF STOCKPILING CASH

Still, executives may be tempted to pour money down black holes because the money isn't theirs—it's the shareholders'—and because they often measure their eminence and success by revenues rather than profits per dollar invested. As long ago as 1934, Graham and Dodd, writing on dividend policy, said that reinvesting a substantial part of the earnings must be clearly justified *to the shareholders* on the basis of concrete benefits exceeding the value of the forgone dividends.[5] Even if the retention of earnings is a necessity, they added, stockholders should be advised of that fact. And that was said at a time before so many companies had set off on programs of random diversification away from the very business—the only business—in which the shareholders had consented to invest. With any decent regard for those owners, a company that makes steel would not have turned itself into a jobber of pharmaceuticals without consulting them.

The problem may go deeper still. Cash sitting around for any length of time can be unbearable, *even if it's your own*. We all would like to create a notable business or product; we would all like to head up a large company rather than a small one. Perhaps it's not the money. Perhaps it's the game that counts. Indeed, the profit motive may be little more than a cover, a rationalization.[6] We want to run a global enterprise, we want to create something significant to put on our psychic tombstones, and, yes, sometimes we just enjoy trying to beat the odds and conquer an uncertain world. The Hunt family of Texas and others, too, have squandered Texas-sized fortunes searching for personal fulfillment or just excitement. The odds that Robert Campeau would win his overleveraged bet on Federated Department Stores were terrible from the start. But the game itself is almost irresistible even if its generic name is *speculation*. Being enthusiastic—and sometimes manic—we tell shareholders and ourselves, too, that the bold new merger will be very profitable, at least in the long run. That's why the projections in those strategic long-term plans go straight up.

Impatience is the other part of the problem. There is a proverb that genius is patience, and CEOs are not geniuses any more than the rest of us. It is painful to sit with a pile of dollars, doing "nothing," looking like a coward, with security analysts yelling "Jump," even if what you might jump into looks suspiciously like a black hole. Good finance executives recognize the problem and try to protect against it. At one paper company, the financial chief squirreled money away as an "investment" rather than showing it as cash so that the CEO would not think of it as spendable money. (It worked.) Exxon has a conscious plan not to "stockpile" dollars but instead to pay dividends and to repurchase stock lest impatience get the best of them. But it takes discipline.

Patience may seem foolish in an era of random takeovers when cash is still something of a dangerously hot item. But for companies with the means to ward off takeovers, and ultimately even for those that don't, investment decisions should not be made hurriedly. Good opportunities do not necessarily come along every year or even every two or three. Ford Motor, which at the beginning of the 1980s had lost all its working capital and was in acute financial distress, engineered a solid turnaround. Still, just a few years later, it was being severely criticized for holding onto $9 billion of cash despite the fact that its routine capital expenditures were running $4.7 billion a year and the industry once again seemed headed for hard times.[7] Soon after that, the company, either stung by the criticism or, more likely, having lost patience, allowed the swelling cash to burn a hole in its pocket. Toward the end of the 1980s, it spent about $8 billion on the Jaguar nameplate and some other acquisitions peripheral to its core business. By the end of 1990, the company was short of earnings *and* cash and could respond only weakly to reports that it would have to sell assets and delay new models.[8] For those who do not have a friendly control shareholder, and even for those such as Ford who do, cash may be impolitic, but it is not sinful.

No doubt the management of National Intergroup produced "solid" projections for each new business that it bought, but, given the dismal record, the board of directors should have assessed the projected results for new investments by the poor performance of the old. (One wonders where the National Intergroup board of directors could have been during these years of inept management. On paper, it was a picture board, one that included senior executives of several major corporations and banks, the president of a university, the dean of a major business school, and other "distinguished" people.) Note, of course, the past performance that matters is not the overall, average results, which may still be benefiting from some spectacular but old winners. A supermarket chain, for example, may be quite successful and still be unable to find new locations that do not cannibalize existing stores. Without suggesting a preoccupation with any one year's results, only an analysis of recent store openings will reveal whether sufficient new opportunities are being found.

Graham and Dodd had it just right. A decision to retain and reinvest a significant part of the earnings should be explained to shareholders, and shareholders should insist on more than the usual bromide that dividends will "keep pace" with earnings. (See chapter 11.) Think of it in this way: companies make money in order to distribute it (eventually) to shareholders. Assuming that the business is successful, some of the money *must* be kept to protect the business and to comply with legal and social obligations. Still more money *may* be kept if the company can reinvest it more profitably than the shareholders can manage on their own. Beyond that, however, the dollars should be distributed. The choice is the simple one of allocating capital, of deciding where it can be better used: by the company or by its owners. (If the latter, then the distribution might take the usual form of a cash dividend or it might be done by share repurchase, which for tax and other reasons can be an extraordinarily attractive alternative. Stock buybacks are explored in chapter 8.) The crossover point, the one at which money should be paid out rather than retained by the company, is an issue that will be discussed. But whether the number is a bit lower or higher is not significant. What matters most is to see the issue in the proper framework.

JUSTIFYING THE DIVIDEND–VERSUS–REINVESTMENT DECISION: THE HURDLE RATE

Finance people in and out of industry are accustomed to thinking about new projects in terms of the cost of capital, sometimes called the hurdle rate. That cost is the minimum amount that must be earned to justify the investment. What is meant is not literally the cost, because the debt portion, for example, may have been borrowed years ago at much lower interest rates. And to calculate the "cost" of retained earnings is almost impossible. Instead, we define the cost of capital as the *opportunity* cost. Money is valuable, whatever its source, and a good measure of that value is what the money would earn in whatever other comparable opportunities are available. In this context, it means that a company should not reinvest earnings in discretionary projects unless it reasonably expects, and has demonstrated its ability, to earn at least as much as history tells that the shareholders could, on average, earn on their own if only the money were paid out.

Defining the cost of capital in these terms is quite consistent with the traditional view of dividend policy. Companies were not expected to expand just for the sake of it, and it was commonplace to distribute earnings, even all the earnings, to shareholders. That's what investments were about. For the first quarter of this century, there were speculators, to be sure, but the line between them and investors was much more sharply drawn than today. Investors were not supposed to think in terms of price appreciation, or "total return" as we now call it. They bought securities for income—interest or dividends. While a corporation might retain its earnings, the burden of proof, so to speak, was on management.[9]

Some people in management still think in these traditional terms. Charles R. Sitter, senior vice-president of Exxon and its chief financial officer, believes that debt and equity are alike in the sense that in both cases the company is simply the custodian of investors' money. Shareholders, like creditors, have given the company only the temporary use of their funds. If the available opportunities are not sufficiently attractive, the company should have no greater compunction about returning money to shareholders—paying dividends or buying back stock—than it would have about prepaying debt. The trick, he said, is not to be "macho" about building a large cash kitty and then stretching to find uses for it.

You won't find anything that resembles Sitter's views in today's finance literature. The only similar discussion is in the 1984 annual report of Berkshire Hathaway, where the chairman, Warren Buffett, concluded that if a company's internal rate of return does not at least equal that available to investors in the financial markets, the money should be distributed to shareholders. Otherwise, he said, the company might be investing to earn 8 percent when shareholders could on their own buy stocks with an average annual return of, say, 10 percent. In a world where the dollar that a company keeps won't be worth a dollar in the market price of its shares unless it can produce a return of 10 percent on that dollar, dollars invested at 8 percent will soon be marked down in market price, and the shareholders will have suffered a loss. His conclusion, stated in terms of long-term market values, was:

> Unrestricted earnings [roughly equivalent to "available cash flow"] should be retained only when there is a reasonable prospect—backed preferably by historical evidence or, when appropriate, by a thoughtful analysis of the future—that *for every dollar retained by the corporation, at least one dollar of market value will be created for owners.*[10]

Buffett went on to note that senior managers rarely impose on themselves the same dividend policy they expect of their corporate subsidiaries:

Many corporate managers reason very much along these [disciplined] lines in determining whether subsidiaries should distribute earnings to their parent companies. At that level, the managers have no trouble thinking like intelligent owners. . . . But if [the CEO's]own long-term record with incremental capital is 5%—and market rates are 10%—*he is likely to impose a dividend policy on shareholders of the parent company that merely follows some historical or industry-wide payout pattern.* Furthermore, he will expect managers of subsidiaries to give him a full account as to why [earnings should be retained] rather than distributed to the parent-owner. But seldom will he supply *his* owners with a similar analysis.[11]

In short, don't expect to find many companies with the necessary discipline. The corollary is that companies that over time demonstrate a genuine concern for their shareholders are highly valued by security analysts and investors.

CREATING A DOLLAR OF VALUE FOR A DOLLAR OF RETAINED EARNINGS

What does it mean to create a dollar of market value for a dollar of retained earnings? There is a Delphic quality to that standard. If for several years our mythical drug company, Middle American, has been earning over 20 percent on equity, should we reject any proposals that would dilute that record? At first blush, it might seem so. The current price of the stock probably reflects the market's expectation that the company will continue to produce 20 percent returns or something close to that. If instead the company now "settles" for projects with only a 14 percent expected annual return, the price of the stock may well drop. Would those new projects create market value of a dollar for a dollar, or would they erode the value?

A drug company with exceptionally high returns on equity is admittedly special. But the stocks of most other public companies also sell above their book values. While industrial companies earn about 13 percent on their common equity, investors in stocks earn, over very long periods of time, a compounded total return (dividends plus price appreciation) of only about 10 percent a year.[12] And they are quite pleased with that. *In other words, while investors have come to expect management to produce a better than 10 percent compounded return on equity capital, they, as investors, are content with a 10 percent return, and so they mark up the average industrial stock to a price above book value.* That's a very important concept. Shareholders assume that industry can do better managing money actively than they can do passively. And history confirms that, on average, they are right. A number of factors could affect the relationship, notably inflation, but until now, on average, a dollar left in the business, and not distributed in dividends, has created, say, $1.30 of market value for shareholders if, as has been the case, the business could earn on that dollar of equity a 13 percent return.

Now suppose that an average company—not just an exceptional drug company but one that has been earning 13 percent on its common equity—sees that the opportunities for a 13 percent return are drying up, and the problem is more than a passing episode. Shareholders will suffer a permanent loss of market value no matter what the company does, because the market price probably reflects a more optimistic set of expectations.

That's not very appealing. From the CEO's point of view, the prospect of investing capital in projects that yield less than 13 percent is also not very appealing. Why would a CEO want to have a business epitaph that he or she was content to dwell in the bottom portion of the class?

The answer may not be appealing to an ambitious CEO, but it's realistic and a major improvement over some of the alternatives. The answer is that while no one *wants* to be below average, approximately half of American industry has no choice. Entire groups, ranging from airlines to oil drilling equipment, have shown returns consistently below average. Banks, too, few of which consistently earn 13 percent on their equity. To insist we all be first or second in each segment of our business, as General Electric (with some shuffling of the cards) has largely succeeded in doing, is not a useful standard for the community as a whole unless we want to legislate away the half that lives on the "other side" of the tracks. A minimum hurdle rate of 13 percent is simply too high as an absolute cutoff.

To paraphrase the Duchess's advice to Alice, there must be an acceptable hurdle rate somewhere, if only we can find it. We can—by looking at the problem in terms of dividend policy. In other words, if with the dividends they receive shareholders can invest in other stocks and if on average those investments produce a 10 percent compounded annual rate of total return, including appreciation, that so-called opportunity cost represents a highly suitable threshold or cutoff point for companies faced with the decision of whether to retain earnings or to distribute them. Only if the company can do as well or better should it reinvest.

We must be careful not to fall into the trap of trying to quantify this cost of capital precisely. There is no magic at 10 percent. For example, the *compounded* total return from stocks has been 10 percent a year; the *average* annual return has been about 12 percent.[13] The difference is so large because of what Martin L. Leibowitz of Salomon Brothers calls "volatility drag": the greater the fluctuations in the annual returns of a stock (or group of stocks), the more the compounded annual rate of return, which is how portfolios are generally measured, will fall below the average annual return.[14] Since investors as a whole cannot go in and out of the market, I prefer the more conservative compounded 10 percent return. Even that number does not represent an irreducible minimum, however. We can justify a figure even lower than 10 percent by taking into account the personal income tax that individual shareholders, for example, would have to pay on a dividend. Assuming the ability and integrity of management are unquestioned, that may be the right thing to do. Eight dollars, for example, would ordinarily be an inadequate return on $100 of shareholders equity, but it would represent a respectable tax-equivalent yield on the $65 which would be the after-tax proceeds of a dividend to a taxable shareholder.

There is no one number that is so compelling as to exclude all others; precision is an illusion. We are talking about hurdle rates that are to be applied by people who are working within a complex, often highly political setting—people who get bored, go on vacation, or just want to (dis)approve a project in order to have done with the issue.[15] Using a different method from the one used here, one that among other things blends the cost of both debt and equity, Quaker Oats' hurdle rate for new investments was a little over 11 percent and Coca-Cola's was 12 percent. (The discussion of risk as an element in the calculation of the cost of capital or hurdle rate has, for convenience, been left for chapter 10.) Those are useful numbers and they are the product of extensive experience. In the interest of stability, Coca-Cola's rate was allowed to remain unchanged for at least four years despite fluctuating interest rates. But however arrived at, in today's financial and economic climate, a hurdle rate, or assumed cost of capital, in the 10–11 percent range seems quite appropriate. It is somewhat below the 13 percent return on equity currently enjoyed by industry as a whole and so is suitable as a *minimum* rate of return. To be sure, if interest rates were to rise significantly and for a sustained period, the minimum would have to be set higher; otherwise shareholders would no longer be getting a full dollar of market value per dollar of retained earnings.

Does that mean that companies should accept any and all projects that walk in the door offering an 11 percent return? Obviously not.

Companies approve first all new projects that offer a rate of return above the hurdle rate. Highly profitable companies may well exhaust their available funds long before reaching the 11 percent proposals. It's only for the marginal, tail-end project, after the better ones have been approved, that this cost-of-capital concept has any bite.

It's true, of course, that companies like Coca-Cola enjoy high price-earnings ratios because they have heretofore been able to deliver high returns on invested capital. But it's easy to draw a wrong inference from that fact. It's true that if Coca-Cola cannot do better than 11 percent, its stock price will soon drop. But it does not follow that because Coca-Cola has been so successful up to now in finding better than 11 percent opportunities, an 11 percent project today should necessarily be rejected. While a high price-earnings ratio reflects an expectation on Wall Street that the company has bright prospects, Wall Street may simply be wrong. If so, the business operations should not be distorted by the fact that expectations and outcome may be destined to differ for reasons wholly beyond management's control. If in fact the security analysts' expectations are wrong—if there is a continuing dearth of high-return opportunities—that high price-earnings ratio will ultimately have to be corrected. Management has not guaranteed the current stock price. Or to put it somewhat differently, any proposed new project needs to be analyzed on an independent, stand-alone basis. The fact that a company now owns an extraordinary business should not deter it from investing in an ordinary but still satisfactory one. If the ordinary one will produce returns of 11 percent and is the best available, then in the current economic climate, the investment should satisfy the principle of a dollar of market value for each dollar invested.

PAYING DIVIDENDS IS NOT AN ADMISSION OF FAILURE

If a company does not earn a decent return on its newly retained earnings over time, and many do not, then the money should be paid out so that investors can put it in one that does. Some companies are in industries that are growing and profitable, and some are not. In a mature economy, the fact that a great many companies do not have exciting prospects is a truism. The question is, How ready are managers to acknowledge that reality? Companies that have only meager opportunities should not also be frozen, as Ben Graham described those that keep all their earnings. Dividends are important. Over time, they affect the allocation of capital by society. Setting a floor, a hurdle rate, *somewhere* is a step forward for all concerned. Such a test would have dictated a much higher dividend payout by Hecla Mining, for example, a company that over a nine-year period reinvested almost all of its earnings with very little to show for it. Nortek falls into the same category.

A higher payout is not a confession of failure. Dividends are often an act of managerial candor that mark the company as a corporate all-star. Perhaps the payout should take the form of share repurchases rather than cash dividends. But however the money is returned to shareholders, managers must recognize that they sometimes run out of good opportunities. The ancient Greeks knew better than to go to war when the gods were not smiling on them and the odds were poor. It seems more difficult in business, perhaps because our corporate warriors have read less history. Exxon is one of a growing number of exceptions, willing to acknowledge that acceptable projects are not always available. In addition to substantial dividends, Exxon bought back out of excess cash flow during the 1980s over $15 billion of stock, which not only served shareholders well but maintained an essential aspect of corporate discipline.

LIMITATIONS OF ANY PURELY FINANCIAL OR QUANTITATIVE ANALYSIS

A central theme of this book is that the importance of finance—and, of course, finance teachers—has been greatly exaggerated. That applies also to this discussion of whether available cash flows should be retained or paid out. Unless a company decides to abandon a business altogether, the fact is that many of the expenditures are obligatory; management simply has no choice. We have seen, for example, that short of liquidating the company, Caterpillar had an array of investments that it had to make if it was to maintain its competitive position, particularly in relation to Komatsu, the Japanese intruder. *No financial analysis could add very much.* Perhaps years ago the company should have gone into the electronics business, but instead it went into earth-moving equipment. That is where it is, and an enormous investment and goodwill have been built around that decision. Just about all of the stepped-up capital expenditures at Caterpillar appear to have been "no-brainers," meaning that they were designed to lower the cost or increase the quality of the product rather than to increase overall capacity or go off in new directions. Absent a decision to liquidate the business—either immediately or by milking it over time—there was virtually no issue as to most of these expenditures.

Coca-Cola has formalized this distinction by exempting from the hurdle rate any projects that are not "optional" by its standards. Exxon, Liz Claiborne, and FMC do pretty much the same thing.

For easy reference, Munger divides investments into several rough categories. To begin with, there are lots of *no-brainers*—investments that must be made if the business is to continue with any chance of success. Others may not be very profitable in their own right, but they produce synergies or positive trade-offs elsewhere in the product line. Still others may be desirable because the losses that would flow from *not making the investment* would be unacceptable. In addition to these no-brainers, there are also gold mines, cash traps, and cash cows. *Gold mines* are few and far between, but if we think of owning one of the network television stations (or the dominant newspaper) in Chicago a few years ago, the concept is clear. A gold mine is a business that is expected to produce substantial earnings for a long while and without depleting the source. Hecla Mining seems to have been a *cash trap.* All the money that came out of those silver and gold mines, and more, ended up going back into the ground. The profits should have been paid out to shareholders, except for some minimal amounts necessary to limp along. In that case the mines might have been reasonably valuable as *cash cows:* the cash flow would have been maximized, though eventually it would have dried up.

The relevance of this once-over-lightly view of Munger's analysis is that it underscores the fact that nicely calculated financial hurdle rates and costs of capital have little to do with real-world business and dividend decisions. If we push the analysis of a project far enough, it is true, we could produce some numbers that could then be subjected to a cost-of-capital test. But what would it add? We are talking about investment returns over long periods of time, and the numbers soon get fuzzy. Economists like to talk about making all investments that show a positive net present value, as if even small positive numbers are a significant signal. If that were so, then it might be useful to calculate the cost of capital to a tenth of a percentage point. But it is not. As Exxon found, the effort to fix the cost of capital with any precision is a waste of time because it is soon overwhelmed by the uncertainties of the business. In projects affected by oil prices, for example, the company uses at least two different crude oil scenarios, one likely and one pessimistic, and the difference in the expected returns between those two can be as much as ten percentage *points.*

As we saw in chapter 6, Quaker Oats learned the same lesson—the hard way.

Calculating its cost of capital for 1988, Quaker Oats fixed the cost of the equity component at "approximately 14.3 percent," a seemingly precise figure.[16] I am skeptical about the value of this highly quantitative approach. The analysis of a proposed capital investment depends so much on the context of the industry, the nature of the competition, and other imponderables. Beyond that, managements should always leave a reasonable margin for the inevitable error of optimism. As William H. Schumann III, treasurer of FMC, commented, the optimism usually takes the form of not realizing that the competition is probably deciding to expand its capacity at the very time that you're deciding to expand yours, and once again you end up waging war at a time when the gods are not smiling. (Every inventor in a garage likes to think that the other garages house only the family car.) In capital budgeting, it is the analysis and the discipline that are valuable, not the close tweaking of the numbers. Companies such as FMC and Coca-Cola recognize this reality by not changing hurdle rates often. Exxon does so by defining its cost of capital only within a range of one to two percentage points. The company's chief financial officer, Sitter, summed it up well: while the theory is that you stop investing when the lines cross at X.X percent, "the lines are not lines but bands, and the investment return band is frequently quite a wide band."

SOME CONCLUDING OBSERVATIONS ON DIVIDEND POLICY

A YARDSTICK FOR DETERMINING DIVIDENDS: CASH FLOW VS. EARNINGS

How much money is available for dividends? Companies frequently say that they pay out 40 percent or so of earnings, but it is an answer that has not been thought out. It implies a certain consistency, which is what shareholders want, but why at 40 percent and not some other level, say 80 percent?

Certainly earnings are important, but a better starting point would be the cash flow from operations, a useful concept but one that needs definition. There is no single definition of operating cash flow, but it is customary to add back to a company's net earnings from operations several noncash items that were charged to earnings in the income statement, the most important of which are (1) depreciation, (2) amortization, if any, of intangible assets (typically those that arise from a business acquisition), and (3) increases in deferred taxes, to the extent they are likely to be permanent. (That is how the term "operating cash flow" is used here.) Depreciation is usually the largest of these items. It is an accounting proxy for the wear and tear and the obsolescence of a company's existing assets.

Operating cash flow is sometimes treated as if it were freely disposable income, but that is a serious mistake. We are entitled to think of cash flow as a source of dividends *if and only if* we first deduct those obligatory expenditures that must be made simply to enable a company to maintain its existing, stand-in-place business and competitive position. (Forklifts do wear out, and machine tools do become obsolete.) If the core business is a black hole, one into which dollars disappear, never to be seen again, those no-growth expenditures should be reexamined, but otherwise they are obligatory. Deducting them from operating cash flow leaves the amount that is realistically available for dividends, expansion, business acquisitions, prepayment of debt, and so on, referred to here as available cash flow.[17]

The *operating* cash flow will invariably be larger than the earnings, but often the *available* cash flow is not. Indeed, in a capital-intensive business there may be times when the cash flow that is available after obligatory expenditures is a negative number. At the end of the 1970s, for example, Ford Motor enjoyed a large and positive *operating* cash flow (earnings plus depreciation and amortization), but its *available* cash flow was either negative or at least not large enough to cover the dividend. Ford was reinvesting heavily to make its cars more fuel-efficient, an investment that had to be made if only to protect market share. Earnings in 1979 of about $1.2 billion were substantial, and depreciation and amortization of equipment added $1.6 billion more to cash flow. But net capital expenditures totaled $3.4 billion. While operating cash flow was $2.8 billion, available cash flow was negative as much as $600 million. On top of that, Ford paid a cash dividend of $470 million. Although the earnings and operating cash flow covered the dividend, the *available cash flow* did not. The dividend should have been dropped. Instead, the company paid out over $900 million in dividends in the years 1979–1981. It did not eliminate the dividend until 1982, by which time its working capital had been seriously eroded.

Much the same pattern could be seen more recently at Caterpillar, where, despite its already discussed, costly fight for survival, the company was maintaining in 1990 and early 1991 a dividend rate that was unsupported by available cash flows.

There is frequently a debate over which is more useful as an analytic tool: earnings or cash flow. The answer is that both are useful, and neither one alone tells you all that you need to know. Since both earnings and cash flow statements are required by the SEC, I have never understood the need to choose between them, except for those people who are unable to work with more than one number at a time. Cash flow statements, however, do show more readily that, even apart from capital expenditures, some businesses are more capital-intensive than others and are likely to have less freely available cash. Department stores are a good example. They require large amounts of capital to carry the necessary inventory and accounts receivable. Supermarkets, by contrast, require much less capital because they have no accounts receivable and their inventory turns over so much more rapidly that very little money is tied up. Often they are able to operate with negative working capital.[18] These differences in cash flow characteristics are enormously important.

It is inadvisable for companies to contemplate paying dividends on a regular basis except out of available cash flow. One of the few aspects of dividend policy on which there is widespread agreement is that a dividend rate, once established, should not be cut casually. Consistency, where practicable, is important. Leading corporations encourage individual investors, in particular, to think of a dividend as income that can be spent freely in day-to-day living without impairing their real, (that is, inflation-adjusted) capital.[19] Since investors typically do arrange their budgets so that their living expenses are covered by dividend, interest, and other ordinary income, once a dividend has been set, companies have an implicit responsibility to maintain it through the normal vicissitudes of a business cycle— that is, through bad years and good. Otherwise investors will be forced to rearrange their financial affairs at what may be the worst possible moment. Unless the regular dividend is set at a level within the expected available cash flow, the company will be borrowing to pay it in the best of times; and when earnings drop, the dividend will soon be cut or dropped altogether. On the other hand, companies that shape their dividend policy properly are demonstrating their loyalty and respect for shareholders in a concrete way.[20] That is not to say, however, that the dividend may never exceed the available cash flow but only that it should not do so on a regular basis. Because there may be exceptional years, the word *regular* is key.

TO BORROW OR NOT TO BORROW, THAT IS THE QUESTION

Many companies regularly enjoy significantly positive available cash flows because those cash flows reflect only the investments necessary to enable them to maintain existing positions. What if a company has in addition a variety of other attractive investment opportunities? Should it still not pay a dividend? Or should it borrow to pay dividends? On the assumption that any borrowing would be within reasonable bounds, the usual answer is to go ahead and pay a dividend. True, it sounds imprudent to borrow with one hand to pay dividends with the other, and in a closely held corporation management might be less inclined to do so. But for public corporations, history argues that if there is available cash flow, dividends should be the norm, even in the face of major capital expenditures. There is too much evidence, both anecdotal and systematic, that corporate executives who keep all the money tend to get sloppy.[21] Obviously there are exceptions. Emerging high-technology companies that are already starved for capital do not need the discipline of going to the bank to borrow the next quarter's dividend to keep them on their toes. There are exceptions, too, for brilliant CEOs with already impressive records. But that is the point: they are exceptional.

There are, however, large numbers of dividend-paying companies with shareholders who have come to expect dividends even though they are being financed by floating new debt or stock issues. In reality the companies have committed themselves to dividends and growth—cakes and ale—regardless of whether the available cash flow is sufficient to cover the dividends or whether interest rates are high or low. Are the managements being candid with shareholders about the source of the payout?

Southern Company was a typical utility of the late 1970s and 1980s. During the nine years 1975–1983, shareholders received total dividends of about $3.7 billion, well in excess of the company's earnings and cash flow after deducting the capital expenditures necessary just to sustain the existing operations. Where did the money come from? The company issued over $5 billion of new securities to replace the dividend payments, as well as to invest. The so-called earnings from which the dividend was implicitly being paid were a myth. Shareholders who thought of those dividends as ordinary income were misled because they were largely a return of capital. Over that nine-year period, book value per share of common stock fell by 5 percent in nominal dollars and in inflation-adjusted dollars by more than half.

Southern Company was a public utility and arguably had a mandate to invest in new generating capacity even if it was unprofitable to do so, but it did not have a mandate to pay dividends out of non-existent earnings—a problem of the company's own making. It, and other utilities like it, had catered for too long to a crowd of dividend junkies—shareholders who wanted a high "yield" even if there was no substance to it. Married to that group of investors—the better ones had long ago left—the company was caught in a catch-22. The business was not producing a real income sufficient to pay the dividend. But if the company had sought to switch to a rational dividend policy or even to explain the foolishness of this one, it would have jeopardized its ability to sell the new shares that enabled it to replenish its cash reserves. A lesson or two in corporate finance early on might have helped.

DIVIDEND REINVESTMENT PROGRAMS

Having raised the possibility of paying dividends out of something other than available cash flows, some mention should be made of the increasingly common practice of declaring dividends on the one hand and asking for the money back on the other. These dividend reinvestment programs, under which shareholders are entitled to buy additional shares with their cash dividends, sometimes at a discount from market, have become quite popular—and not just with the odd-lot holder, for whom they are a convenience. The sales pitch is that shareholders can build up their stock holdings in this fashion,[22] although obviously their real investment in the company would have been "built up" much more cheaply if the board had declared no (or a smaller) cash dividend. Graham and Dodd long ago pointed out the foolishness of paying out a taxable dividend and then urging shareholders (or their look-alikes) to use the 65 percent or so of the money that's left to buy more shares.[23] To the cheers of the Internal Revenue Service, over 1,000 companies have ignored that advice.

A FINAL WORD ABOUT DIVIDEND NONSENSE

The central issue of dividend policy is how well a company uses its resources compared to the available alternatives, notably those available to shareholders. That point of view, however, necessarily tends to ignore other, short-term considerations, such as day-to-day happenings in the stock market. A great deal of ink has been spilled by scholars who believe that dividends are useful as a signal to the market of management's expectations about future earnings. A higher dividend is said to signal its conviction that the earnings are real and will continue to grow, and this signal, in turn, is expected to produce a higher stock price. None of this makes much sense to me. Dividends can give inaccurate prophecies, as happened at Ford in 1979–1981, as well as accurate ones. But prophetic or not, if a company allocates capital intelligently and if it communicates those decisions with candor, dividend signals are irrelevant. Dividends are too important a *business* issue to be relegated to the role of (trivial) news carrier for the stock market.

SUMMARY

At the beginning of chapter 6 we saw a memorandum written to the board of directors by the chief executive and financial officers of our mythical company, Middle American, outlining the major issues affecting that company's, or any company's, dividend policy. The memorandum may have been "real" at Middle American, but I doubt that anything like it has been written at more than a handful of real companies. The dividend is usually an afterthought. It appears on the board agenda at the very beginning of the meeting—to have done with it—or at the very end, when the directors have spent their energy on more important matters. Rarely is dividend policy linked to investment policy. Management submits its capital budgets and dividends are paid out of what's left, even at companies with a proven knack for wasting money.

Of the various issues raised in that memorandum, we have dealt with all but one, the exception being share buybacks which are treated in the next chapter. But over and beyond this specific issue or that, the primary object has been to persuade the reader that dividends do matter; indeed they matter very much. They are at the heart of the difficult choice that managers must make in allocating their capital resources: reinvesting the money within the company or distributing it to shareholders. The crux of the analysis is fairly simple: reallocate the capital internally to noncompulsory uses only if the opportunities are better than those available generally to investors or, as it is sometimes put, only if the expected returns from the available investments exceed the opportunity cost of capital. That opportunity cost cannot be fixed with any precision, but looking at the compounded returns available to shareholders over long periods, a number in the range of 10 to 11 percent seems appropriate in the early 1990s. Interest rate fluctuations and other factors would cause it to change. This cost of capital represents only the minimum hurdle rate and so would affect only the tail end of the projects on management's list.

8

Corporate Share Repurchases

CONSIDER THE ALTERNATIVES

MEMO

TO: Board of Directors of Middle American Corporation
FROM: Phineas Nance, Senior Vice-President, Finance

Management will bring before the upcoming board meeting a proposal for repurchasing over time, in the open market, a substantial number of shares of common stock of the company. The buyback program to be submitted will be the first such proposal the board has considered. With that in mind, Charlie [C. E. O'Rourke, the company's chairman] has asked that I prepare this background memo for you.

As will become apparent at the meeting, management is quite enthusiastic about the prospect of buying back somewhere between 5 and 10 percent of the outstanding stock—depending, of course, on the price. In our view, share repurchase programs should be an integral part of a company's capital allocation process, one in which management weighs reinvestment opportunities not only against the alternative of cash dividends but also both of those alternatives against a third alternative, the buyback of common stock. This company has always formulated its cash dividend policy in those terms, accepting only internal projects that promised a return better than that available to shareholders on their own. Unless we can create value internally, dollar for dollar, we should return those dollars to the shareholders.

In one sense, share repurchases are simply another form of dividend because money is distributed to (some) holders of the common stock. And that is a common way of looking at share repurchases. But, on reflection, they are more than just a variation on the theme of cash distributions because the company has not just paid out cash; it has gotten something in return, its stock. Depending on the price and value of the shares, something quite unique, something quite dynamic, has been introduced into the capital allocation process. Tax savings are a part of the picture, but taxes alone do not explain the attraction of share buybacks.

A CHANGE IN ATTITUDE

Until a few years ago, not many companies repurchased their shares. In some quarters, it was barely respectable. There was a general sense that having once issued shares to raise money, there was no reason to buy them back. As one CEO said, his company was not in business for that purpose. In a sense, he was right. If a company buys another company's shares, it has an asset that it can book as such and even borrow against. But if it buys its own shares, what does it have? Certainly not an "asset." A stock repurchase shrinks the company's assets by the amount of cash paid out, it reduces the company's borrowing base, and it reduces the shareholders' aggregate equity. One might say that a buyback resembles a lizard lunching on its own tail. It seems unnatural. One wonders not just at the sight but how the tail could possibly be tasty.

People still remember the futile efforts by banks and investment companies in the late 1920s to shore up confidence and the price of their stocks by secretly buying their own shares in the open market. Beyond that, many people wondered why there was nothing better to do with the money. But those sentiments no longer express the prevailing mood. Fashions change. As recently as 1981, American corporations bought back just $2.5 billion of their outstanding shares. In 1982, when stocks were depressed, they still bought back only a meager $2.2 billion worth—or about 1/10 of 1 percent of the shares outstanding. Then, just a few years later, the pattern changed. Goodyear retired 48 percent of its shares, Union Carbide 55 percent, and others did much the same thing. During the years 1986–1988, buybacks averaged $48 billion a year.[1]

"PLAIN VANILLA" STOCK REPURCHASES

The proposal to be submitted at the board meeting contemplates what might be called an everyday, "plain vanilla" buyback, one in which a company has the simple, single purpose of reducing significantly—say, by 5 percent or more—its outstanding shares. Such a buyback can take place either by a tender offer to all shareholders or by purchasing stock day to day in the open market. At first blush, it may seem to be just another form of cash dividend because the company is distributing cash to shareholders. But even from the shareholders' point of view, there are major differences. Some shareholders receive cash and some don't, and those who don't will have increased their proportionate stake in the continuing business.

Some companies fund stock repurchases with cash on hand, some use borrowed money, and some who borrow have as their primary goal a reconfiguration of the company's capital structure so as to increase the proportion of debt to equity. Changing the debt-to-equity ratio may be a reasonable thing to do, but that is not what we have in mind here. It's not "plain vanilla," and for purposes of the board discussion, our purposes will be better served by a single-minded focus on buybacks that have no such secondary agenda. As you probably suspect, they are troublesome enough.

Some buybacks may look superficially like plain vanilla, but they are in fact quite different. Likely as not, they arise in response to a real or feared takeover bid. In recent years, for example, Phillips Petroleum, Carter Hawley Hale, and many others were drastically restructured as part of a plan to preempt hostile bids. Typically the company sold assets and borrowed to the hilt, all with a view to offering shareholders a premium price for their shares. These restructurings are in substance more like leveraged buyouts than the plain vanilla buyback that we will propose. For example, in 1985, Phillips Petroleum was faced with hostile bids from two different sources. In response, it took several defensive steps, one of which was to tender for 20 million of its own shares at a total cost of $1 billion.

Buybacks that are open only to a particular group, and not to shareholders generally, are also "nonvanilla." Companies such as Texaco, Holiday, Ashland Oil, and Bally Manufacturing have paid greenmail to hostile suitors such as the Bass brothers, the Belzbergs, and Donald Trump. By paying a premium for the raiders' shares, the companies remove the raiders from the scene.

THE ABUSE OF EVEN PLAIN VANILLA BUYBACKS

Having put to one side greenmail, one might think that the garden variety of buyback would not raise significant problems. It's quite the other way around, however. Greenmail payments to a raider, made at a premium over the predawn price, are obviously unfair to the company's remaining shareholders. Managers with even a schoolyard sense of decency don't do it. By contrast, a plain vanilla buyback is an ambiguous transaction. As is often said, companies are in business to operate stores, build airplanes, or whatever, and not to "trade" in their own capital stock or to "shrink" the company. The most common criticism is that a buyback is an admission that management has failed to find good uses for capital.[2] Good managers, it is claimed, should not have to fall back on this sort of financial maneuver. Let the company pay a cash dividend; shareholders can do their own buying if the stock is cheap.

Buybacks are also suspect thanks to the CEOs who try to manipulate markets. In the 1920s, when the disclosure rules were more lax, companies often bought in their shares to conceal bad news. From the shareholders' point of view, it was a case of double jeopardy: their own money was being used to deceive them. In the days before deposit insurance, banks bought in huge amounts of stock, hoping to keep up appearances and avoid a run on the bank.[3] On the heels of the 1929 crash, being less than clairvoyant, some banks continued to buy in their shares, chasing the market on the way down. Like Alice following the White Rabbit, they disappeared down a deep hole.

Today the primary fear is that companies buying in their shares may be concealing good news rather than bad. Believing, perhaps, that earnings are about to move up, managers are tempted to use buy-ins to flush out an unsuspecting public on the cheap.[4] Or, if not that, the insiders, trying to soak up stock that might otherwise fall into hostile hands, may be entrenching themselves at shareholder expense. Whatever the specific fear, underlying them all is a widespread conviction that the process is inherently suspect; for a company to repurchase its stock amounts to "shoveling around pieces of paper," as one critic said.[5]

The critics have often been right. Datapoint, a mid-size manufacturer of computer networking equipment, sustained losses of $125 million in the three fiscal years 1985–1987. Its U.S. revenues fell during the three years from $123 million to $51 million, reflecting competitive pressures on technology, sales volume, and price. Having already bought back 12 percent of its shares, thus reducing the total to 18 million, the company exchanged a new 13 percent preferred stock for an additional 8 million shares of common in 1987. True, the common was exchanged for preferred stock, not debt. But what conceivable corporate purpose could have been served? The company continued to lose money, and unlike the common, the preferred cost the company $10 million a year in dividends. Meanwhile Datapoint slid further downhill. A year later, a possible purpose for all this "shoveling around" of financial paper emerged. The chairman of the company, Asher Edelman, one of the more visible corporate raiders of the day, offered to buy the balance of the common stock. Having cut the number of common shares in half, he had succeeded in reducing the out-of-pocket cash cost of acquiring absolute control.

Like Datapoint, Tektronix is a high-tech company that was weakened by substantial stock buybacks. Mid-size technology companies are usually in the wrong stage of development to shrink their capital. Tektronix, which makes test and measurement products and computer equipment, had experienced flat to declining sales for several years. Having bought back 3 million shares in 1986–1987, the company borrowed heavily in 1988 and retired still another 9.5 million shares at a cost of $346 million, or an average of $36 a share. That same year, the company lost money. In 1989 it turned a modest profit, but a third of its staff had been laid off, and the backlog was down. And despite a strong stock market, the stock was trading below $20 a share, barely half the level the company paid just a year earlier.

It is surprising how often companies are willing to acknowledge that propping up the price of the stock is a reason for their buybacks.[6] Some, such as Tandy, have been quite candid. A Tandy official has said that with the company's business in a "transition period"—aren't they all?—buybacks were an important defensive device. Indeed, to get more bang for a buck, the company preferred to buy shares over time rather than by a one-shot tender offer. And to get still more bang, he added, it gave the commission business to brokerage houses whose analysts wrote up the company affirmatively.[7] For a time at least, it is true, such defensive tactics will soak up stock that might otherwise be accumulated by an unfriendly holder, but they are deceptive, if not fraudulent.

The most obvious risk is that the company will take advantage of inside information. Even with no specific developments in the offing, CEOs often have much better insights as to the value of the company. That nose for value is not something that an insider ordinarily has to share. The law probably insists—it's not all that clear—that when a company uses money that belongs to all the shareholders to buy out some of them, it has an affirmative obligation to disclose its intentions.[8] At best, however, the public shareholdeers are kept pretty much in the dark. It is not easy to distinguish bad buyouts, where management is not acting in good faith, from well-intentioned ones. Figuring the proper value of a share of stock is no simple trick. Should shareholders keep their shares or should they tender? There is usually a range of values, and the shareholders get no help from management.[9] Like Comprehensive Care, which shrunk its stock by one-fourth in fiscal 1987, companies generally say something bland— such as that the repurchase is in the best interests of all the share-holders—and very little else.[10]

THE RULE ABROAD

Outside the United States, the law generally reflects this fear of abuse. Much as they did here, for example, banks in Germany had tried to prop up the price of their stocks in the late 1920s and 1930, sometimes eroding their capital base by more than half.[11] In most European countries, buybacks are now either prohibited, as in Sweden, or severely restricted, as in Germany. In the United States, where regulation is divided between the states and the federal government, there are some modest disclosure requirements and some safeguards against overt market manipulation, but that's about all. The British, somewhere between these two extremes, no longer prohibit share repurchases but do require prior shareholder approval of the amount to be bought, the price to be paid, and other aspects that American companies would regard as cramping their legitimate freedom.[12]

In sum, the potential for abuse is there, and, sadly, that potential has often been realized. Does that suggest some ambivalence in our recommendation that Middle American commit substantial funds to the program? Charlie will have more to say about this at the meeting, but the answer is "no." Very few financial concepts or tools are inherently good or bad; any blade will cut in both directions. A company's business and prospects, its financial strength, its sense of moderation, all play a role. In the right hands, with the right perspective, we believe that share repurchases often represent an outstanding use of capital.

Nance was right, there are often good reasons for a buyback program, at least in the hands of a thoughtful management. Sometimes a repurchase of shares is clearly better than a cash dividend, better than investing the same dollars back in the business, and better than doing nothing at all. But it requires of management a patient analysis, a high degree of objectivity about the company and its prospects, and a fair amount of intellectual integrity about one's own role there and the rights of shareholders. That's no small threshold.

Despite the possibility of error, the rewards for a soundly conceived share repurchase program can be enormous. One of the rules of finance offered in the Introduction of this book was that it is difficult to reinvest the retained earnings of a good business successfully. With rare exceptions, managers fall victim to the unrealistic expectation that they can find another business just as good as one they now have, or that they can make it as good, or that having found a good one, it does not much matter what price they pay. Share repurchases often offer them the opportunity to buy more of a good business, the one they already own, at a price that makes the purchase either attractive by any standard or at least better than the next available alternative.

BARGAIN PURCHASES

The most obvious occasion for a plain vanilla repurchase is where the company can buy stock at a substantial discount from intrinsic value. That may sound straightforward, but intrinsic value is a slippery concept. Along with a few others such as "maximizing shareholder value" and "strategic planning," "intrinsic value" is one of the most abused phrases in the financial vocabulary. It has nothing to do with the next turn (or even two) in the stock market. It has nothing to do with the stock price last month or last year or with the price the company's stock would enjoy if it sold at the same price-earnings ratio as the industry average. If the airline industry is selling at twenty times current earnings, it does not mean that Delta's stock is selling below intrinsic value because its price-earnings ratio is somewhat less. Such discounts may be important to traders who hope to capture them in the next few days or weeks but not to companies considering whether to retire stock.

All of those so-called discounts are based either on where the stock market has just been or on expectations of where it is about to go. They have nothing to do with intrinsic value *because they look to the stock market not just for a good opportunity to buy, which is sensible, but for the ultimate reward, which is not*. The stock may in fact rise, but for a stock buyback that's about as meaningful as saying that the investment in the East Asian market by our fictitious company, Middle American, was a brilliant move because ultimately the common stock went up. It confuses cause and effect. It confuses the real success of an investment with the mirror of it in the stock market.

CALCULATING THE INVESTMENT VALUE OF REPURCHASED SHARES

A stock repurchase should be analyzed, just as any other investment would be, on the basis of the projected stream of income and cash flow over time. On that basis, there are sometimes splendid opportunities. In the late 1970s, for example, when I was president of Supermarkets General, a leading food chain, its stock was selling at about five times its current earnings and at an even lower multiple of projected earnings for the next three to five years. Even at five times earnings, the buyback promised a return after taxes of 20 percent a year, well above the company's internal benchmark for investments in the business itself. Better yet, the company had sufficient capital resources so that there were no hard choices to make. It could build and support whatever new stores were available—good sites are hard to find—and it could (and did) also buy back over 5 percent of its shares. In buying those shares, the company was capturing for the continuing shareholders a stream of income, much as it would in a tangible investment. And unlike some of the other "opportunities" available to the company, this one was in an already profitable business, the one that management knew best. It already knew that the accounting was honest, and the bills had all been paid on time.

In the 1980s, when I was no longer at the company—which may have been the reason—Supermarkets General's stock rose sharply. Everyone was delighted, but that is not why the earlier decision to shrink the number of shares was a good idea.

It is true, of course, that shares of its own common stock were not an "investment" for Supermarkets General in the usual sense. They could not be booked as an asset. (Once upon a time the accountants allowed such tricks, but no more.) Supermarkets General, the company, was poorer, not richer, for having made this "great" investment. (A cynic might say that too many such successes would have undone the company.) Still, a buyback should be analyzed as an advantageous investment, if—and it is a big if—management is looking at the long-term welfare of all the shareholders and if it can increase the intrinsic value per share outstanding after the transaction. For the continuing shareholders, a share repurchase is often a particularly exciting concept, with high prospects for advantage.[13]

Buffett succinctly captured the excitement of share repurchases in the 1984 annual report of Berkshire Hathaway. The stock market, he said, is not as efficient as many economists and business school professors would have us believe; sometimes bargains do exist. Companies that seize those opportunities have demonstrated their "pro-shareholder leanings" more directly than any glossy, four-color annual report or handout:

> The obvious point involves basic arithmetic: major repurchases at prices well below per-share intrinsic business value immediately increase, in a highly significant way, that value. When companies purchase their own stock, they often find it easy to get $2 of present value for $1. Corporate acquisition programs almost never do as well and, in a discouragingly large number of cases, fail to get anything close to $1 of value for each $1 expended.
>
> The other benefit of repurchases is less subject to precise measurement but . . . [by] making repurchases when a company's market value is well below its business value, management clearly demonstrates that it is given to actions that enhance the wealth of shareholders, rather than to actions that expand management's domain. . . . Investors should pay more for a business that is lodged in the hands of a manager with demonstrated pro-shareholder leanings than for one in the hands of a self-interested manager marching to a different drummer.[14]

BARGAIN PRICES: FAIR OR UNFAIR?

Buying back stock for 50 cents on the dollar of intrinsic value may not seem controversial, but like everything else about buybacks it is. One fear is that what is good for the continuing shareholders is, by definition, bad for those who have sold their shares back to the company. Why would anyone knowingly sell "dollars" for 50 cents? There must have been some deception, or else the sellers would not have sold. In short, the critics suspect that at the heart of any bargain purchase there inevitably lies an unfair advantage.[15]

The implicit assumption is that a stock repurchase program is a zero-sum game; whatever one group gains, the other loses. And behind that assumption lies another important one: in substance a company's shareholders all have the same investment goals or horizons. If Middle American were privately owned, with only twenty or so shareholders, that second assumption would be essentially correct. None of the twenty could trade in and out of the stock. The shareholders would have little choice but to measure their personal profit in terms of the company's profits and dividends. But for a public company, the assumption that all the shareholders are patient holders who have held the stock for years and expect, or at least are willing, to leave it to their children is obviously unrealistic. Trading has soared since 1960, when a pokey 3 million shares a day changed hands on the New York Stock

Exchange. Now the turnover is 150 million shares or more a day. (Indeed, much of the total trading goes unreported in those numbers.) It's not Uncle Bill in Peoria who's doing all that trading. Many of Middle American's shares are held at any given time by a wide array of professionals with hyperactive tendencies:

- Traders who are in the stock for a few hours and who readily concede that they never pay (and probably should not pay) attention to fundamentals.
- Traders who are in the stock for a few weeks or until the stock moves up a few points.
- Money managers who bought the stock without looking inside the package, because it is in the drug industry and they believe that the industry as a whole will move up against the market in the next ninety days or so.
- Money managers who set a target of 30 percent or so price appreciation and at that point will kick out the stock regardless of fundamentals. (That members of this group are sometimes called fundamental-value investors reveals how little money managers sometimes understand about value investing.)
- Program traders who are ready to buy or sell this and all the other stocks in the Standard & Poor's 500 Stock Index because of an arbitrage opportunity but may not be able to "unwind" the transaction for several weeks.

In fact, even among professionals, very little money is managed on patient, Graham-and-Dodd, fundamental-value principles. (Institutional money management is discussed at greater length in chapter 11.) A few years ago I did a very unsystematic survey and came up with 5 percent as the amount of money being managed on a genuine long-term basis. Most business people already know that intuitively. They have all seen security analysts sell off their company's stock in a near panic anytime a quarter's earnings disappoint them. And a variety of research that is much more thorough says that my little survey was either correct or as correct as need be.[16]

Because shareholders come in so many different versions, with such different interests, a share buyback is not a zero-sum game but rather one that everyone can win, according to individual goals. *Because their goals are so different, it is not true that a company can capture a bargain on behalf of the continuing, nonselling shareholders only at the expense of those who do sell.* An example may help clarify the concept. In a bid for tenders in May 1984, Teledyne was offering $200 a share for 5 million shares of its common stock—about 25 percent of the total then outstanding.[17] Before the announcement, the stock was selling at about $156 a share. Those who did not tender, including management (which already owned about 12 percent of the stock), were presumably holding Teledyne for the long pull. Obviously they thought the intrinsic value of their investment would benefit. But those who were in Teledyne for the short run were apparently ecstatic at the prospect of a quick 29 percent gain. The 5 million share offer was promptly oversubscribed, and the company ultimately bought all 8.7 million shares that were tendered at a total cost of over $1.7 billion.[18]

Teledyne, which had bought back stock all during the 1970s and early 1980s, had some long-term, value investors who were unwilling to sell a "dollar" at a discount. Investors who held their shares throughout those years saw the stock rise from $8 a share (adjusted for splits) in the early 1970s to over $250 in the second half of 1984. Those who sold into those buybacks also did well, but the nonsellers did even better.

In a leveraged buyout, the shareholders are given no meaningful choice—either tender your shares now or see them redeemed in a freezeout merger three months later. But in a buyback there is a choice, at least where management makes adequate disclosure of business developments and prospects. The issue for a shareholder is whether to take the money and run or be patient. Not everyone can be patient; not everyone wants to be.

What is adequate disclosure? In a share buyback, a company should reverse the usual emphasis. Instead of being especially candid about negative information, the company should be absolutely sure to disclose all the potentially cheery news. Nor should management stop at disclosure only of the hard news. There are often a variety of so-called soft data relating to plans, appraisals, or prospects that may be quite problematic but are capable of having a significant impact. Managements don't usually like to release these cheery projections. There is an ingrained tendency to be cautious about these matters because ordinarily they are reluctant to disappoint investors. But this is not the ordinary case. That is particularly true for companies where management owns a substantial part of the stock and therefore has a palpable conflict of interest.[19]

SHOULD SHAREHOLDERS DO THEIR OWN BARGAIN HUNTING?

It is sometimes said that, taxes aside, a self-tender is neither better nor worse than a cash dividend. Teledyne could simply have paid that

$1.7 billion as a cash dividend—the equivalent of $200 a share for the over 8 million shares acquired in the 1984 tender offer—and let shareholders buy additional stock for themselves. Tax-exempt investors, in particular, could have increased their proportionate ownership exactly as did those who elected not to tender.

What is overlooked is that there are some unique benefits to a properly conceived share repurchase plan. First, while it is no doubt correct that shareholders, on receiving a cash dividend, *could* reinvest in the company, the reality is that they don't—or at least there is no reason to expect that they will. Shareholders—particularly individual shareholders who, after all, still own most of the shares—do not get up every morning, or even every Monday morning, and reassess each of their holdings. True, a sinking stock price should stimulate investors to consider buying additional shares. Often, however, it has the reverse effect of inducing them to sell and cut their losses. By repurchasing shares, a conscientious and loyal management, aware that the stock is at a discount, in effect is capturing the bargain for all rather than for the few. It should be congratulated for doing so.

The more basic flaw in the "taxes aside" argument against share repurchases is that for most shareholders, taxes do count. It is a mystery, in fact, why so many thoughtful finance books open the discussion of a problem by saying "taxes aside."[20] In a discussion of finance, it's a bit like saying "money aside." (Hitting aside, I might have been a good ballplayer.) A shareholder is taxed fully on a dividend but on a sale of stock only to the extent that he or she has a gain. With a combined federal and state income tax rate of, say, 35 percent, taxes count a whole lot. And for long-term holders who do not tender any of their shares back to the company, there is a major additional tax advantage: all taxes are deferred for an indefinite period, a superb result whose benefits are not often recognized, and about the best that a tax planner could hope to do.

SHARE REPURCHASES: GOOD SENSE EVEN WITHOUT A BARGAIN PRICE

Fifty-cent dollars are not always lying around for the asking, and as the discount shrinks, so do some of the unique attractions of a stock buyback. But bargain or no bargain, the basic issue remains the same. What can management do with the money as compared with what shareholders can do with it for themselves? We saw that same tension in the discussion in chapter 7 of cash dividends, and it applies fully as much to a share repurchase. My own corporate experience was that, once some cash began to accumulate, the urge to be creative with it was almost irresistible. What peerless leader wants to admit to managerial impotence? A former executive of American Standard, John L. Grant, captured that urge marvelously well. Picture yourself, he said, in the executive suite and imagine how the boss is likely to regard a buildup of cash in the company's coffers. He should, Grant said, consider repurchasing stock, but the thoughts really going through his mind are the following:

- "If we don't find more investment opportunities and show we can grow, our excessive liquidity will make us a takeover candidate and all my plans for the future may be shattered."
- "We need growth to maintain a good image in the investment community, as well as to attract and hold able employees."
- "Our cash gives us a means of diversifying and making our business less subject to the ups and downs of the business cycle."
- "We need to grow because there's a higher margin of safety in bigness. Also, it's nice to see our name rising on the *Fortune* 500 list."[21]

It may not sound very bold to walk down the hall at corporate headquarters and tell people that we're giving money back to the shareholders. How will that help to attract and hold good managers? As Grant suggested, the shareholder response ought to be simple: we don't need you to diversify or buffer the business cycle. We expect mature companies such as this one to generate cash rather than spending it on extraneous acquisitions, which do not assist present businesses, have only average potential, considering the prices paid, and require new business skills for wise control. The response of a thoughtful employee ought not to be very different because companies that waste money rarely provide either long-term opportunities or security. In short, it is not immoral to hold cash until you have something useful to do with it, and it is not a shameful retreat to pay dividends or repurchase stock.

Audio/Video Affiliates is a case in point. In the late 1980s the company operated over a hundred consumer electronics stores, primarily in small cities. It was conservatively capitalized and could have continued to open new outlets, but with VCR sales flattening out and no new products coming on stream, most electronics retailers were doing poorly. The company's sales fell by 15 percent during the two years ended January 1989, to $195 million; profits fell by more than 50 percent. A proposed buyout of the company failed, and although it had the resources, the company decided not to invest further in the business at that time. Instead it offered to all shareholders an opportunity to sell back to the company, pursuant to a tender offer, about 30 percent of the outstanding shares at a price well above market.[22] As one director put it, the company decided to return its excess capital to shareholders and to do so in a tax-efficient way.[23]

A critic might have said that Audio/Video should have found better uses for the money. But in reality, with the industry marking time, the only alternative was to diversify. When one company buys another, it often ends up in a bidding contest, with the so-called winner paying top dollar. The buyer's shareholders lose. In a well-conceived plain vanilla share repurchase, there need be no losers.

THE BASELINE CASE

Even so, at some point the market price may be so high that a share repurchase plan does not make sense. The "return" on the investment in treasury stock may become so low that any excess cash or untapped borrowing power might better be used to pay cash dividends. But the price at which that happens is higher than is usually realized. Assume, for example, that a few years from now the stock of our fictitious drug company, Middle American, is earning about 20 percent on shareholder equity—down from 25 or so percent previously but still excellent—and that it is paying out 40 percent of its earnings as dividends. Earnings would be growing at a 12 percent compounded annual rate. (With a 20 percent return on equity and with dividends equal to eight percentage points, the equity would grow by 12 percent a year and so, therefore, would earnings.) That's not bad, but let's assume that by then the company has available to it fewer attractive opportunities for new business investments. Let's assume also that the stock is selling at three times its book value— roughly normal for a good drug company. At that price, and given our assumptions about profits and the dividend payout ratio, the company's stock would be selling at a price that would produce an earnings yield of slightly more than 6 percent, or about one-third of the 20 percent yield on book value. Stated the usual way, the price-earnings ratio would be 16—the reciprocal of 6+ percent— and the company would be paying annual cash dividends amounting to 2.67 percent of the market price.

For a company to buy back its stock at a price that produces an earnings yield of less than 7 percent on the investment seems too low to make it worthwhile. Certainly the stock would not look like a 50 cent dollar. But wait. If that 12 percent growth rate and the price-earnings ratio are sustainable—an extremely important "if"—a share repurchase program may still be attractive. If the company continues to earn 20 percent on equity, which in turn is growing 12 percent annually, the nonselling shareholders will enjoy a total return of 14.67 percent annually, consisting of 12 percent in stock price appreciation and 2.67 percent in cash dividends, as the following figures show:

Return on equity (book value)	20%
Dividend payout ratio	40%
Annual growth in book value and earnings	12%
Ratio of market price to book value	3 X
Average annual growth in market price per share	12%
Average annual dividend yield on market price	2.67%
Total annual return to shareholders (market appreciation plus dividends)	14.67%

Of course, such assumptions, *on average*, tend to be too good to be true. Over a fifty-year period, stocks (including stocks that started out at high prices reflecting the high returns then being earned on equity) have earned for investors a total return of about 10 percent compounded annually.[24] But even an annual return of 10 percent from a share repurchase program may be acceptable for a nontaxable investor, such as a pension fund. After all, such an investor demonstrates, by holding on to a company's shares, that it prefers investment in this company, at its present share price, to investment in the marketable shares of other available companies. And the continuing, fully taxable shareholder should have a *much* better result from share repurchases. The taxable shareholder, by forgoing a dividend in exchange for corporate use in share repurchases of the same funds, gets to earn money on the taxes that would have been paid currently on a cash dividend—taxes that are put off until, much later, the sale price for the shares is enhanced by the, say, 10 percent–return investment the company made on his or her behalf when it repurchased stock.

The arithmetic can get interesting when repurchases continue over a long period, allowing large effects from compound interest. If you earn 10 percent per year on your money, pay taxes each year at a 33.3 percent rate, and invest the balance at 10 percent before taxes, you will earn 6.67 percent per year after taxes and will, after compounding, increase a $10,000 investment to about $100,000 after taxes over thirty-six years. If I, on the other hand, invest $10,000 at a

10 percent compounded annual rate, before taxes, and pay no tax until cash-in time, thirty-six years later, when I will pay taxes at the same 33.3 percent rate, then I realize $309,000, pay $103,000 in taxes, and have left $206,000, more than twice as much as you have. My $206,000 has given me an annual, compounded-rate, after-tax return of 8.77 percent, compared with yours of only 6.67 percent. The difference is entirely due to my pay-later arrangement with the income tax collector. And, besides, under current tax law, neither I nor my transferees may ever pay any income tax on my gain because I may die with my stock, give it to my favorite charity (in ways that avoid the alternative minimum tax) or others who can use its full economic value without taxation.

Thus, buying in shares of Middle American at sixteen times current earnings might not be a great bargain for nontaxable shareholders, but it can provide a satisfactory result for them, and a great result for taxable shareholders, even if Middle American cools down enough to provide only a 10 percent return for existing investors. Moreover, the result, even if modest, may be a great deal better than that available from throwing money at acquisitions stimulated by fee-receiving advisers.

This description of Middle American resembles somewhat the experience of Merck. Over the years 1984–1987, Merck bought back about 11 percent of its common shares for about $1.9 billion, reducing the number of shares from 444 million to 394 million (adjusted for a stock split in 1988). While the company's return on book value and price-earnings ratio were somewhat different, the averages were about the same as those of Middle American.

SOME BETTER-THAN-BASELINE CASES

If from time to time bargains are available and if a company is willing to buy stock aggressively, the rewards will far exceed the baseline case. During the 1970s, the Washington Post company bought in stock, shrinking the number of shares outstanding from about 19 million at the end of 1974 to about 14 million at the end of 1981—more than 25 percent. The company's net earnings grew from $14 million in 1974 to $33 million in 1981, compounding at an annual rate of 11.89 percent. But the earnings per share grew over that period from $.78 to $2.32, a compounded annual increase of 16.85 percent. What would have been in any event an excellent result for shareholders was transformed into a superb one. The extra ingredients were the substantial amounts of stock that the company was willing to buy, plus the fact that during the mid- to late 1970s, it was able to do so at "discount" prices of seven to eight times current earnings. For a shareholder who bought 1,000 shares at the beginning of 1975 and *did not sell*, an investment of about $12,500 became one of about $125,000, which, because it had never been taxed, was still there seven years later. In a good company, in a good industry, augmenting important assets *per share* is the key.

Now, continuing our little study of the effects of compound interest, consider a taxable shareholder who also bought 1,000 shares of the Washington Post company in 1975 for $12,500 but instead of holding them sold out at year end and reinvested the after-tax proceeds in a company just as successful as the Washington Post. Assume, being astute, that she repeated the process each year, and assume further that this pattern continued not for seven years but for a somewhat longer period of fifteen years. In short, assume that she defied the odds and found each successive year, fifteen times over, still another equally good company. Assume, too, that her federal and state capital gains tax averaged 28 percent a year. By mid-1989, ignoring dividends and commissions, she would have had $355,000 worth of stock, which is not bad but not nearly so good as the $1.2 million that a do-nothing, nonselling, continuing shareholder would have had. When we speak of someone having the patience of Job, we forget how profitable it can be.

THE FINANCIAL TIGER AT EXXON

Exxon has had the largest repurchase program of all. During the six years 1983–1988, it bought back (net of resales and adjusted for a stock split) 524 million shares at an aggregate cost of $14.5 billion— $4.1 billion in 1988 alone. Everything that Exxon does, of course, is on a larger-than-life scale, but the scale here was large even for Exxon. By the end of 1988, the company had retired 28 percent of the 1.81 billion shares that had once been outstanding. Exxon generates large cash flows from operations—about $10 billion a year from 1983 to 1988. Jack F. Bennett, the senior vice-president of finance during those years, would later say that compared to the alternatives, share repurchases had been the most advantageous use of excess cash flow for shareholders. The company was already paying substantial dividends, he said, and shareholders are reluctant to see the dividend rate fluctuate. They are much readier "to accept volatility in share repurchases than dividends," so if a major opportunity had come along, the company would have felt free to stop buying stock. In addition, the company took into account the tax advantages for many shareholders of a share repurchase program over cash dividends.

It is tempting to see Exxon as simply having bought back oil on the cheap, but Bennett rejected that. The program was conceived, he said, on essentially the same return-on-investment basis as any other capital expenditure—the same basis recommended all through this chapter.[25]

Stated differently, while the company continued to invest about $6 billion to $9 billion a year in its oil exploration and other operations, it was unable to invest more—by buying oil reserves, for example—without dropping below the company's hurdle rate. Since it refused to do that, buying back stock was a happy alternative. (How many other companies have fudged the numbers just to invest in dubious projects or acquisitions?) The price of oil had dropped sharply in the early 1980s, depressing the price of all oil company stocks, and as Bennett drily observed, the company presumably had higher expectations about the company's eventual prospects than did the marginal seller of stock. (For years, the stock of Exxon, a company with huge oil reserves and established market positions, sold at six times earning or less.)

Bennett apparently felt free to halt the program from time to time, depending on market conditions, but he sought board approval for continued purchases each quarter.

SHARE REPURCHASES VERSUS DIVERSIFICATION: EXXON VERSUS AMERICAN EXPRESS

Charles R. Sitter, Bennett's successor at Exxon, rightly fears, as he has said, that companies with strong cash flows will "let the money burn a hole in [their] pockets" if they don't distribute the excess. Diversification is a seductive trap. The fact that you can run one type of business well, he explained, doesn't prove that you can also run something else—or, he might have added, overcome the burden of having paid too high an entry price.

Sitter did not name any companies that had embarked on misguided diversification programs, but one that fits the description marvelously well is American Express, a company that dissipated more than half of its likely value in this fashion. American Express owned a great business, better than Exxon's, called Travel Related Services (TRS), which included the company's credit card and traveler's check operations. The American Express credit card was the prestige card in the industry and commanded a loyal following despite its higher charges. Traveler's checks were an even more attractive operation because customers received no interest for depositing large amounts of money with the company—$24 billion of checks were issued in 1989—which the company could then lend out at high rates. During the 1980s, TRS's net income (after taxes) grew at a 20 percent compounded annual rate—from $177 million in 1980 to $830 million in 1989. TRS consistently earned 27 percent or more on shareholders' equity. Exxon, on the other hand, deals in a commodity, whose pricing is erratic and subject to political and other factors over which Exxon has no control.

In a sense, the success at TRS may have been the problem because it emboldened management to suppose that it could repeat it elsewhere. The company used the entire stream of profits from TRS, and much more, to stitch together the pieces of what became Shearson Lehman Hutton, hoping to make of it the keystone of a diversified financial services supermarket, a global one at that. American Express bought other businesses, too, but the Shearson operation was by far the largest and most grandiose. As of June 30, 1990, the company had invested about $4 billion in Shearson, not including capital raised directly by Shearson itself. It began with the purchase of Shearson for $1 billion in shares of American Express in 1981 and concluded with more than $1 billion of additional investments in late 1989 and early 1990 to staunch the hemorrhaging at Shearson. To put that $4 billion in scale, at the beginning of 1981, the year the first segment of Shearson was acquired, American Express's entire net worth was $2.2 billion, and the total stock market value of the company was $2.9 billion. Shearson built lavish offices around the world, including a $25 million conference center–ski resort in Colorado, but the so-called synergy from a global financial services business was never more than a mirage; it shone brightly in the prose of American Express's annual reports but then disappeared on a closer look. Even in the salad years 1987–1988, Shearson failed to earn a return of more than 6 percent on equity. From 1981 through mid-1990, taken as a whole, and after allocating corporate overhead expenses, the business did not make so much as a single dollar. In the language of an Exxon, it was a dry hole.

American Express bought a variety of other businesses, and on some of them it made money, but overall the results there too were mixed at best. In 1987 and 1988, for example, a banking subsidiary, Trade Development Bank (now merged with American Express Bank), took huge losses on $1.6 billion of Third World country loans, and half again as much remained on the books. At the end of the 1980s, of all the major businesses it had bought under the incumbent management, only one was still there *and profitable*: IDS Financial Services, a business that was earning about 14 percent on shareholders' equity but which will always be for American Express a relatively small one. It would be difficult to unravel all of these bold moves to see what American Express would have looked like today if it had possessed the discipline of an Exxon, except, of course, that it would have been a great company. But it is not too difficult to do so just with Shearson, to see what American Express might have looked like in June 1990 if it had reinvested the TRS profits back into the well managed TRS business by buying back stock, instead of ploughing money into a historically troubled industry in pursuit of an imperial dream.

The company began the decade with 285 million shares outstanding. Using the Shearson monies to buy back stock would have reduced that to perhaps as little as 188 million. Instead, management allowed the outstanding shares to balloon to 445 million by mid-1990. James D. Robinson III, the chairman, seemed oblivious to the fact that each newly issued share represented a dilution of the shareholders' stake in its existing businesses, including the wonderful TRS. Almost all those shares, including the 27 million sold in June 1990 to make good the losses at Shearson, were sold at low multiples of earnings. It was little short of criminal. American Express, which owned the outstanding TRS business, was selling (parts of) it on the cheap. (Peter Lynch, who ran the Fidelity Magellan fund, has coined a crude but apt term for such acquisition programs, *diworseification*.[26])

It is true that Wall Street, at least, applauded the purchase of the first segments of Shearson Lehman Hutton. And it is surely possible that if American Express had not been so taken with the ambitious model of a financial supermarket and if Shearson had continued to be run in the same penny-pinching, prudent style as before the acquisition, the outcome would have been acceptable. But as much as half of the ultimate investment in the Shearson financial supermarket came as part of, or in the wake of, the purchase of Hutton, and by then the applause had dried up.

More telling than any cheers or boos from the gallery was an incident that took place in the summer of 1985. Sanford I. Weill had been the CEO of Shearson when it was acquired in 1981, and in 1983 he became the president of American Express itself. By 1985, having left the company, he offered to buy its insurance subsidiary, Fireman's Fund. At a meeting of the American Express board of directors to consider his offer, Weill appeared and so, too, did Warren Buffett, the chairman of Berkshire Hathaway, who was to have provided some of Weill's capital. Buffett had once been a substantial investor in American Express and knew the company well. He was sitting on Weill's side of the table but, even so, offered the board some advice. Regardless of whether they sold Fireman's Fund to Weill, he said, they should sell it to someone. Buffett described TRS as an exquisite franchise, which to him meant that TRS operated in a market and with products that, like few others, did not have to compete primarily on price. American Express should sell all its other businesses, because, he said, they were fuzzying up this great franchise. According to one of the participants, Buffett's comments had an "electric impact" on the board, particularly on Howard L. Clark, Sr., the retired CEO of American Express. It might have been hoped that these comments would stimulate some reexamination of the American Express diversification program, and for a time they seemed to have had some effect. The company sold off portions of Fireman's Fund, not to Weill but as part of public offerings in October 1985 and May 1986. But by 1987 Robinson was back on the diworseification trail in a serious way, throwing the ill-fated Hutton log on the Shearson pile.

Table 8–1 gives values for American Express—both actual and as it might have looked had it never heard of Shearson. Let's assume that American Express had not issued the 85 million shares of stock (adjusted for stock splits) used to buy Shearson in 1981. Assume, too, that using the $3 billion in cash it later invested in Shearson, it had retired stock at a price equal to the highest price in each of the years those monies were disbursed. Valued at the same multiple of twelve times current earnings at which it was actually selling in mid-1990, the stock of this "what if" American Express would have traded at over twice the price at which it was in fact trading. True, the actual price previously paid to repurchase shares in the open market might have been higher, but then too the price-earnings ratio for the "what if" company might also have been higher. Assuming that those two factors balance each other out, it seems altogether likely that the shareholders would have been at least two times richer. An American Express

Table 8–1

American Express: What Was and What If

	Actual American Express	"What If" American Express
Earnings per share		
12 months ended June 20, 1990	$2.49[a]	$5.74
Average for 3 years, 1987–1989	$2.11	$3.82
TRS contribution (three-year average) to		
Revenues	45%[b]	65%
Earnings	79%	85%
TRS compounded annual earnings growth rate, 1980–1989	20%	20%
Shares of American Express issued to buy Shearson (millions, adjusted for stock splits)	85	n.a.
Dollars invested in Shearson/dollars used to buy back shares ($ millions)[c]	$3,024	$3,024
Shares outstanding (millions)		
December 31, 1980	285	285
June 30, 1990	445[c]	188
Stock price at June 30, 1990 at 12 times current earnings	$30¾	$68⅞

[a]Excludes charges in first quarter of 1990 for restructuring and change in accounting practices.
[b]Shearson revenues exclude interest.
[c]Does not reflect either the public sale of a portion of the Shearson stock by the company in 1987 or the retirement of those shares in exchange for additional shares of American Express in August 1990.

reconstituted without Shearson and with a greater focus on TRS, and with a far stronger balance sheet too, would have been a much more attractive company. Instead of selling, as it did in mid-1990, at twelve times its earnings, a below-market multiple, the stock might well have sold above fourteen times earnings, the market average.

There is a slightly different way of looking at American Express, but it confirms our conclusion that the diversification program was a fiasco. In 1981, on a per-share basis, the earnings from businesses *other than TRS* accounted for about 80 cents per share of the company's earnings. By 1989, adjusted for stock splits, the per-share earnings accounted for by the TRS division were three and a half times what they had been eight years earlier. But the earnings of all the rest, including Shearson, still represented only about 80 cents per share. All that money and nothing to show for it. In the meantime, the company's long-term debt had mushroomed from $1.1 billion to $11.7 billion, more than half of which—precisely how much more is unclear—had been incurred to finance diworseification. Long-term debt, once modest, now far exceeded shareholders' equity. This company, which should have been awash in the earnings and (except to finance credit card receivables) the cash flow from TRS, was instead forced to issue new shares in June 1990 to bolster its weakened credit.

NO FREE LUNCH HERE?

If you happen to be passing through Yale, the University of Chicago, MIT, or most any other B-school or economics department, you could probably hear a don argue that, even with buybacks on the scale of $15 billion, Exxon was spinning its wheels. They worry that the increased earnings per share enjoyed by the remaining shareholders as a result of such a program do not add real value to their holdings because the improvement is offset by added risk. The contention is that while the earnings per share may rise, ordinarily the improvement can be achieved only by increasing debt and therefore risk. The financial markets, it is said, will compensate for that added risk by reducing the price-earnings ratio (and therefore the value) of the common stock. In short, there is no free lunch.[27] The company is what it is, and value cannot be added simply by jiggling the capital structure.

Whatever its conceptual appeal, however, the theory misses a lot. Some companies have cash on hand and so do not have to borrow at all. Their cash and net worth will shrink by the amount of the buyback, but the cash was not earning much and the stock market rarely values cash dollar for dollar in the price of the company shares.[28] For still others, those that must borrow, the tilt in the debt-to-equity ratio, the added leverage, may be temporary because they have substantial continuing cash flows and will quickly pay down the added debt.[29] During the relevant years, Exxon, for example, had sufficient earnings to pay all interest charges at least 8.5 times. For a company so conservatively capitalized, where was the added risk, or if there was more, what was the harm from it? During the years 1986–1988, when the oil industry's average return on equity was a modest 10.8 percent,[30] Exxon was reporting 17.8 percent, very high for the industry. For the decade 1980–1990, Exxon's shareholders enjoyed a sparkling total return (dividends plus price appreciation) of 18 percent a year—more than twice the industry median. Realistically, the company and its continuing shareholders did enjoy a free lunch on their share repurchases, or at least they ate haute cuisine at McDonald's prices.

It is true that not all companies are like Exxon. Ralston Purina also bought back a great deal of stock but was unable to do so without a major increase in corporate debt. Having spent over $2 billion to buy in shares, the company's earnings before interest and taxes (from continuing operations), which had covered interest charges nine times in 1982, covered them only three and a half times in 1989. According to the risk/reward, no-free-lunch theory, the company's share price should have reflected the added risk, which was significant. In the debt-tolerant climate of the 1980s, however, the stock rose from about 12 in the first quarter of the 1982 fiscal year to about 80 at the end of fiscal 1989, and the price-earnings ratio more than doubled. The 1980s were a good time for food companies but not that good. It was a time when leveraged restructurings were being *rewarded,* not penalized.

More fundamentally, however, the debate about whether share repurchases can directly affect the market value of an enterprise is simply beside the point. While share repurchases, it is true, do take place in the stock market, properly conceived they are a company operation, not a stock market one. Why do so many people—in and out of academia—miss the point? *It is the business effects that matter, not the near-term stock market effects.*[31] If the business decision is correct, if the "investment" in the retired shares has been well conceived, the stock market—often wise, often not—will eventually sort itself out.

Who cares if a share repurchase "signals" better profits, as so many Wall Street analysts and others, obsessed with market performance, like to ask?[32] For twelve years Teledyne bought back its stock, paying over $2.7 billion.[33] Stock repurchases on such a scale are not primarily a signal to the market of some other event, such as higher profits. Buybacks are the "event," a major event, with a direct impact of their own, and should be scrutinized as such.

A MODEL WITHOUT A MODEL

The lessons at Exxon and elsewhere are that buybacks are sometimes clearly better than either the available reinvestment opportunities or a cash dividend. Still, a good many questions remain. Suppose there is not enough capital to approve all good projects and also to buy back shares. Which comes first? Should a company forgo profitable business investments in order to make even more "profitable" investments in its shares? If the shares are very cheap, does that mean that the company should forgo or even eliminate cash dividends? I don't have answers to such questions, and I am wary of analyses that assume there are single-best, definitive responses.

The reasons I am so wary may help to explain the inherent fallacy of many of the algebraic formulas that delight B-school people. If a company has available a large number of excellent projects with a projected return of 16 percent or better, should it abandon some of them in favor of buying back shares on which it will expect to "earn" 25 percent? The most sensible answer, I suggest, is that the answer is unclear. Sometimes, yes, it should postpone the investment in tangible assets in favor of a buyback. The latter might be an opportunity that is unlikely to last very long. Perhaps the business opportunity—the ability to build a new alumina reduction plant—will still be there in a year, and the year's delay will not matter. By allowing additional time for research on the refining process, the delay might even help. On the other hand, for a local retailer to reject six terrific new store sites may be downright foolish if those stores would be occupied by a competitor. And on the further hand—I wish I had three hands—perhaps the tension is not all that great, either because the company can do some of both or because it can borrow. Companies with a wealth of good projects are often already successful ones. Such companies usually have a good measure of untapped borrowing power, in part because they know that rare good opportunities sometimes do come along—particularly for well-run, successful companies. By utilizing that borrowing capacity, the hard choice between business projects and buybacks may not be very hard at all.

This process of complicating the issues could go on and on, but I hope the point is clear. True, it's difficult to imagine circumstances in which a company would disregard the expectations of shareholders and suddenly omit its cash dividend in order to buy back stock, but I have no formula. Anyone who does may be missing the main point.

THE RECENT SURGE IN SHARE REPURCHASES: NOT ALL TO THE GOOD

At the beginning of this chapter, we saw that share repurchases soared in the 1980s. Some part of the increase can be explained by a generally better understanding of the benefits of plain vanilla buybacks. Call it "maximizing shareholder values," one of the catchy phrases of the day. As recently as 1982, Exxon's management was saying that it had no plans to retire shares,[34] but by the end of the decade it had repurchased $15 billion worth. Still, there have not been enough plain vanilla buybacks to account for anything like the more than $140 billion of stock that corporations bought back over 1986–1988. It would be nice to report that everyone at the Business Roundtable and American Manufacturers Association has been thinking about shareholder value, assiduously taking notes, but it isn't so.

Of the tens of billions of equities repurchased in recent years, fear of takeovers was the most important factor. To thwart a bid, for example, Carter Hawley Hale, owner of a mediocre collection of retailing businesses, bought stock in the open market at prices 50 percent higher than they had been a few weeks before. Seeing how frightened they were, investment bankers regularly beseeched corporate clients to buy back shares in order, as one said, to "close the value gap between current market value and 'break-up' value before the company becomes a target."[35] In short, many share repurchases had little to do with the creation of long-term business values and the judicious use of cash flows.

The surge in share repurchases closely followed the surge in mergers and acquisitions. Only now that the threat of takeovers has visibly subsided will we begin to see to what extent corporate managers have learned to think, like Exxon, of share repurchases as a recurring, normal, nondefensive part of their corporate strategy. The belief here is that some of those lessons have been learned. Bigger is not always better. Managers speak more comfortably now about the need for a focused mission, and many of them no longer see acquisitions as the obvious use of excess cash flows. Perhaps even American Express has learned a thing or two.

A WORD OF CAUTION

At the outset of this chapter, I said that plain vanilla buybacks are not for everyone. But I then went on to explore how attractive they can sometimes be. In the general prosperity of the 1980s, it often seemed easy to borrow money, buy back shares, and soon after see that decision vindicated in the stock market. But the combination of a share repurchase program and added leverage is like driving water through a small nozzle at high speed. It's dangerous and in any event works well only in strong hands.

It behooves outside directors to adopt an independent posture toward share buybacks. The board should review any proposals with particular care, but it should also encourage management to consider one when the circumstances seem propitious. It is difficult to think of many other issues on which outside directors can so clearly earn their keep.

In a share repurchase program, the company is inescapably making a judgment about the value of its business. It is trying to buy in a portion of its equity at a bargain price but without the unfair, illegal advantage of trading on inside information. By definition, the company may be rejecting the current valuation of its stock on Wall Street, not because it has better information but rather because it has a more thoughtful, longer-term view of values. At the least, it is saying that the price is reasonable; it is not paying more than a dollar for a dollar's worth of stock, measured by business values. For many businesses, these are little better than guesses—guesses made more difficult by the natural optimism of CEOs who are accustomed to challenges and expect to win. If they were cautious by nature, if the future didn't usually look good to them, they would probably be elsewhere.

Tempting as it may be to swing into action, management often needs to be patient, and that can be very difficult. Analysts and others will criticize the company for sitting on cash, as if it were indecent to expose any significant amount of money to public view. But in a stock market that swings from manic to depressive, from pricing à la Tiffany's to Filene's Basement, with remarkable frequency, opportunities will arise. History tells us that, as someone said, stability itself may eventually be destabilizing by encouraging a false sense of confidence and renewed speculation.[36] It's the inability to know when those opportunities will arise that makes waiting so painful, particularly if in the interim the stock moves higher rather than lower.

Given the temptation to use the money sooner than later, given too the temptation to use buybacks for a variety of inappropriate purposes, the operation may easily turn out badly.

No doubt the management of Comprehensive Care, for example, had great expectations when the company shrunk its stock by over 25 percent in fiscal 1987, buying back over 4 million shares at $13 a share. The company develops and manages programs for drug abuse and psychiatric treatment. Patient days in existing units had declined sharply; profits were falling and unfortunately they continued to fall. The balance sheet eroded with them. Debt, more than half of it attributable to the buyback, soon exceeded shareholders' equity. The banks imposed credit constraints. A year and a half later, the dividend was omitted, and a loss was reported. Not long after that, in 1990, the company, which by then had lost financial flexibility, saw its stock fall below $2 a share.

Price Communications retired over $100 million worth of common stock in 1986–1988, shrinking its stock by more than half. Why it did that is something of a mystery, given the company's poor prospects. Price, whose total revenues were only about $90 million, lost $12 million to $24 million in each of those three years. The company owned various broadcast and newspaper properties, but it had paid top dollar and was soon liquidating assets to stay a step or so ahead of the sheriff. By the fall of 1989, with a smaller revenue base, the company had $400 million of debt. With annual interest charges of over $45 million, over half its total revenues were dedicated to interest payments.[37] (Despite the continuing losses, the company had split its stock five-for-four at least once every year beginning in 1985.[38]) One possible explanation for the share repurchases was that the president and CEO, Robert Price, held a class of junior stock that would become convertible into common stock if the price of the common rose above a stipulated level for a period of time. It's impossible to say whether Price, a former investment banker and former deputy mayor of New York, had that in mind, and in any event the conversion privilege was not triggered. But for a company awash in hard-to-service debt, it was reckless to spend $100 million on buybacks.

In the fall of 1990, with Price Communications hovering on the edge of bankruptcy, the president blamed the company's problems on the credit crunch. No mention was made of the company's own lack of judgment.[39]

Buybacks are not for everyone. It's hard to separate the saints and sinners, however. Even when we tell the saints to line up on the right and the sinners on the left, everyone in the class moves in the same direction. What to do? In the United States, we leave the issue to the business discretion of corporate managements and directors. The courts are reluctant to intervene. Perhaps, somewhat like the British, we should insist that whenever a company intends to buy back shares in the face of a pending or threatened takeover or whenever the proposed repurchase is from a particular, designated seller (rather than by tender offer or open market transactions), the matter should be put to a vote of the shareholders. The mere fact of such a requirement, together with the accompanying disclosures, would make at least choirboys, if not saints, out of a few sinners.

As if that were not enough, one further note of caution needs to be struck. Most stocks, including our fictitious Middle American, usually sell at prices well above their book values. For a company to buy back a share of stock, therefore, means that the excess of the purchase price above the book value of that share reduces the book value of the remaining shares. The buyback may be beneficial for the continuing shareholders, but the book value of their shares will suffer as a result. Still, most shareholders probably would not notice or care.

Book value as such may not matter, but buybacks by companies whose stocks are selling above their book value can significantly distort some of the usual yardsticks for measuring the profitability of the business and management's compensation. In this respect, buybacks are very much like the extraordinary write-downs that some companies take to reduce the balance sheet values of operations whose prospects have soured. Net worth is reduced in the one case by the amount of the buyback and in the other by the amount of the write-down. The result is that a financial operation, such as a buyback, can make the business henceforth seem more profitable and efficient than is in fact the case because it will inflate the company's return on equity for future periods. And it will do that long after the buyback itself has been forgotten.

Gillette is a good example. It happens to be a very profitable company, but in the process of buying back about 22 percent of its stock in the 1980s, it completely eliminated shareholders' equity. With a book value per share of less than $8, the company bought back stock in 1986 at $29 a share and subsequently in 1988 at $45 a share. As a result, shareholders' equity became a *minus* $133 million. Net income for 1987 (adjusted for the buyback) declined, of course, but only by about 17 percent—from $230 million to $192 million. With the company's equity rapidly disappearing, however, return on equity rose from about 18 percent in 1985 to about 39 percent in 1987. Then it leaped to infinity in 1989. Gillette's business was very good, but it was not infinitely good.

Similarly, compare two companies in the food industry, Ralston Purina and H. J. Heinz. Ordinarily one might have assumed that Ralston Purina, which showed a much higher return on equity in the late 1980s, was the more profitable company. Wrong. Heinz was the stronger of the two, with generally better market positions and higher profit margins. Ralston Purina, however, had bought back much more stock than Heinz, thus boosting its return on equity. The usually good yardstick didn't work. As one thoughtful money manager, Seth Klarman, has said, not every company that seems to be earning a 25 percent return on equity is equally profitable.

LEGAL AND ACCOUNTING CONSTRAINTS OF SHARE REPURCHASES

While the legal restrictions on plain vanilla buybacks in the United States are relatively few, there are some. Moreover, there are significant tax implications for shareholders. For a corporate manager, rather than a lawyer or banker, these factors can be summarized without doing them much injustice.

The central business question is whether to buy stock in the open market or by a tender offer. Open market purchases will be at prevailing market prices, and while the announcement of a repurchase program will have some positive effect on the market, it is often minor and ephemeral. Open market purchases are usually the least expensive route; the mechanics are relatively simple and inexpensive. An investment bank or brokerage firm buys stock for the company within the company's price guidelines, at about the same commissions applicable to institutional investors. Although there is no explicit requirement that a company disclose its buyback program, the antifraud rules, particularly the rules against insider trading, apply. Because the buyback itself may constitute significant information, it would be the rare company that did not announce its intentions. And if the company has material inside information apart from the buyback itself, that should also be disclosed. Earnings projections that the company had intended for use only in capital budgeting or for other internal purposes should be examined for the assumptions on which they were written. If the company expects a banner year, better than the Street expects, some further disclosure might be required.

The federal securities laws also restrict the manner in which shares are acquired. To prevent manipulation, the SEC has established a safe-harbor rule (Rule 10b-18) under which, in general, company purchases may not exceed 25 percent of the average daily trading volume, may not be made at the beginning or end of the day, and may not be made at prices over the market. Although the rule is nominally only a safe-harbor provision and therefore not mandatory, adherence to it is close to universal.

Open market purchases are the low-cost, usually sensible route. But for companies eager to buy back large amounts of their stock and to do so quickly, or for companies that fear the price may soon move up, they may not be the answer. Depending on the level of trading in the company's stock, the volume limitations under Rule 10b-18 may be too restrictive. Block purchases are exempt from those limitations, but they cannot be used as mere conduits for circumventing volume limitations. Companies seeking to buy back in a short time a large portion of their shares should consider a tender offer.

In a self-tender, the company commits to buy a minimum, typically substantial, number of shares pursuant to a formal tender offer document that it files with the SEC and distributes to shareholders. In a conventional tender offer, the company offers to buy shares at a fixed price. Recently, however, there has increasingly appeared the modified Dutch auction in which shareholders are asked to set the price, within limits set by the company, at which they individually are ready to sell. The offer states the quantity of shares to be bought. Assuming the requisite number of shares are tendered, there will be a lowest price at which the company can purchase that quantity. All those who tendered stock at or below that price will have their shares purchased at that one price. The shares of those whose offers were at a price higher than the purchase price will not be bought in the tender offer.

In 1981 Todd Shipyards was the first to use a Dutch auction in this way. The advantage to the company is clear: shareholders interested in selling are forced to compete. Concerned about the possibility of manipulation, however, the SEC has set some limitations, notably by insisting that the company state beforehand the number of shares to be purchased.

A still more recent invention are the "put rights" used by Gillette and others. In 1988 Gillette was under pressure from a hostile group to sell the company and thereby to realize values that supposedly were not being reflected currently in the stock price. A bargain was struck under which Gillette agreed to repurchase one-seventh of the company's outstanding shares at a price 40 to 50 percent over the market price that had prevailed shortly before. The concern was that the price might be "too fair," that is, too high, which would have been unfair to those who, as some inevitably would do, failed to tender. The company solved the problem by issuing to all shareholders rights to sell stock to the company at $45 a share, at the rate of one share for each seven owned. Being transferable, the rights traded at the value the stock market fixed as the difference between the $45 put price and the expected value of the stock after the offer expired. Thus, even those who did not sell any shares could capture their pro rata portion of the premium by selling off their rights.

Put rights are interesting, but as the Gillette case suggests, they are intended for situations where the repurchase price may represent a premium over intrinsic value and, rather than accede to a hostile bidder's greenmail demands for a premium for one shareholder, the company pays a "premium"—in effect, a dividend—to all.

TAX CONSIDERATIONS

For shareholders, a corporate stock redemption raises the possibility that the proceeds will be taxed as a dividend. Although the federal tax rate for the moment is the same for both ordinary income and capital gains, there is a substantial difference in the overall result because a dividend is taxed in its entirety (to the extent of the corporation's current and accumulated earnings and profits) and a capital gain only to the extent of the gain. The argument has sometimes been made that stock redemptions should be universally treated *as if* the company had paid a cash dividend to all the shareholders, with the continuing shareholders then deemed to have bought the shares of those who, in fact, sold their stock back to the company.[40] Whatever the theoretical merits, the law does not treat buybacks generally as the equivalent of a dividend. Instead, only shareholders whose proportionate interest in the company is essentially unaffected by the distribution are taxed on sales of stock to the company as if the company had paid a dividend. Control shareholders who have sold their entire holdings or reduced their proportionate interest by more than

20 percent, and those noncontrol shareholders of a widely held corporation who reduce their percentage ownership by any amount, are taxed only to the extent of the gain.

For shareholders that are themselves corporations, the issues are the same, but here it is usually a benefit to have the transaction treated as a dividend because of the preferential treatment accorded under the tax laws to intercorporate dividend payments.

While there are some arcane aspects, the fundamentals of the tax law are such that noncorporate investors should be able to ensure themselves of capital gains treatment, and corporate investors of dividend treatment, if they so desire.

ACCOUNTING EFFECTS

Years ago, when a substantial number of companies were still acquiring other companies in exchange for common stock of the purchaser, it was common to remind people that the ability to account for the acquisition on the acquiring company's books as a so-called pooling of interests might be jeopardized by a significant buyback program within two years of the acquisition. That could be important if the acquired company was being purchased for more than its asset values. For example, unless pooling treatment was available, a substantial goodwill item might be added to the books of the purchaser, and under the applicable accounting rules, that goodwill would be charged off against future earnings although it would not be deductible for tax purposes. The pressure of hostile takeovers in recent years, however, has made the leisurely pace of acquisitions for stock almost an anachronism.

This brief summary of legal and other factors affecting buybacks applies only to the more limited, plain vanilla versions. For share repurchases that involve a drastic corporate restructuring, the greenmailing of a hostile bidder, or a freezeout, there are significant other issues under both state and federal law.

9

Stock Splits and Stock Dividends

LOOIE KNOWS BEST

The CEO of Middle American, Charles E. O'Rourke, was scheduled to make a presentation before the New York Society of Security Analysts, and he was being put through his paces by several colleagues who had prepared questions, trying to anticipate those that would be asked at the meeting. In part they played security analyst, but they also threw in a few curve balls of their own, the kind that would have been impolitic to ask directly. How soon might the Food and Drug Administration approve the new cold remedy? What will next year's capital budget look like? Toward the end of the session, Phineas Nance, the chief financial officer, asked whether the company was considering splitting the stock now that it was trading at over $90 a share. O'Rourke pulled up short. "Phin, I don't know," he said. "It's not the kind of thing companies signal in advance. When we're ready to split the stock, we'll do it, that's all."

The company's presentation at the Downtown Club went well. What analysts hate most is being sandbagged by unexpected bad news, and O'Rourke knew not to do that. Toward the end of the meeting, sure enough, the analyst from Third Chicago, Ben Focus, asked about a stock split. "Let me tell you about Looie's pizza," O'Rourke replied. "Sam walks into Looie's, asks for a small pizza, and Looie says, 'You want it cut into four pieces or eight?' Sam says, 'Naw, just four. I'm not hungry enough for eight.'" The audience laughed, and the question soon got lost.

Stock splits and stock dividends are very much like pizza. Everyone agrees that a company worth $100 million taken as a whole is not worth any more or less if the pie is cut into 1 million shares or 2 million shares. There are no meaningful tax consequences, so why bother?

But companies do bother. In a "good" year, such as 1983, 20 percent of the companies listed on the New York Stock Exchange make stock distributions of one sort or another.[1] In the early 1970s stock dividends were more popular than stock splits, and now it is the other way around. But allowing for minor changes in the style, stock splits and dividends have been a part of corporate financial policy since the early part of the century.[2] Even so, the question persists, Why bother?

Although stock splits and stock dividends are alike in that in either case there is still just one pizza, they are used and perceived quite differently. Technically the dividing line is drawn at distributions of 25 percent or more. According to the major stock exchanges, any distribution under 25 percent is a stock dividend, and anything of 25 percent or more is a split. Why the distinction? Why do we need rules as to the number of slices? The answer is that small stock dividends are often announced by companies *as if* they represented a distribution of current earnings, thus encouraging shareholders to treat them *as if* they were a current cash dividend that could be sold without diluting one's personal capital. In the 1960s, in particular, it was common for growth companies to pay small or no cash dividends and to substitute small periodic, even quarterly, stock dividends that mimicked cash payments. Small variations in the size of a stock dividend were considered important. Stock dividends of less than the year's full earnings were sometimes said to indicate a "cautious" attitude by the board about future earning power,[3] as if it cost more to print a 4 percent stock dividend than a 2 percent one. The whole process of paying something that didn't cost the company any money but looked like money and could be turned into money proved to be too tempting, of course, and abuses set in. Recurring stock dividends were paid even when the market value of the shares distributed far exceeded the reinvested earnings for the year or when there were no earnings at all. Like the smile on the Cheshire cat, many of these dividends were all smile and no substance.

Under the current stock exchange and accounting rules, any stock dividend must be accompanied by a transfer of the market value of the shares from earned surplus to the capital accounts.[4] Stock splits, on the other hand, are essentially unregulated. (Repeated stock distributions in the range of 25 to 100 percent suggest not very subtle attempts at market manipulation. Price Communications, for example, despite continuing losses and a low stock price, split its shares five-for-four for five consecutive years, beginning in 1985, by which time it was on the brink of bankruptcy.)

STOCK SPLITS

The phrase *stock split* has its conceptual origins in the nineteenth century, when the par value of a share was still considered important. Well-regarded companies typically issued stock with a par value of $100 a share so as to assure creditors and shareholders alike that something of substantial value had been received for their shares. (It didn't work, of course. U.S. Steel, American Can, and others issued watered stock by the simple expedient of overvaluing the assets received for them. Only the public, buying for cash, paid full value.) A so-called split-up of the stock therefore entailed a splitting of each "old" share into, say, three new ones, and at the same time a reduction in par value. In the modern era, par values have lost whatever slight meaning they once had, and a stock split can be effected either by the traditional technique—splitting the stock much like an amoeba—or by distributing, say, two new shares as a dividend in respect of each old share, in which case it is known as a stock split in the *form* of a stock dividend. Regardless of the procedure, in each case shareholders will have three shares for each one they had before.

The reason usually given for splitting a stock is to bring the trading price down to a more "convenient" range of, say, $25 to $50 a share. Because stocks are traded in round lots of 100 shares, some individual shareholders who would buy 100 shares of a $50 stock might resist buying 50 shares if the price were $100 a share. There is some truth to this, although at a time when professionals account for the preponderance of trading, there can't be very much. Still, people do talk of a $100 or $200 stock as being too expensive, just as they speak of very low-price "penny" stocks as being cheap.[5] Looie knows that it's only a question of how many cuts he makes in the pizza, but stocks are intangibles, with a life and perception of their own.

The only substantive difference between one share of a $100 stock and two of a $50 stock is that the seemingly cheaper stock in fact costs more to trade because standard commission costs are based not just on the dollar amount of the transaction but on the number of shares. The so-called regular commission on a trade of 200 shares of a $50 stock is $143, as against $81 for 100 shares of a $100 stock. But in an era when brokers' commissions are fully negotiable, that difference quickly evaporates, particularly for institutional investors. And apart from commissions, there are only matters of perception, style, and attitude. Very low-price stocks are considered flimsy and speculative; very high-price ones are classy, stodgy, or just expensive.

The notion that Looie might be smarter than an efficient stock market intrigues financial economists, who wonder whether underlying these stock distributions something significant might be going on. In a fully efficient market, the market price should not change until new information comes along because all the current information is already reflected in the price. Accordingly, they have carefully studied the possibility that stock splits, especially those coupled with a dividend increase, are an oblique way for management to communicate good news to the market.[6] In addition to those meetings at the Downtown Club and the corporate departments of investor relations, perhaps stock splits also serve as a useful signal.

If there is a signal, it is quite crude. With the benefit of hindsight, we can see that in some cases, good things were about to happen, but in still others, the split was followed by a severe price drop within a year or two. The stock splits were celebrating last year's success rather than signaling the next. Or, as sometimes happens, knowing that stock splits will attract some speculative interest, companies use them for manipulative purposes.

Anchor Glass, for example, did an initial public offering in the spring of 1986 at an (adjusted) price of $10.25. The following year the stock was split two-for-one, and the price dutifully rose for a short time thereafter. For the year 1987 as a whole, however, earnings declined, and by year-end 1988 the stock price had dropped back to $9.75—barely more than half the $18.50 price at the time the split was announced.[7]

Studies show that stock prices do move up for a few days after the announcement. Are they moving up because traders expect each other to buy, thus confirming for a time their own expectations, or because of something of enduring substance? It's hard to say.

To see if the short-term price increases are sustained over a more substantial period, I took a random sample of a dozen companies that had declared two-for-one stock splits in 1980 and examined them again at the end of 1983.[8] Table 9–1 lists the twelve companies, together with their stock prices two trading days before the announce-

Table 9–1
No Coherent Signal from Stock Splits

	Price of Stock Two Trading Days Before Split Announcement[a]	Price on Dec. 30, 1983	Percentage Increase (Decrease)	Percentage Point Difference from S&P 500
Advanced Micro Devices	9.0	33.6	273.3	229.8
Alaska Interstate[b]	19.4	13.6	(29.9)	(73.4)
Albertson's	9.4	27.1	188.3	144.8
Alcan Aluminum	29.4	39.8	35.4	(8.1)
Amerada Hess	26.5	29.0	9.4	(34.1)
American Standard	34.6	31.5	(9.0)	(52.5)
Anixter Bros.	7.8	24.3	211.5	168.0
Atlantic Richfield	45.9	43.3	(5.7)	(49.2)
Baker International	28.3	19.3	(31.8)	(75.3)
Barry Wright	16.1	30.0	86.3	42.8
Burlington Northern	33.3	99.0	197.3	153.8
Butler International	14.1	20.5	45.4	1.9
S&P 500	114.9[c]	164.9	43.5	. . .

[a]Prices adjusted to reflect splits.
[b]Enstar Corp. after May 1982.
[c]Value as of midyear 1980.

ment of the split, the adjusted price three-plus years later, at year end 1983, and the percentage change in price during that time. The table also includes the mean average of the Standard & Poor's 500 Stock Index for 1980 and the value at year end 1983. No adjustments were made for cash dividends during the interim.

The median price appreciation for all twelve companies was 40 percent for the period ending December 30, 1983, which was not very different from that of the index. But the median tells almost nothing about the group as a whole. The numbers are a random walk, with gains of over 200 percent and four companies showing losses. For traders and economists, neither of whom have much respect for the other, stock splits may be important, but for the rest of us, they seem rather empty.

Graham and Dodd suggested that for a company seeking to treat its shareholders evenhandedly, the best course is to announce before-hand that it will split the stock "at least 3 for 2 if (a) the price has [remained] above $100 per share for more than a year, and if (b) the company can expect to pay [an increased] dividend."[9] That would leave the stock split, when ultimately it is announced, with nothing that would surprise, signal, or manipulate shareholders. But as we have seen, neither O'Rourke nor any other CEO seems to have heeded the advice.[10]

Until a few years ago, that would have wrapped up the discussion of stock splits. Companies believed that there's nothing bad about them and that they often give the stock price a quick boost and stimulate interest on the part of small investors, who might otherwise feel left out. Buffett and Munger at Berkshire Hathaway, however, have reawakened interest in the problem by refusing to split the company's shares despite a very high price. Having acquired control of the company in 1964 at a price of about $16 a share, they have never paid a cash dividend. They have not split the stock either, and by 1990 the share price had risen above $8,000, causing market computers to hiccough. Adding a little interpretive gloss, their reasoning is roughly as follows:[11]

1. While irrational price swings create opportunities for Berkshire to own stock of other companies at favorable prices, they are not helpful for the stock of Berkshire itself, where investors should be able to come and go—hopefully not too often—at prices reasonably close to intrinsic value.

2. The regular commission for an $8,000 share of Berkshire is no more than for a $100 share elsewhere. So the popular view of shareholders as people who might buy 200 shares of a $40 stock but not one share of an $8,000 stock is that of a shareholder who does not care to read financial statements and in any event is not as smart as Looie.

3. Since no company needs all investors, the object is to attract the best rather than the most. ("All of our policies . . . are designed to attract the business-oriented long-term owner and to filter out possible buyers whose focus is short-term and market-oriented."[12])

4. There are only a few things a company can do to pick its own

shareholders. Like any other merchandising problem, a company needs to know its market. Issuing annual reports with wonderfully analytic letters from the chairman and without pretty pictures helps. Not putting a popular price on the shares may also help to weed out those for whom a lower, "cheaper" price would be significant.

There is very little turnover among Berkshire shareholders, but it's hard to measure how much of that loyalty is attributable to an intimidating stock price and how much to other factors. Institutions trade more than individuals and in that respect tend to dilute the quality of a company's shareholder base. For whatever reason—it's hardly the stock price—the institutional ownership of Berkshire was about 12 percent, of which more than half was held by one Florida bank.[13] With an investment that had compounded at an annual rate of over 25 percent, investors simply may not have cared whether the pie came in large or small slices.

Most corporate managers split their stocks because they are eager to increase the trading. It is an article of faith that there is no such thing as too much liquidity. Underlying that widespread belief, however, is a profound confusion between trading efficiency and economic efficiency, between what feeds stockbrokers and what feeds shareholders and the nation. Trading or operating efficiency means that trades can be executed at small cost and quickly, partly because of technology—notably the Exchange's high-speed computer system—and partly because of the large volume of transactions. But when economists speak of an efficient market, they are usually, and correctly, speaking of efficiency in the more profound sense that the market mechanism allocates goods and capital to their best uses by adjusting prices. As we watch the troubled Soviet economy, we can appreciate the importance of that market function.

The usual assumption is that no matter how much trading takes place, no matter how rapidly investors exchange their stocks, the real goals of the stock market are being advanced. Is that so, or at some (ill-defined) point does additional trading impair the object rather than advance it? What are we to make of a market whose primary allocative purpose is to find new sources of capital if for each dollar of cash raised by the issuance of new common stocks, it spends a dollar or more just to trade the old ones?

As I wrote in 1989:

When institutions trade the same shares over and over again, there is only duplication and waste, not gain. . . . In the early 1960s, the turnover of shares of New York Stock Exchange companies was about 14% a year. Including trading in NYSE stocks in other markets, the turnover figure for 1987 was about 95%. The total cost of all this activity—commissions and other trading expenses—was about $25 billion, according to the Securities Industry Association. That $25 billion equaled more than one-sixth of all corporate earnings. It was also more than the average annual value of all new common stocks issued for cash.[14]

Liquidity is like crack: the more you rely on it, the greater is the craving. In defining their shareholder base, therefore, companies should reject, as best they can, trading junkies. When stocks were still turning over at an annual rate of 14 percent, no complaints were heard that the New York Stock Exchange lacked liquidity. Strip away the ideological free-market fix, and the only advantage of the extra liquidity in today's markets is to reduce the spread between bid and asked prices. But in 1960, when investors were holding their stocks for seven years on average—the reciprocal of 14 percent turnover— they did not expect to sell out on a moment's notice. Despite the larger spreads, their total trading costs were less, not more.

True, no one wants to be locked in. Better answers come, however, if we think less about how to get out than how to make better decisions on why and how to get in. Those who expect to sell out quickly and cheaply are more likely to buy for speculative or foolish reasons and to act as uninformed owners in between times. They are less likely to know their companies or the products, just as those who rent houses for the summer don't take the same interest as those who own.

How many shareholders does a company need? A stock split might attract additional interest in the stock, but it would come from investors who think that two shares of a $60 stock are "cheaper" than one share of a $120 one. Are those the investors your company wants—investors who will soon sell out and will sell for reasons no better than the one that brought them to you in the first place? Think instead in terms of attracting the best shareholders, not the most.

STOCK DIVIDENDS

However little there is to be said in favor of a stock split, there is less for a stock dividend.

For years Ben Graham tried to make a case for stock dividends. It was not so much that he attached real significance to the process but rather that he was aghast at the spectacle of large, growing companies paying substantial cash dividends on the one hand and then financing their expansion by the sale of new securities, including common stock. Shareholders received a generous dividend, but they were concurrently called upon to put the same money, *tax diminished,* back into the business. It seemed pretty dumb. (It was.) Over one seven-year period, AT&T paid out over $2.5 billion in dividend⌐ and then received back from shareholders, or their transferees, an equivalent amount through rights offerings. Apart from the substantial tax loss to investors, the company incurred large costs in the elaborate financings that were involved.[15]

Graham proposed that companies such as AT&T keep the dividend money and instead distribute to shareholders an equivalent amount of stock, valued at market. He fully recognized, of course, that his proposal, however logical, violated the norms of the financial community, which treasures cash dividends at least for their effect on stock prices, if not for their own sake. Graham lost that battle. He didn't succeed in convincing many corporations, and those that he did were soon forced to retreat to the conventional wisdom of the marketplace. Companies that tried to substitute a stock dividend policy along the lines he suggested saw their stock prices fall (as did Caterpillar's in 1953) or were forced to rescind it (General Public Utilities in 1968).[16] Institutional investors explained their open hostility by saying that stock dividends blurred the distinction between capital and income in the administration of trusts, but something more deep rooted was at work.

With a stock dividend, the shareholders receive something that can be "cashed" almost as easily as a check while the company keeps the dividend money. The problem, as Graham recognized, is that the practice has always lent itself to recurring manipulation and deception. In 1929 North American Co. paid quarterly stock dividends of $2\frac{1}{2}$ percent, with an aggregate market value of $12.70 per share, even though the year's earnings were only $5.03. That potential for abuse is still there. Sixty years later, in 1989, Triton Energy declared a 3 percent stock dividend that may have nominally complied with the requirements of the New York Stock Exchange, but nonetheless was misleading. The company had lost large amounts of money during the three prior years, and even in the first quarter of the current fiscal year, when the stock dividend was declared, the company showed a loss. A 100-share stockholder who sold those three "new" shares to buy groceries would have been spending capital, not income.

Quantum Chemical, a leading producer of polyethylene, had been restructured at the beginning of 1989 by paying a cash dividend to shareholders of $50 a share, funded by an increase in long-term debt to more than $2 billion. The celebration was barely over when product prices plunged, and the company was forced to skip its quarterly cash payment. It substituted a 1 percent stock dividend, as if to cushion the blow, and announced its intention to "continue" the stock payments the following year. (Overcome with enthusiasm, the company increased the dividend to 2 percent in 1990.) Examining a company with a heavy burden of debt, no net worth, and continuing losses in an industry beset by overcapacity, an intelligent investor would have concluded that the stock "dividend" was a sham. First Executive, the now-defunct insurance company with a notoriously large portfolio of junk bonds, paid several stock dividends in 1987 and 1988 even while its stock price was already low and sliding sideways or lower. The same happened at Denison Mines in 1988 and 1989.

With the growing institutionalization of the stock market, the appeal of stock dividends seems to be wearing off. In 1988 thirty-four New York Stock Exchange companies declared stock dividends, compared to ninety-nine in 1973.

Even when a stock dividend is not misleading, there are no significant advantages. The theory is that shareholders can sell those additional shares without impairing capital. But if the retained earnings are real, shareholders can do the same by selling a few of their existing shares, declaring a so-called homemade dividend. For the holder of a 100-share round lot, that would mean being left with 97 shares or so, depending on how large a dividend he or she decides to "declare." That may seem untidy, but so what? The capital would remain intact just as much as if the holder had received shares in a stock dividend and sold them. For investors the critical issue is whether the retained earnings represent free cash flow that can be used to finance real growth. If so, a "homemade dividend" is appropriate enough, and it should not matter whether the 3 shares to be sold are 3 of 103 or 3 of 100.

Until a few years ago, the 97-share holder, when eventually he or she sold, would have had to pay an extra odd lot commission of 1/8 or 1/4 of a point, but now the New York Stock Exchange has made it possible to escape that charge. (All odd lots at the specialist's post at the opening of the market now trade at the same price as round lots.) In any event, with institutions accounting for the bulk of the trading, it is difficult to believe that the odd lot commission should be a factor affecting corporate financial policy.

Stick with it, Looie. Four slices or eight, the quantity and the quality are the same.

10

Capital Budgeting, Risk, and Return

THE CAPITAL ASSET PRICING MODEL

The value of a capital project or other business investment is determined by estimating the future stream of income to be derived from it and then discounting it to a present value. In chapter 7, we saw how difficult it is to estimate the returns, and in this chapter we will look again at the discount rate. Discounting is a necessity. A dollar tomorrow is not as valuable as a dollar today, because there is a time value to money and also because of the risk that the expected returns or payments won't materialize. The discount rate for Company X, therefore, is a function of a "pure" riskless cost of capital—usually the rate the Treasury would have to pay—plus an adjustment for the fact that the Treasury is the only "business" whose promise to pay is absolutely guaranteed. (It owns the printing press.) All the rest of us should, and do, pay more for capital than the government. The more remote and uncertain the payoff, the more we pay.

How much more? An intriguing question, it is the central inquiry in this chapter: how to adjust, if at all, a company's cost of capital for risk. The question is not trivial. Under the laws of compound interest, if my cost of capital is 11 percent, I will proceed with many long-term projects that you cannot afford if your cost is, say, 15 percent. To a large extent, you will be confined to projects with quick paybacks, where the high cost of capital is less of a burden.

As we will see, almost half of American industry tries to capture the risk factor by using an ambitious financial model, the capital asset pricing model (CAPM, pronounced "Cap-M"). CAPM began as a de-

188

vice for building and analyzing the portfolios of outside investors, but it is now regarded as a basic business tool, in as well as outside of industry. What started out as a "basic" tool soon became, in fact, *the* tool. That's too bad, because very few of the corporate managements who use CAPM, or who rely on consultants who use it, understand it well enough or realize what a mischievous piece of work it is.

RISK AND RETURN

CAPM is designed to measure risk and to calculate the trade-off between risk and expected returns, whether for managers of passive stock portfolios or managers of businesses.[1] Simplifying a bit, at one end of the risk spectrum is a short-term U.S. Treasury note, at the other a wildcat oil drilling operation. In between, there are long-term government bonds, where there is no risk of default, but there is a risk of price fluctuations as interest rates move up and down. There are also corporate bonds, where there is indeed a risk of default. As a group, common stocks are riskier still, in two respects: the eventual outcomes vary considerably, and whatever the eventual outcome, in between times the prices will fluctuate a great deal. The second of these two risks, the volatility factor, can be seen from the following list, which for a sixty-year period shows the standard deviation—a common statistical tool for measuring variability—of the annual returns of these various securities:

Treasury bills	3.4
Long-term government bonds	8.2
Corporate bonds	8.3
Common stocks	21.2

The higher the standard deviation the more the annual returns deviate from the average over time. Even T-bills fluctuate.[2]

The fact that the prices of common stocks are highly variable does not, however, mean that stocks are less likely to be profitable than bonds over time. At least in the past, the returns from common stock investing have been far better. What we mean by "risk" in finance is the likelihood of a broader range of outcomes rather than the most likely or average outcome. Think of games, as every finance teacher instructs students, or in this case, two games. In both games there are only three possible results and the results are equally likely. In the first game, the three outcomes are 20-40-60. In the second, they are

0-20-100. If each game is played once a day for a year, the average outcome will be 40 for both, but the *range* of outcomes on any given day is obviously far greater in game 2 than game 1. It is in this sense that game 2 is said to be riskier and that we intuitively realize that common stocks, however profitable over the long term, are riskier or more speculative than high-grade bonds. The distinction is important because the value of an investment depends not just on the likely or average returns but also on the likelihood of an extreme outcome—a bust or near-bust—on any given project.

That difference between expected average return and risk is graphically shown in chart 10–1. The expected returns on investments A and B are the same, but B is a good deal riskier.

Wise people, says one B-school text, don't run risks just for fun.[3] Under the no-free-lunch principle, businesses with more than ordinary (range-of-outcome) risk must offer more than ordinary profits to

Chart 10–1

Possible Outcomes of Two Independent
Investments

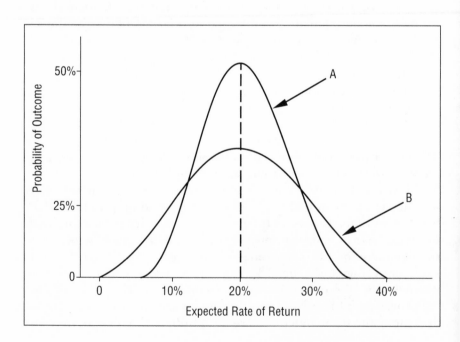

investors. Common stocks must on average earn more for investors than investment-grade bonds, or they will not be bought. With that introduction, let's look at how the risk concept enters into the calculation of the cost of capital—first the cost of debt and then the cost of equity.

RISK-ADJUSTED COST OF DEBT

For any particular company, the cost of capital is usually said to be the after-tax cost of its debt and the cost of its equity blended in proportion to its targeted debt-to-equity ratio. (It is more practical to use the target ratio than to adjust for all the month-to-month or even year-to-year variations.) Assuming the target ratio is realistic, the cost of debt is relatively easy to calculate, particularly for companies with bond issues rated by one of the major rating services. A call to an investment banker will get them a quick answer. The risk factor is already reflected in the bond company's rating—BBB, or whatever else it happens to be—which takes into account not only the character of the business but also the company's capital structure and other so-called financial risks. It may be, of course, that the company does not need to borrow in order to make the investment in question, but that does not matter. Whether the dollars invested in a project are new dollars or old dollars, the company is using capital, a portion of which was borrowed, and all capital has an *opportunity* cost. If nothing else, the company could presumably have used the available dollars to pay down existing debt, thereby using the opportunity to reduce its interest charges.

Calculating the after-tax cost of debt is fairly easy, but still it is not a mindless exercise. Usually, for example, there is no reason to second-guess the prevailing interest rate structure. In the early 1980s, however, the Federal Reserve Board was for a time squeezing inflation out of the economy and interest rates were abnormally high. At one point, the prime rate reached 22 percent and a current-cost test for long-term debt would have closed the door to most capital projects. Should, say, Ford Motor have abandoned the enormous product development program then underway because the hurdle rate was too high? Hardly. If it had done so (and, of course, it did not), what would its product line have looked like a short while later when rates began to fall? Many companies therefore use a mix of current and projected interest rates. In either case, they are trying to fix the opportunity cost of that borrowed money only within some reasonable,

192 / Sense and Nonsense in Corporate Finance

not very precise range. Some fuzziness about the cost of long-term capital is inescapable and in any event, assuming that a decent margin of safety has been built into the capital budgeting process, not important.

Less-than-prime corporate borrowers, those with a weak credit rating, also present a problem. The bond market is simply not open for them in all seasons. One of the twelve cardinal rules suggested in the Introduction to this book is that you can run out of almost anything, except money. An investment-grade rating—BBB− or higher on the Standard & Poor's rating scale—is valuable partly because a company can borrow more cheaply, but much more important, because credit will almost always be available. Money will be there if you need it. In the mid- to late 1980s, when money was astonishingly easy to come by, companies became quite casual about the importance of an investment-grade rating and the need for reserve borrowing power. A guidebook on finance by senior staff at the consulting firm of McKinsey & Company, for example, contained a table showing the latest interest rates for different maturities for various Standard & Poor's bond ratings from triple-A to single-B. (In the summer of 1988, according to the authors, the interest rates for thirty-year bonds, say, ranged from 6.82 percent for triple-As, at the high end of the quality scale, to 10.10 percent for single-As at the mid point, and on to 11.02 percent for double-Bs and 12.96 percent for single-Bs, at the low or junk bond end.) The authors' advice was that except for some minor adjustments and the inevitable rate fluctuations, those rates represented the cost of debt capital for each of the ratings, including the junk.[4] Having casually accepted the notion of perfect or complete markets, they had not stopped to consider the possibility, as in fact happened, that even before the book appeared in 1990, the market for junk bonds of any kind, regardless of the interest rate, would close down.[5] Under efficient market theory, markets would not close down! But a more cautious, less ideological view of the bond market, one more in tune with history, would have recognized that the existence of a market for secondary issuers, much less one with a narrow interest rate spread between single-A and junk bonds, is not dependable—as a great many companies soon found out.

Even with these qualifications, however, the cost of debt capital is much easier to calculate than the cost of equity. Being the senior capital of a company, with a maturity date and with the interest usually fixed in amount and covered by earnings several times over, there are many fewer variables.

RISK-ADJUSTED COST OF EQUITY: CAPM

Determining the cost of equity on a risk-adjusted basis is far more difficult. The very concept is murky, and the popular definitions can produce dubious and even silly results.

One simplistic way to determine the cost of equity would be to follow the technique for determining the cost of debt: using a company's current price-earnings ratio or its dividend yield. A stock selling, say, at $20 a share and earning $1.20 a share has, on a current earnings basis, a "cost" of 6 percent. But while that may tell us something useful, it is not nearly as informative as a bond price or rating. The problem is mainly that, unlike with a bond, we do not know what the "coupon"—the earnings or dividend—will be on a common stock next year or the year after that. A high price-earnings ratio, for example, may suggest that the earnings are temporarily depressed, so that at almost any price, the P/E ratio will be high. Or in some unquantifiable fashion it may instead be telling us that this is a red-hot growth stock. Unfortunately, there is no statistical way to separate the two.

Enter the capital asset pricing model, which is said to define *and even to measure* the cost of equity capital on a risk-adjusted basis. While there are others, the following is a popular version of CAPM and the one we will use. Take (1) the current rate of return on Treasuries, usually short-term bills, the most risk-free, least volatile investment. To the current T-bill rate add (2) the *average* annual return that investors in common stocks as a group—using, for example, the Standard & Poor's 500 Stock Index—have enjoyed over long periods of time as a premium over and above the then T-bill rate. According to a widely used data base, the average annual premium, adjusted for inflation, has been about 8.4 percent, meaning that while the T-bill rate and the stock premium vary, the stock premium has averaged about 8.4 percent a year. This premium is said to be the reward that investors receive for accepting the inherently greater volatility of stocks compared to the risk-free T-bill rate. The volatility of that average common stock, as measured by the S&P index, is a mathematical value called the "beta" and by convention is set at 1.0. (The beta for T-bills is zero.) For any particular company, the final step in calculating its cost of equity capital is (3) to adjust the premium, upward or downward, for the beta of the stock of the company in question.[6] Stocks that are more than ordinarily volatile *relative to the index* have betas above one, which raise their cost of equity to an above-average level, while less volatile ones have betas below one, which reduce their cost of equity to a below-average level.

An illustration may help. Let's take a specific company, Consolidated Papers. The following is a CAPM computation of the cost of equity (as distinguished from the cost of all capital) as of mid-1989 for Consolidated Papers, a highly successful paper company with strong market positions. All the "costs" are expressed in terms of annualized rates of return. At the time, the T-bill rate was 8 percent, so that the cost of equity capital for the *average* S&P 500 company would have been 8.0 plus 8.4 percent, or 16.4 percent. Since this company had a beta of 0.95, slightly below the market average of 1.0, its cost of equity capital in mid-1989 was slightly less than the market average of 16.4 percent:

Current risk-free, Treasury bill rate	8.00%
Plus: average long-term returns from a market basket of stocks in excess of risk-free rate[7]	8.40
Minus: adjustment for the company's beta of .95 (8.4% × .05 = 0.42%)	−0.42
Total cost of equity capital for Consolidated Papers (8.0% + 8.4% − .42%)	15.98%

USES OF CAPM

What do we do with this approximately 16 percent number? According to capital asset pricing theory, it represents the opportunity cost of equity capital, adjusted for risk, which we can use in two quite different situations. CAPM calculates the cost of equity capital for (1) those investors who buy the shares of Consolidated Papers and also (2) the company's management in evaluating proposed investment projects. That means that for the outside investor, if, for example, at the current share price the expected total returns (dividends plus price appreciation) from buying or holding the shares of Consolidated Papers are less than the 16 percent available from other companies with similar risk (beta) profiles, then the price of Consolidated Papers will have to decline until the balance is restored. No one knows what the actual returns will be; it is the (long-term) expectation that counts. For Consolidated Papers' managers, CAPM says that after they have exhausted any better opportunities (and only then), they should still invest in projects arising out of their existing line of business—the only one reflected in the company's beta—that promise a return of at least 16 percent on the equity portion of the capital employed. (For a project in a different line of business, they would have to select the appropriate beta.) In other words, given the risks of this company's business as measured by the volatility of its stock, there is no point in its investing for a return of less than 16 percent. Because Consolidated Papers is debt-free and apparently content to remain that way, the cost of its equity is in effect the cost of all capital. (If it did have debt, the beta of the project would be unchanged, but CAPM says that the beta of the stock would be higher because leverage would increase the risk/volatility of the stock.) And since, according to the theory, expected returns that high are available in the marketplace with no greater risk, the company should not accept any internal project for which the expected returns are less than 16 percent. To be sure, when the project is up and running, the actual results may be better or worse, but that is only to say that results do not always match expectations. But for Consolidated Papers, with a beta of 0.95, the expectation of a 16 percent return should be there.

That is the model. It is an exciting model because there seems to be a direct, easily computed relationship between the beta of a stock— its short-term price volatility relative to the market as a whole—and the ultimate, long-term rewards of owning it. The higher the beta is, the higher the expected rewards must be or else investors would not buy it. (In fact, there is said by many economists to be an approximately linear, one-to-one relationship, so that in order to achieve a 10 percent higher than average profit—above the T-bill rate—one must buy a portfolio with a 10 percent higher than average beta, that is, a beta of 1.1.[8]) What is so exciting is that the risk factor now appears to be measurable. For many investments, the payoff will be postponed for years or even decades. It is difficult to estimate what those future returns will be, but it also difficult to decide at what discount rate those future returns should be valued. A dollar twenty years from now, discounted at 15 percent, is worth only 6 cents today. CAPM purports to provide the otherwise elusive key to fixing that discount rate.

ASSUMPTIONS UNDERLYING CAPM

Now let's look at the assumptions that underlie CAPM. It is important to understand those assumptions because they are so controversial and because many companies have adopted CAPM. First, the model assumes that the stock market is efficient in the sense that the stock prices incorporate all the publicly available information about those companies and that the prices have been set by professional investors who are very wise, or at least as wise as can be. This market efficiency assumption is crucial but, I suspect, not all that well understood. Without realizing the inconsistency, many a chief financial officer who has adopted CAPM for capital budgeting purposes has observed that the stock market is often irrational and that his own stock fluctuates much more than does his business. In any event, without a high degree of efficiency, a stock could fluctuate for extraneous as well as appropriate reasons, in which case the beta of a stock would have little relation to the fluctuating fortunes of the underlying business. Second, scholars generally believe, and the model assumes, that in an efficient market, investors wanting to own stocks can do no better than to buy the whole market, or at least some broad group of stocks such as the Standard & Poor's 500 Stock Index. In other words, so-called wise investors will reject the traditional Graham and Dodd approach of a careful selection of a handful of stocks on the basis of price and value. The effort would be doomed. It's like the old joke about the two economists who are walking across the campus, when they see what appears to be a $20 bill on the ground. As the younger one stoops to pick it up, his older and wiser colleague restrains him, saying that if it were really a $20 bill, someone else would already have picked it up. So, too, in an efficient market there are no bargains that are perceptible beforehand because someone else has picked them up. Looking at stocks, therefore, we might as well buy the whole works.

The third assumption focuses on the risk-weighing role of CAPM and betas. It is impossible, of course, to measure risk directly, because risk is a measure of what is unknown or uncertain. The very notion of "measurable risk" seems like an oxymoron. It suggests that there exists a reasonably large and homogeneous group from which statisticians can calculate probabilities, much as actuaries do their work. It's one thing to estimate the statistical life expectancy of a woman age twenty-eight, but obviously it is much more difficult to quantify the uncertainties of a complex, competitive industrial and commercial world. Instead the scholars adopted as a proxy or surrogate for risk the variability or volatility of the market returns from different securities.[9] T-bills, as mentioned, are assigned a risk character, or beta, of zero. The Standard & Poor's 500 Stock Index has an assigned beta of 1.0. Standard statistical tools are then used to determine the volatility of other stock prices over discrete short periods, such as weeks or months, and the cumulative results over a span of a year or more are then compared with the weekly or monthly returns for the market index. If, as in the case of Consolidated Papers, a stock's volatility is slightly less than that of the S&P 500, its beta will be 0.95. For a public utility, with even less volatility, the beta might be as low as 0.60.

One more assumption or definition in CAPM needs to be explained. If this explanation seems tedious, the answer is that while CAPM is in general use by corporate America, very few of those using it have an adequate understanding of it. True, most of us don't have a good understanding of how our car's fuel injection system operates, but driving the car tells us that in fact it does work. Economics, on the other hand, is a social science. Since economic theories are much less susceptible to direct measurement, it is important to open up the hood and take a more careful look at how they are put together.[10]

This last assumption of CAPM starts with the noncontroversial premise that the volatility of even a modestly diversified portfolio of stocks is a good deal less than that of almost any of its components. The reason is clear. Stocks don't move in lockstep. When the group as a whole is going down, some go down less than others, and some even go up. Thus in a model that assumes that the ideal stock portfolio consists of all stocks, or a close facsimile, the volatility risk of any given stock can be thought of as having two different aspects. One is the extent to which that stock moves more (or less) in sympathy with the market basket. If, for example, there is an economic recession and stocks generally fall, stock X can be expected to drop, too, but will it drop more or less than the average? That is called market risk, or systematic risk, and *this is the only sort of risk that is connoted by a stock's beta.* As one popular text put it, the beta "measures the amount that investors expect the stock price to change for each additional 1% change *in the market.*"[11] Nothing matters under CAPM except the extent to which a stock moves in sympathy with general economic conditions as they in turn are reflected in the market.

To be sure, there are other risks in a business. These other risks, called unique risks, refer to stock price changes that are independent of the market as a whole. If Apple Computer threatens to wipe out IBM's business in personal computers, that's a unique risk. Explosions, a change in management, a strike, and discoveries of new products are all elements of unique risk that, either as gains or losses, will affect a company's stock price in a way that cannot be correlated with the movements of the market as a whole. The distinction is important because for purposes of CAPM, it is assumed that in any well-diversified portfolio, the unique risks will offset each other and therefore *need not be counted*. As that same text said, "The risk of a well-diversified portfolio depends on the market risk [beta] of the securities included in the portfolio."[12] Tattoo it "on your forehead," the authors said. The risk that matters, they say, is market sensitivity risk because under CAPM it is the only risk that investors will get paid for.[13]

What does this mean for capital budgeting and dividend policy? Why are not all risks important? For a passive investor trying to track the stock market by owning an index fund, perhaps market risk may be all that matters. (After all, if the index is large enough, it becomes the market, and thus there is no "risk" of deviating from the market.) But how does that help the management of Consolidated Papers? The answer is that modern financial theorists—plus a host of consultants who use it to define their "value drivers" and other computerized solutions—assume that in making their internal investment decisions, Consolidated Papers's management is aware of the "wise investor" preferences, which, according to CAPM, determine stock prices. Knowing that they will not be rewarded in the stock market except to the extent that they follow the CAPM set of instructions that are embedded in stock prices, they should make their managerial decisions as to hurdle rates and the cost of capital with a regard only for the company's market risk and not its unique or total risk.

All this technical talk is no small matter. How we fix the discount rate is important because projects that are viable at one rate will fall by the wayside if the rate moves up even a few percentage points. It is said, for example, that the Japanese were able to invest profitably in many projects that Americans rejected because their costs of capital were much lower. Put it this way: during much of 1989–1990, CAPM said that the cost of equity capital for the average large public company (the S&P 500) was about 16 percent, a very high hurdle. Taken in conjunction with the high cost of debt capital in the United States, many American companies, relying on CAPM, may have been passing up some worthwhile opportunities, leaving them to financially less "sophisticated" competitors in Japan and Europe, who for this and other reasons were working with a lower set of costs.

NONSENSE REVISITED

CAPM is a mathematically elegant attempt to quantify risk and to describe the trade-off between risk and return for publicly traded stocks. I doubt, however, that it helps in determining the proper internal rates of return for capital budgeting purposes. On the contrary, with their desire to emulate the quantitative precision of the natural sciences, I fear that economics and finance teachers have done a good deal of mischief, advising us to tattoo on our foreheads a CAPM prescription—invest only in projects that beat the beta[14]—that potentially puts us at a competitive disadvantage. It fixes too high a cost of capital for some companies that should be encouraged to reinvest more freely, it fixes far too low a cost of capital for others, and it gets the right number for still others only by coincidence. But scholars and consultants have promoted it extremely well. (I know of no current finance textbook that does not follow it almost religiously.[15]) Few corporate executives understand the radical assumptions underlying CAPM. And yet, relying on the scholars, who are often wearing their consulting hats, approximately half of corporate America has adopted the model, with minor variations, as a basis for decision making.

Does CAPM have value in the selection of stocks by outside investors? I don't believe so, but valuable or not, our concern here is limited to CAPM's supposed utility as a tool in allocating corporate capital, and the belief here is that corporate finance managers should not pay even lip-service to capital asset pricing theory. Fire those CAPM-peddling consultants. Go back to a world where there are no simple solutions, but at least there are no simplistically wrong ones.

What's wrong with CAPM? The assumptions underlying it are faulty.

1. *The market does not know your business better than you do.* The finance scholars are telling Exxon and Consolidated Papers that they should buy a beta book from Merrill Lynch in order to know the market sensitivity risks of their new investments. The market, they are saying, knows how sensitive a company's business is to changes in the general economy, *and* the market knows this better than the company itself. The company should pick from the Merrill Lynch booklet the beta that is applicable to the particular project under consideration, and whichever number it picks, CAPM assumes that the market has at least as good information about the volatility of that project relative to the economy as the company itself. Hold on! That is a radical assumption because it elevates efficient market theory, and the wisdom of investors, to a level never before accepted. (The "wisdom" of institutional

investors is discussed in chapter 11.) The notion that the stock market has consistently good access to inside information, not just publicly available information, is called the strong form of market efficiency theory. While scholars generally accept the version of efficient market theory that argues that the stock market correctly reflects all publicly available information, even they reject the notion that the stock market has access to confidential, inside data. Yet in arguing that a company should determine the risks of a new project from a beta book, that is what they are saying.

Consider an apparel company, such as Liz Claiborne, that was contemplating an entirely new line of clothing for the working woman, similar to its existing collection but designed for those who wear larger sizes. (The author is a director of Liz Claiborne, Inc.) How profitable would the new business have to be to justify the cost of capital for a company that, as a whole, even in 1990 had a very high beta, 1.60? Would the new business be more volatile simply because it was new? Or would it be less so because it built on the goodwill of the existing lines? Claiborne's management studied the risks of the new business carefully: the depth of the market and who else was in the business (unique risks) and how stable the business was likely to be through the economic cycle (market risks). The company paid no attention to the volatile history of its stock price for a variety of reasons, one being that management was confident that it knew a good deal more about the volatility of its *business* than did the stock market. (Remember that no matter what the theory, the volatility of the company's stock would be significant for a corporate manager only insofar as it correlates with that of the business itself.) Management ignored the beta, and for good reason. Having been tagged early on as a growth company, trading at times at a price-earnings ratio as high as 30, the Claiborne stock had been exceptionally volatile, far more so than the business itself. In the industry down-year of 1988, the company's earnings fell by 4 percent from the year before, but the stock price dropped by 60 percent from its previous year's high. Samuel M. Miller, the chief financial officer, says today that he sees nothing in that history to inspire confidence that the stock market knows the Claiborne business better than does the Claiborne management.

Miller makes sense. Remember that capital asset pricing theory was developed for use by investors working with a virtually unlimited array of choices but, of course, no ability to affect the ultimate outcome of those investments. It is one thing for a pension fund manager to accept the historical verdict, the beta, as to the risks of a passively held stock portfolio and quite another for business executives whose very job it is to monitor, manage, and, if need be, adjust and readjust the risks and goals of a project as it unfolds. The capital budgeting process is dynamic. That is not to say that a clothing company can be made to look like a power company, but it is to say that risk can be managed. Why should the passivity of a portfolio manager be the model?

2. *The instability of the equity risk premium.* Under the popular version of CAPM, we are supposed to take the current T-bill rate and add to it the 8.4 percent premium for the Standard & Poor's index, with its beta of 1.0. We are then to adjust the result for the beta of the company in question. The presumption in the finance literature is that a long period of history is the best proxy for expectations about future returns, and so 8.4 percent, the average equity risk premium for the sixty years ended 1985, is considered an approximately right number to use today.[16] (The possibility that this number is no longer the right one is acknowledged in passing, but it is not explored.[17]) The theory is that stocks and bonds constitute a single, seamless, highly efficient market and that the substantially higher returns from stocks can be explained *entirely* by their tendency to be much more volatile over the short term.

The reasons that the premium might *not* remain stable are so numerous that one can only wonder why the scholars have assumed otherwise. Let's consider just a few. For example, while the bond and stock markets have moved much closer together in the last twenty years, for much of that sixty-year period they were quite separate. Many of the bond buyers were by law or convention barred from buying stocks with their bond money, and those restrictions and other inhibitions broke down only gradually. Even if we were to assume that bonds and stocks trade in a single market, with no significant barriers, it is not clear why we should assume that the equity risk premium is a function solely of the greater volatility of stocks. For much of that sixty-year period, inflation was a minor factor, unlike today. The average T-bill rate was 3.5 percent, not 8 percent as it was in 1989. The impact of unexpected inflation on stocks and bonds is quite different, making it treacherous to add mechanically a historically high fixed premium to a more recently high T-bill rate. We should never forget the possibility that trend may not be destiny. Finally, if in fact stocks do produce far better returns over time than do fixed income securities, investors willing to hold stocks throughout the cycle should have recognized long ago that the beta is only an aggregation of short-term fluctuations and that at almost any time in the past there was a huge profit to be had for those willing to ignore market volatility risk.[18]

On Wall Street, the idea of a fixed 8.4 percent equity risk premium has been discredited for some time. According to Leibowitz at Salomon, the market no longer uses a figure as high as 8 percent and rarely even 7 percent. The usual estimates of the equity risk premium are in the range of 4 to 6 percent, and occasionally as low as 3 percent. The difference between a premium of 3 percent and one of 8 percent is stunning. It can be as big as the difference between a 10 percent and a 15 percent total cost of equity (a 7 percent T-bill rate, plus the premium). Compounded annually for twenty years, a dollar becomes $6.73 at 10 percent and over two times that much, $16.37, at 15 percent. Any model that can happily encompass results as different as $6.73 and $16.37 is not a useful one.[19]

3. *CAPM produces some astonishingly foolish results.* The assumption that in calculating the cutoff point for new investments a business should rely solely on market sensitivity risk can lead to some quixotic results. The argument is that in calculating discount and hurdle rates all that matters is the volatility of this business in relation to the volatility of the average business. True, for companies having a beta equal to the average of 1.0, the model often produces a reasonable result. The cost of equity capital, using the method on page 194, would be about 16 percent. Assuming that half of a company's capital consists of debt and that the after-tax cost of its debt is about 6 percent, the weighted cost of the two combined would be about 11 percent, a reasonable cutoff point under almost any theory. That is not surprising; almost any model should work well enough at the midpoint. If, however, we look at companies with low betas of 0.65 or thereabouts, the model often breaks down. Some of the companies are the ones that we would expect to find, such as the electric power companies. The stock of an electric company does not respond as much as most other stocks to a business downturn because the business does not respond as

much. So far, so good. Therefore, it's reasonable to encourage utilities to invest at lower-than-average rates of return. But for some others with low betas, such as gold and sugar companies, the results are absurd. Homestake Mining, for example, has a beta of only 0.60, and Savannah Foods, the country's largest sugar producer, has one of 0.65. These companies are not at all what we would expect of ones with low betas. Because the consumption of gold for jewelry and other commercial uses is steady but modest, gold prices respond primarily to speculative demands that are not steady. The price is largely a function of what traders today think traders tomorrow will be expecting traders the day after tomorrow to pay for gold.[20] Sugar also is a speculative commodity. The reason that Savannah Foods' stock does not move as much as the market as a whole, that is, the reason it has a low beta, is twofold: in an economic downturn we still put sugar in our coffee, and, more significant, the United States has adopted a protectionist policy that shields American producers (in 1990, for example, it guaranteed them 22 cents a pound, compared to a world market price of 15 cents).

What does that mean for capital budgeting purposes? The low Savannah Foods beta tells us about life in the sugar business as it exists behind a protectionist barrier, nothing at all about life without the barrier, and nothing about the probability that the barrier will be lowered, as indeed it might.[21] But despite this constrained view of "risk" in the sugar business, CAPM would have us draw from that low beta the "lesson" that Savannah Foods should invest more aggressively in its business than most other companies do in theirs, or at least at lower rates of return than most. It tells us to do this even though the president might decide tomorrow that we should no longer deny access to the U.S. sugar market to the developing countries of the Caribbean Basin and the Philippines. (The theoretical explanation is that investors, at least, have adequately hedged by buying Asian and other sugar company stocks.)

For a gold company, the CAPM lesson is equally implausible. The Homestake beta suggests a business at least as stable (relative to the economy as a whole) as that of the best of the utilities, thus encouraging its management to plough money back into its gold mines at relatively low rates of return on equity. No sensible manager would do that. For as long as one would care to consider, Homestake's earnings have been systematically unstable. In fact, the Homestake beta itself is unstable, as shown in the following

figures calculated, using data from Value Line, by regressing three
years of weekly returns of the Homestake common stock against
the weekly returns of the S&P 500:[22]

1980	0.65	1985	1.20
1981	0.75	1986	1.10
1982	1.05	1987	0.65
1983	1.15	1988	0.65
1984	1.20	1989	0.65

Despite the fluctuations in the Homestake beta, and despite a dismal profitability record, based on the early 1990 beta of 0.60
CAPM is counseling the Homestake management to keep sticking
more money into those mines even at below normal expected
rates of return. The wisdom of that is hard to fathom.

4. *Unique risks are probably more important than market risks.* I
could extend these criticisms of CAPM further, but one more specific point, and then one general observation, should suffice. Statisticians say that of the total risk of a business, only about 30 percent is market risk.[23] The rest are the "unique risks" already
mentioned, mostly the risks that the competition will, or will not,
eat your lunch. (The prototype of a low-unique-risk business is a
dominant newspaper in a major city, say, the *New York Times*.
Which newspaper is going to eat their lunch?) CAPM says to ignore unique risks in computing the cost of capital; I believe
CAPM has got it exactly backward. The important risks for management to consider are precisely the unique ones—that the
product is lousy and the like. The market risks, those related to
the interim ups and downs of the stock market and the business
cycle, can be accepted with much better aplomb *because the critical concern for management is how well the business performs on
average and over time.* Like Graham and Dodd, I think that except
for short-term traders and those without sufficient resources to
stay the course, the short-term volatility of stocks is not important
even for outside investors. But in capital budgeting, I have essentially no doubt at all. Interim volatility risks should be largely ignored assuming that the company has the resources to weather
the usual (and even unusual) storms. They should be ignored, because the implicit assumption of most capital expenditures is that
the company expects to stay with that business for a long time,

through the ups and downs, which in any event are unpredictable. What matters is the strength of the business, the unique risks, over the cycle as a whole. Will the company gain market share or lose it? Indeed, a downturn may present opportunities to increase market share, even if the immediate consequence is to exaggerate the effect of the downturn and thereby to increase the company's beta. That is how companies should do their budgeting, and I suspect that is how truly wise investors would prefer to have them do it.

Academic finance people sometimes note in passing that all risks—unique as well as market risks—do enter into the capital budgeting process. But to preserve the purity of CAPM, they say that the unique risks should be factored into the expected annual returns, not into the discount rate where risks would ordinarily be reflected.[24] The effect is to fudge and obscure the otherwise recognized and important distinction between risk and expected returns. In other words, if we think of building 100 gas stations, experience and analysis tell us that the expected returns on capital will be, say, 14 percent, on average. In addition, we want to know how risky or dispersed those returns are likely to be, whether they will vary all over the lot, even while averaging 14 percent overall. This dispersion, the so-called risk, will affect the value of that 14 percent expected average return because we do care about the short-term volatility and the ultimate dispersion of the individual results that make up that 100-station average. (How much we care is not all that clear, but we do care somewhat.) According to the CAPM model builders, however, we should include in the risk-adjusted cost of capital only those risks, the *market volatility risks*, that are congenial to their model. The risks of, say, a higher gasoline tax or other factors that are not common to the economy as a whole should, they say, be put somewhere else in the equation. Those risks should be used to adjust upward or downward the 14 percent expected average returns. According to CAPM, these "adjusted" expected returns would then be discounted by a cost of capital that has been calculated with an eye only to the remaining, now "purified" set of risks, the market volatility risks, that are the centerpiece of their analysis.

Many business school people, having built important consulting practices around these models, have a considerable stake in them. By introducing a seemingly consistent and systematic method of risk analysis into the strategic planning process, they have produced highly saleable products.[25] But expected returns are one thing and the volatility or dispersion of those returns is quite another. Confusing the two is not consistent with good scholarly practice. Nor does it serve the needs of business clients, many of whom recognize that estimating expected returns even in the normal, unadulterated way is difficult enough.

In this and other ways, scholars have thoroughly confused long-term business or outcome risk and short-term volatility or quotational risk. A few years ago, I tried to capture that distinction in a simple chart that compared the total returns of the S&P 500 Stock Index, including dividends, over one-year and five-year periods for the years 1946–1985 (chart 10–2). The fluctuations of the five-year average annual returns closely follow the earnings of the index group of companies. As one would suspect, the five-year line on the chart is relatively stable, showing a loss of more than 1 percent only once. By comparison, the volatility of the one-year returns is a grotesque exaggeration of the experience of a five-year investor. But the fluctuations—the betas—on which financial economists rely in building their capital asset pricing models resemble the one-year returns on that chart much more closely than the five-year returns. (In fact, betas are the aggregated weekly or monthly prices, which are even more short term. Although it strains still further the assumption that stock price volatility matches true business risk, the economists were eager for more data points, which in their mathematically modeled world would yield a more "accurate" set of calculations.)

THE SCIENTIFIC PRETENSIONS OF CAPM

The concluding and general observation on CAPM is drawn from a Nobel Memorial Lecture by Friedrich August von Hayek in 1974, entitled "The Pretence of Knowledge."[26] (One can cite a Nobel economist to support either side of almost any debate. The trick is to pick the right one.) Although von Hayek was dealing with macroeconomic issues, his observations are applicable here too.

Economists, von Hayek said, have strained too hard to mimic the quantitative precision of the physical sciences, and in doing so they have ignored the fact that they are dealing with a complex social science in which quantitative data will be hard to come by. Describing their techniques as "scientistic," meaning that they have only the appearance of being scientific, von Hayek concluded that economists

Chart 10–2

Annual Percentage Return on S&P 500 Index
Through Year End

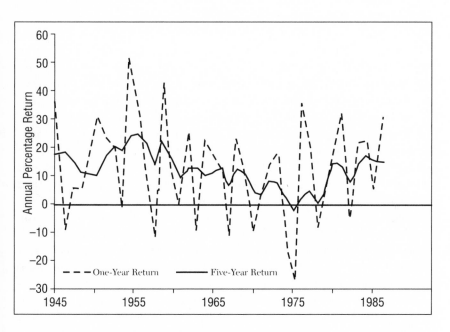

have too often been tempted to measure that which is measurable
rather than that which is important.

> Unlike the position that exists in the physical sciences, in economics and
> other disciplines that deal with essentially complex phenomena, the as-
> pects of the events to be accounted for about which we can get quantita-
> tive data are necessarily limited and may not include the important ones.
> While in the physical sciences it is generally assumed, probably with good
> reason, that any important factor which determines the observed events
> will itself be directly observable and measurable, in the study of such com-
> plex phenomena as the market, which depends on the actions of many
> individuals, all the circumstances which will determine the outcome of a
> process . . . will hardly ever be fully known or measurable. And while in
> the physical sciences the investigator will be able to measure what, on the
> basis of a *prima facie* theory, he thinks important, in the social sciences
> often that is treated as important which happens to be accessible to mea-
> surement. This is sometimes carried to the point where it is demanded that
> our theories must be formulated in such terms that they refer only to mea-
> surable magnitudes.[27]

Von Hayek's lecture was a succinct criticism of the forces driving so many of the currently fashionable ideas in corporate finance. What a pity that in the more than fifteen years since he gave that lecture, it has not had more impact.

CONCLUSION

There is general agreement that it would be beneficial to adjust the cost of capital to reflect the risks of a project, meaning the likelihood that the actual outcome will vary from the average or expected one. A 14 percent expected return from 100 new McDonald's outlets is a good deal more predictable, and so more valuable, than the same returns would be from a nuclear reactor or a novel genetic engineering project. As Exxon, for one, recognized,[28] the effort to correct the cost of capital for risk is likely to be unproductive. Disappointing as it may be, there is no valid basis on which to reduce to a statistical function that which is inherently uncertain and immeasurable. Within limits, the choice of the proper discount rate for a capital project, like the choice of the proper price-earnings ratio for a stock, is arbitrary. There are programs that will provide such answers, but that tells us more about our vulnerability to packaged solutions than about the measurability of risk and uncertainty.

We do need to be aware that some capital projects are riskier in the sense that, whatever the estimated average outcome, the range of results within the group is likely to be quite large. How much we care about this dispersion factor is not clear, however. As we saw in chapter 7, the capital budgeting process is fraught with uncertainty from beginning to end. The analysis of a proposed investment depends on so many variables, such as what the competition is doing, that any important expenditures should always leave a substantial margin for error. Truly good investments are hard to find. In the end, however, it is the analysis, and the discipline that it imposes, that are useful, not the close massaging of the cost of capital or hurdle rate.

11

Shareholders and Management

Thomas A. Murphy, the former chairman of General Motors, recently wrote to a friend describing "many so-called 'investors' [as] nothing more than predators, opportunists, speculators, traders, arbitragers, scavengers, even black-mailers, whose focus is on nothing more than trying to capitalize on the short-term . . . profit to them, regardless of the consequences" to others. Not accepting the responsibilities of ownership, Murphy added, they do not deserve consideration as true owners of the enterprise. Being retired, Murphy could be blunt, but any CEO still in office probably has views that are not much different.

Once upon a time, the world was safe for the managers of large public corporations—safe at least from shareholders. Ownership of the stock was so fragmented that effective control rested with the management rather than the nominal owners of the enterprise. Shareholders elected the directors, as legally they must do, but there was no substance to the process. Management had picked the candidates beforehand, and over 99 percent of the time there was no opposition slate.

At a publicly owned corporation, unhappy shareholders are free to come and go at any time. This market liquidity is an attractive aspect, but until recently, if a company was doing poorly, selling out was all that investors could do. It was called the Wall Street Rule: if you don't like management's performance, don't do anything about it; just get out. For years, Ben Graham wrote poignantly about the importance of being an intelligent owner of stocks, not just a good buyer or seller, but no one took heed.[1] For corporate managers, even the underachievers, shareholders remained little more than an abstraction. Managers paid lip-service to their shareholders. They spent an hour or two with them at the annual meeting and then complained about the waste of time.

In the 1980s the pattern broke down, first under the impact of hostile tender offers. Business acquisitions of all kinds, which had totaled only $12 billion in 1975, leaped fifteenfold, to $180 billion, in 1985 and then to $268 billion in 1988, the peak year. Hostile tender offers were the engine driving these mergers. In a sense, the shareholders still did not matter; they were only the incidental beneficiaries of a lottery in which companies, and even whole industries, were targeted for takeover. But their shares now mattered as they had not mattered before because they could be rolled up in a tender offer for control.

The second, and ultimately more important, change was that the ownership of American industry was steadily shifting from the traditional, individual shareholder to institutional holders, notably the pension funds. In 1950 institutional investors controlled financial assets of $107 billion. By 1980 they controlled almost $2 trillion of assets, and by 1990 about $6 trillion. Of the almost $4 trillion of corporate equities outstanding, institutions now own about 45 percent. At Lilly, Nike, Capital Cities/ABC, Whirlpool, and some others, 80 percent or more of the shares are institutionally owned.[2] These changes in share ownership had been underway for years, but for the longest while they had gone unnoticed. Then, in the 1980s, institutional investors began to be noticed and also, noticing themselves, began to flex their muscles as they had not thought to do before.

The concentration of ownership is remarkable. In January 1991 an analysis was made of the S&P 500 companies, ranking them by total market value of the outstanding common shares and then taking every twenty-fifth company in order—twenty companies in all. The Schedule 13Fs filed by institutional investors show that at the average S&P 500 company, it takes just twenty institutional holders to account for 34 percent of the outstanding stock.[3] With a few conference calls, the CEO of an S&P 500 company can reach the control group of shareholders—or they can call him.

Only an ostrich would ignore twenty shareholders who collectively own 34 percent of his company. Managers of publicly owned companies need to think about their shareholders as never before. The question is, What should they think?

A PAGE OUT OF AMERICAN INDUSTRIAL HISTORY: THE BUDDY SYSTEM

Let me suggest an improbable model for management-shareholder relations. I call it the buddy system, like the arrangement for protecting swimmers in deep water. The most celebrated example of it was the minority interest in General Motors that the du Pont company first acquired in 1918 and retained for almost forty years, until the federal government brought an antitrust suit and forced it to divest.[4] The GM–du Pont relationship was unique in the annals of American industry. In many respects, it resembled more the ties we still see in Germany, where even at the largest companies substantial blocks of stock are held, for example, by one of the major banks. In the United States, we say, it is not possible to find investors of the same substantial and enduring quality as in Germany, investors willing and able to play a constructive, but still muted, role. Saddled with high costs and other perverse incentives, our banks have virtually abandoned their traditional ties to their largest and best industrial customers. (Outside the banking system, the American attitude is that if it's worth owning a substantial part of another company, one should insist on owning all of it.) But at least this once it did happen here. And it succeeded so brilliantly that it is a model for what might yet be and, more immediately, a mirror to illuminate our present deficiencies.

Ultimately du Pont profited enormously from its investment, but that was secondary to the enormous benefits to General Motors from which du Pont's profits flowed. During the years after World War I, General Motors was saved from quite probable extinction by du Pont's financial support and its credibility in financial markets. Du Pont brought help to GM internally too, installing new and better financial controls. And during those formative years, when GM was faced with a managerial crisis, du Pont lent to GM for several years Pierre S. du Pont, the best it had, as president.

Du Pont first conceived of an investment in GM as an outlet for its accumulated wartime profits at a time when William C. Durant, the president of GM, was looking for a substantial financial partner. The investment was not an obvious one at all because the automobile business was not yet generally accepted. There were dissenting votes on the du Pont board, but the proposal had the energetic support of Pierre du Pont and Jacob J. Raskob, the company's treasurer. The initial investment, made early in 1918, was $25 million. Raskob had written a memorandum for the du Pont finance committee that showed extraordinary insight into the future of the automobile industry. In Raskob's opinion, General Motors occupied a unique position in the industry and with proper management would eventually show results second to none. Du Pont's ability to sell paints and other products to GM was mentioned in the memo, but that was a minor factor. Du Pont first acquired a 23.8 percent stake. By the end of 1919, du Pont had increased its investment in GM to $49 million and a 28.7 percent interest. With Durant's concurrence, du Pont promptly took control of GM's finance committee, and Raskob was installed as committee chairman.

At the end of World War I, Ford still dominated the automobile industry and it was not afraid to use its muscle when, in 1920, the industry fell on hard times. Faced with excess inventories, Ford slashed prices dramatically, as it could afford to do. Durant secretly tried to support the price of GM's stock by buying on margin and soon was over his head. With swollen inventories and short-term debt, GM was over its head too. Ford's aggressive pricing tactics tightened its grip on market share, which rose from 45 percent in 1920 to 60 percent in 1921, while GM's market share fell from 17 to 12 percent. Although du Pont had not intended to invest anything more in GM, it came to the rescue. It brought in J. P. Morgan to refinance GM, and as part of the process, du Pont increased its own holdings to 36 percent, the highest level they would reach. Except for a minor interest, Durant was bought out. Pierre du Pont, who earlier had transformed du Pont from an old-line cartel to a modern operating company, assumed the presidency of GM for more than two years. His reputation and leadership helped to stabilized the company. Among his many contributions was a recognition of the managerial and organizational genius of Alfred P. Sloan, Jr., and it was Sloan who succeeded him as president. In time, the company prospered mightily.

What a "buddy" was du Pont. It is tempting to think about whether GM would have stumbled so badly in the 1970s and 1980s if the du Pont company had still been there. In the early 1920s, the GM management, with Pierre du Pont's participation, had carefully formulated a policy for creating several well-differentiated grades of cars, from Chevrolet to Cadillac. Sloan, who played a major role in the project, wrote that "each car in the line should properly be conceived in its relationship to the line as a whole."[5] The concept of a complete line of cars, with carefully differentiated price and quality segments, something Ford had not achieved, was central to GM's strategy for half a century. It is difficult to imagine that the du Pont company, as principal shareholder, would not have rebelled against GM's decision in the 1980s to achieve production "economies" by policies that made it difficult for customers to distinguish a Chevrolet from a Cadillac except by the price tag.

In 1957 the Supreme Court forced du Pont to dispose of its investment. The court did not find that du Pont had violated the law. Du Pont had not, for example, imposed on GM a requirements contract for du Pont products, nor had it dictated GM's purchasing policies or practices. Indeed the evidence was that GM retained its independence and that both parties had acted honorably and at arm's length.[6] Instead the decision relied on the potential for abuse, although the connection had already endured for decades. As Murphy, chairman of GM during much of the 1970s, would later recall, the du Pont representatives on the GM board pursued only the interests of GM.[7] Still, this remarkably useful and lengthy relationship was terminated.

In retrospect, there were several keys to the success of the du Pont investment in GM. First, it was quite large—not just for GM but for du Pont as well. Du Pont's stake in GM was not idle surplus; the company needed capital for its own postwar expansion. This was the only investment like it the company would ever make, and the decision was important not just for the du Pont company but in a personal sense for the du Pont family too. Second, du Pont never contemplated owning more than a minority interest. Indeed, in 1923, not long after Sloan had become president, du Pont used over one-fourth of its own GM shares to fund a stock purchase plan for the GM senior management. Du Pont was intent *"on creating a partnership relationship between General Motors' management and itself."*[8] Those words were not some self-serving statement by du Pont; they were written years later by Sloan of GM. Third, partly because it was so large, but for other reasons as well, the investment represented an ongoing, long-term commitment to GM. The rewards would be measured by the returns from the business itself, the dividends, rather than the stock market. Fourth, it helped that du Pont had the financial strength and credibility to provide additional funds, if needed, and to help raise them elsewhere. And finally, it also helped that du Pont, the investor, brought to GM something beside money—in this case, the experience and skills of a successful industrial enterprise and the wisdom and leadership of Pierre du Pont and others.

Those are the defining elements. In combination they align the interests of those who manage a business and those who own it in ways that are wholly missing in the usual shareholder-management relationship. Du Pont's power at GM was impressive, but there was also a remarkable sense of its responsibilities. Unless GM grew and prospered, there would be no profit, except from the sale of paints and such, always a secondary consideration. There was no way to hedge, no puts or calls that would allow du Pont's investment to be saved if GM failed. The very idea of hedging with derivative securities would have left Pierre du Pont incredulous. At times the only sensible course, and the one du Pont followed, was to commit further resources to GM. Just as there would be today, Murphy notes, in the troubled days after World War I there was pressure to dismember GM and to recoup du Pont's investment, as part of what now would be called a "restructuring."[9] Du Pont was able to extend itself, partly because it had the wherewithal to do so but more profoundly because from the outset its decision about GM had been as particular and deliberate as it was significant. Du Pont understood why it invested in GM, and neither the dramatic downturn of 1920, the predatory pricing by Ford, nor the failures of GM's management shook that faith. And somehow neither the initial losses nor the later profits ever blurred the separate identity of the two companies. Du Pont never contemplated merger. But neither was GM just part of a portfolio that could be dumped at the first hint of a quarterly downturn.

The closest current-day example of the buddy system is Berkshire Hathaway, which has invested several hundred million dollars each in Capital Cities/ABC, Gillette, Coca-Cola, and a handful of other companies. The dollars are large for Berkshire, and since Buffett, the chairman, owns 44 percent of Berkshire, they are large for him as well. The continuing relationship and the commitment that were so valuable to GM for seventy years are evidenced at Berkshire today by Buffett's dictum that his favorite holding period is forever. (The author is a shareholder of Berkshire Hathaway.) Buffett's business philosophy—there are very few exceptionally good businesses and fewer still that are available at attractive prices—means that these investments will always be limited in number. And while Buffett's skills are quite different from those of Pierre du Pont, the now-retired CEO of Capital Cities, another Tom Murphy, Thomas S. Murphy, is fond of saying how much Buffett contributes.[10]

Not everyone is a Pierre du Pont or a Warren Buffett, but in a sense that is the point. There is a degree of distance and, therefore, balance of power inherent in a large but minority stock position. The balance is quite delicate, and that alone would discourage many. A 15 to 20 percent shareholder provides significant protection against hostile bids. It is not a perfect defense, but it does raise the ante for a putative raider, who is then likely to look elsewhere. On the other hand, while a buddy shareholder with that significant a stake is not in a position to give strict orders to management, it is very likely that the CEO will, in exchange for this more stable, less distracted working environment, pick up the telephone when the buddy calls—and likely, too, that he or she will consult on major transactions. This delicate balance would be shattered if the affiliate so much as suspects that its powerful shareholder might someday press for full working control.

Looking over the landscape of American industry, one struggles to find anything else quite like du Pont. Corporate Partners, an affiliate of Lazard Freres, and other funds have created so-called white squire pools of money that take significant but still friendly positions in public companies.[11] The fund managers, however, are almost never ready to eat their own lunch by investing a permanent part of their capital, apart from whatever fees they receive. The attraction for the fund managers is the rich stream of income, plus the prospect of a relatively early payoff and the recycling of the dollars into the next pool. *Forever* is not in their lexicon. Once upon a time, it is true, investment bankers did think of long-term relationships with industrial companies as their real wealth, but today the business is almost wholly transactional; it's the fees that matter. Morgan Stanley, long considered one of the best of the bankers, acquired Burlington Industries in an LBO in 1987 and took out of the company fees that eventually totaled $175 million.[12] Three years later, with Burlington seriously wounded but still alive, Morgan sold its voting stock and essentially washed its hands of the company. The first J. P. Morgan liked to say that money exists for situations such as these, but by 1990 Mr. Morgan and Morgan Stanley had little but their names in common.

There is missing at investment banks the permanent alignment of interests, of risks and rewards, that existed for GM and du Pont and was so vividly reflected in the du Pont decision to use its own GM shares as a fund for building a partner's relationship with the GM management group. And while other, more entrepreneurial investors are around, generally they are not credibly content to own only a minority interest. However much they protest, in the end they turn out to be potential raiders.

We have yet to see anything like the buddy system among institutional investors. Because they own so many stocks, no particular one is all that important. Knowing that, as managers, they will be judged by their quarterly or annual performance, they tend to watch the behavior of stocks, and other stock players, as much as or more than the behavior of individual companies. The public pension funds have been the most active participants in corporate governance, but they continue to focus on generic "proxy statement" issues, such as nominating committees, confidential voting, and poison pills. They rarely read financial statements. Too bad. As Willie Sutton would have said, that's where the money is and where a buddy could be most productive. The fact is that businesses usually decline only slowly, and the evidence soon shows up in the easy-to-read numbers of their return on equity, profit margins, and share of market. But the funds almost never dig into these company-by-company "financial statement" issues in any serious fashion.

However attractive it may be, the buddy system will remain a rarity. For some investors, the system raises significant tax and accounting questions. Most of the legal concerns are manageable, such as whether a large minority shareholder might be deemed a "control" person under the federal securities laws.[13] But the tax burdens can be quite serious. If a du Pont company does not own the 80 percent of a GM necessary to file consolidated tax returns, there is an extra layer of taxation, the effect of which is to produce a below-market rate of return, unless GM, the operating company, is in the star class. As we saw in chapter 5, the accounting results may also be dreadful. If the investment does not satisfy the requirements for equity-method treatment, a du Pont cannot include in its own earnings its proportionate share of the GM earnings, except to the extent of dividends. If the shareholding company believes that it depends on earnings that are reportable, its inability to show any meaningful income from, say, a 16 percent stake in another company could be a serious drawback.

It would take a radical tinkering with our laws and industrial culture to have anything much in the United States that resembles the buddy system, and it may be that American society is too individualistic for it. Sharing power does not come easily. American manufacturing companies are trying to emulate the Japanese, but it has been difficult, for example, to achieve stable long-term relationships of collaboration and trust with suppliers in which ideas and money are permitted to flow freely.[14] In short, if we are at GM, we want to remain fully independent and to run our own show. If we are at the du Pont company, we want to own enough of GM to make "sure" that things go right. By contrast, the lines of authority in the buddy system are inherently ambiguous.

There is a price for this individualism. At least the GM–du Pont experience tells us what we are missing. Of course, if by chance a company finds a buddy somewhere, one willing to play du Pont to its GM, one with a deep pocket, a reservoir of patience, and no cannibalistic tendencies, it should recognize just how valuable that can be.

WHY INSTITUTIONAL INVESTORS DON'T KNOW MUCH ABOUT YOUR COMPANY

Much of the scorn for shareholders that Murphy of GM expressed is well deserved. Ever since deregulation in 1975, brokerage commissions have steadily declined. For large blocks, they have fallen by over 90 percent and are now as little as 2 cents a share. The demand for stock trading, it turned out, was quite elastic; when trading became cheaper, institutional investors did more of it. Owning about half of the shares, they are thought to account for 65 to 70 percent of the trading.[15]

One public pension fund holds 1,400 stocks. The obligations of a pension fund can be actuarially measured by decades, so that one would expect to see rather little turnover in the portfolio. Surprisingly, over a five-year period, this fund engaged in more than 8,000 stock transactions a year. Although some of that trading reflected, for example, additional purchases of shares as the fund grew in size, much of it was the result of jumping from one stock to another or one manager to another.

Little of this trading reflects a significant revision of long-term prospects, which almost by definition change infrequently. Talk to anyone on the Street, read the brokerage reports, and the focus is consistently on prospects for a good (or bad) quarter or half-year for this company or industry or, on a more systemic level, the impact of minor changes in interest rates. Pension officers acknowledge that the funds are too short term–oriented. And stock trading is only a part of the picture. Since 1985, the use of stock index futures and other derivatives by pension managers has more than doubled. Corporate pension officers are the worst offenders. Thirty-four percent of them use futures of one kind or another, where the emphasis is not on companies as such but on market timing switches in and out of different sectors, such as bonds versus stocks, oils versus retail stores, U.S. versus foreign, and so on, with very little regard for the constituent companies.[16] According to a recent survey, pension officers themselves agree that pension funds have become too short term–oriented.

A CEO wants to deal with investors who share some of his (obsessive) concern for this one company, someone who knows about the products and their markets. Instead, under prevalent institutional money management strategies, no particular company is looked at very much, matters very much, or matters very long. In 1990, for example, the then chairman of Prudential Securities, George L. Ball, sent a Christmas memo to the officers of that investment bank with advice for the new year. He suggested a half-dozen stocks and a number of guidelines. One guideline, which he called a "key to investment success," was to sell any of the stocks that went down 10 to 20 percent. And don't forget this precept, he added.

It is difficult for a corporate management not to be offended by this sort of nonsense. (The import of Ball's advice was that no matter how undervalued a stock may be, an investor should not expect to profit from it unless the price moves directly upward, with no backsliding, from the day of purchase.) No business is immune from occasional setbacks. But let a company fail to meet some short-term earnings expectations by so much as a whisker, and the stock will often be "punished" beyond any measure that can be explained by long-term expectations or values.[17] Even if it is not dumped immediately, it is likely to be unloaded soon after as part of the "normal" window dressing of the portfolio.

This disenchantment with fund managers became outright horror during the 1980s when the name of a large part of the market game became takeovers and restructurings. As we saw in chapter 4, it was an era when the market value of almost any business could be pumped up, even if the company was left gasping under a mountain of debt. No matter how destructive of underlying business values, institutions, wrapping themselves in the flag of shareholder democracy and shedding crocodile tears about their fiduciary duties, took the money.

In Britain, where takeovers also flourished, it was different. As

Tom Heyes, the respected director of ICI Investment Management, recently noted, one "has only to think of companies like APV, Woolworths, Pilkingtons, the Minorco bid for Consolidated Goldfields and Higgs & Hill, to recognize that the acceptance of a bid is not necessarily the fund manager's automatic reaction."[18] Major British funds often held a collegial inquiry into the efficiency and integrity of the target company management. Rejecting a bid that is far above any likely future price is difficult to do, and under no circumstances should it be an everyday event. But in the United Kingdom, it did happen.

By their finality, with no tomorrow for the management group, takeovers are the quintessentially divisive issue. If in fact institutional investors are obligated by fiduciary duty rules to take any offer at a premium price or even if they merely *believe* that they are legally obligated to do so, then they forfeit a lot of the credibility that their British counterparts enjoy.

Is there really a legal compulsion to accept a tender offer? Almost no one would seriously argue that Dow Jones, for example, must sell its *Wall Street Journal* division simply because it receives an offer, even one at an extravagant price. Although Dow Jones is working with other people's money and has certain fiduciary obligations, management's decision to reject an offer would be fully protected by the business judgment rule. Why, then, could not institutional investors have stated at the time that Donald Trump's 1989 bid for AMR (the parent company of American Airlines), the bid of an acquisitive clown, should be rejected? If there were any such statesmen, they kept the message quite secret.[19] As a matter of prudent judgment, an insurance or investment company, say, could well have taken the position that, just as Dow Jones liked the newspaper business, it liked the airline business, it liked especially the American Airlines market position and management, and, after paying a substantial capital gains tax, it would have been hard pressed to find anything better elsewhere. Where is it written or implied in ERISA—the Employee Retirement Income Security Act—or elsewhere that money managers and other fiduciaries must invariably take the money and run?[20]

The question is only rhetorical. Whatever the law may be, and it is unclear, money managers have unhesitatingly accepted any and all takeover bids primarily because of the pressures of the marketplace. (Or they have sold their shares into the market, fully aware that they are being bought by arbitrageurs who will then accept the bid.) Fund managers, particularly those seeking pension fund allocations, know that they are being watched closely for their performance against the market yardsticks. Unlike the British, they do not seriously consider the possibility of turning down a premium bid.

Corporate managers do not respect shareholders; they fear them. Acting on those fears, they have tried to take away shareholder voting rights, and they have manipulated the state corporation laws so as to thwart not just takeovers but accountability to shareholders of any kind. Some of the defensive measures were wrongheaded, but the fear was not wrongheaded. As Murphy of General Motors had said and as senior staff at the California Public Employees' Retirement System (CalPERS) have acknowledged, major shareholders were unwilling to recognize any responsibility that went beyond immediate market gains. Shareholders lost credibility.

INDEX FUNDS AS CREDIBLE LONG-TERM HOLDERS

A ray of hope in the often grim confrontation between owners and managers was that, stung by the criticism that they had been trading too much and too foolishly, the major institutions began to change their pattern of investing. They had learned, they said, that they were too large and slow afoot to capture the bargains or to escape the bad news. A portion of their equity monies would still be traded actively, but a growing part would now be invested "passively" to buy a slice of American industry as a whole. Almost always they chose the Standard & Poor's 500 Stock Index, buying those 500 stocks in precisely the same proportion as the index itself. The S&P 500 was the most visible and widely used index, the one against which their performance would in any event be measured. The largest of the commercial index fund managers, such as Wells Fargo, reduced their annual charges to as little as two "basis points" (0.02 percent of the monies under management). Hundreds of billions of dollars flowed into indexes, particularly from public pension funds.

No one knows just how much money has been indexed. From $50 billion in 1984, the total is said to have reached about $300 billion in 1990. But the numbers are rough. In addition to those funds that are overtly indexed, large amounts are closet indexed, meaning that the money manager, though purporting to do something more creative—and entitled, therefore, to a better fee—is in fact trying only to track the S&P 500 with some shadow group of stocks. Many pension funds allocate over half of their equity funds to indexes, using an index (or two) as the core around which other, more actively managed pools of money are clustered.

ADVANTAGES OF INDEXING

Indexing has some real virtues. Heavy brokerage commissions and advisory fees are much of the explanation why money managers who follow more "active" strategies mostly turn in sub-par report cards.[21] Indexing virtually eliminates those costs. To be sure, if those managers were very bright and disciplined, more of them could have beaten the averages over time, but the record shows that they do not.

While a handful of exceptionally good investors do beat the averages, it is impossible for any large number of large funds, taken as a whole, to do so. The results for a large group inexorably return to the mean. What one player is buying, another one is selling; the average of a large sampling cannot beat the average. Or to put it more directly, the collective performance of a large group of institutional investors is inexorably tied to the business performance of corporate America. And beyond some minimal amounts, anything spent on trading and management fees is money down the drain.

If indexing won't produce better than average results, it will at least ensure against some potentially embarrassing ones, and that is no small benefit. The Wisconsin state pension funds bought about 3 million shares, over 9 percent of the total outstanding, of Prime Motor Inns, a company whose stock soon collapsed as it veered toward and then moved into bankruptcy in 1990. (Prime was examined in some detail in chapter 5.) It is obvious that no true Graham-and-Dodd-type investor would have bought so much as a single share. Long before the collapse, the "smart money" was selling it short. The $100 million loss in market value was not fatal to a state fund with over $20 billion, but public pension funds elsewhere quickly read it as an object lesson in the pitfalls of straying from the straight-and-narrow path—well, half a lesson. Because it was in the S&P 500 index, many of them also owned Prime (but much less of it than Wisconsin).

Prime Motor Inns sums up the performance virtues and weaknesses of indexing rather well: (1) no loss at all for value investors who, being very choosy, particularly about real estate speculations, would not have bought Prime in the first place, (2) a substantial loss for those intrepid enough to try to be a value investor by buying selectively and aggressively but without the same talent or the patience to dig through footnotes, and (3) a modest loss for an indexer, who bought everything on the list, including the lemons, but no stigma. In short, while one can do better than an index, it is surely possible to do far worse.

Having thus sworn off short-termism for half or more of their equities, pension funds reemerged wearing the mantle of true owners and asking to be treated with the same respect. James Martin of the College Retirement Equities Fund, a major indexer, said: "We're the quintessential long-term investors."[22] Having assumed an added measure of responsibility, they are asking for a correspondingly greater voice in the election of directors and major policy decisions.

The question is, how well does the mantle fit? Does index investing represent a serious answer to the dilemma of how to allocate large amounts of money, or is it just another in the long list of fads that have swept through the stock market, gathering momentum until the day they fade and are replaced? If indexing is only another item in the long, fruitless search for easy answers, and as ephemeral as the rest, institutions have yet to earn respect beyond the bare minimum of the law and the number of votes they can muster.

And there is an equally important second question: even if indexing does prove to be durable, how can formula-driven index funds, simply because they are locked in, claim to resemble a Warren Buffett, who invests Berkshire Hathaway's capital in large sums, in only a handful of companies, each of which he carefully selects and monitors?

Institutional investors, including such heavyweights as CalPERS, have been pushing for changes in the proxy and other rules that now constrain their power. It is on indexing that they rely for their legitimacy. Without it, they know, the claim that they are something more than in-and-outers, just "going with the flow," would be difficult to sustain.

At stake in this debate is the control of the largest, most important companies in the United States. Half the money invested in the S&P 500 Index ends up in just a handful of companies—IBM, Exxon, and the rest of the top fifty. Furthermore, while crystal balls come in different shapes and sizes, it is widely thought, and by some economists devoutly hoped, that indexing is still a growing phenomenon.[23] If it takes only twenty institutions to assemble 34 percent of the shares of an S&P 500 company today, what will the proportion be tomorrow?

And beyond all that, CEOs in particular should consider how well they are running the pension funds of their own companies. Corporate and other private pension funds hold over $500 billion of common stocks.[24] There are, in the appendix to this chapter, some suggestions for how companies might better manage the pension funds they have been so fond of criticizing elsewhere.

With that, let's see, first, just how durable indexing is likely to be, and whether indexing still has plenty of room to grow.

Index Fund Investors: Will They Stay the Course?

An index strategy is widely regarded as conservative, particularly at a time when it has performed so well. It is easily explained: if you can't beat the averages, join them. But indexing is not as simple as it seems, as the following reasons for skepticism about its durability indicate.

- *Will they love me in December as they did in May?* The love affair with indexing is a product of the 1980s. Beginning in 1982, the stock market roughly tripled, so that money managers looked like heroes simply by piggy backing the market. But markets turn down as well as up, and we have yet to see whether these managers will be as keen to match the market in the face of a prolonged or deep downturn. The record is not encouraging. In 1972, when the Dow Jones Industrial Average was over 1,000 and the earnings of the Dow were $67.11, pension managers used all their new money, and more, to buy stocks. Two years later, when the Dow was at 600—these bluest of the blue chips were selling below book value—and the earnings were much higher, $99.04, they put only 21 percent of their net new funds into stocks.[25] (What little interest there had been in indexing was all but extinguished by the bear market of 1974.) The same perverse pattern was repeated in 1976 and 1978 and again in 1980 and 1981. We do not yet know about the 1980s bull market, but on the surface it does not seem different. Unless they have become significantly older and wiser, pension funds may still discard in December what they loved in May, only this time it would be an index group—along with junk bonds and real estate.[26]
- *Timing matters, even for indexers.* The implicit assumption of indexing is that a manager can buy into, or add to, an index fund at any time and still do well. I have never seen it said that the timing matters, as long as the investor is in for the long pull. Historically,

however, that is inaccurate. The price (and value) level of the Dow Jones Industrial Average, for example, has fluctuated widely. Someone who bought the Dow in 1906 and kept it for seventy-five years, a rather long pull, would in real dollars (adjusted for inflation) have lost money, except for the dividends (chart 11–1). The volatility of even this blue chip index tells us that good judgment and some ability to distinguish intrinsic business values from market euphoria and gloom are essential. It would not be surprising, therefore, if the notion that a computer can wisely invest billions of dollars, no matter at what price, lost some of its luster.

- *Indexing is never as passive as they say.* The essential premise of a passively managed index fund is that it is better to buy the "market" as a whole rather than trying to make judgments about individual companies, judgments that are as likely to be wrong as right. But that also is too simple. What market, which index? The most commonly used index is the S&P 500, but others use the S&P 1000, the Wilshire 5000, or even several indexes, to capture a broader piece of the market. With the dollar slipping, as it was in 1990, they go abroad, using country funds, some indexed and some

Chart 11–1

Dow Jones Industrial Average in Constant (1987) Dollars

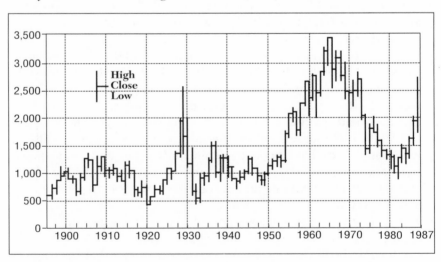

Source: Dow Jones; Bureau of Labor Statistics.

not, to buy slices of foreign markets. Some critics have argued that the S&P 500 is too heavily weighted with financial stocks, and to cure that or some similar problem, they buy so-called tilt funds, which "tilt" in favor of small companies, or away from high-tech ones, or whatever. And so it happened that pension funds began to speak in serious tones of their *actively* managed *passive* investments, as if that were not an oxymoron.[27]

Funds talk about passive investing, but like kids in a candy store, they look around and are tempted to buy some of this and some of that. Apart from an index fund, a prototypical multimanager system is likely to include small growth-stock managers, major growth-stock managers, industry specialists, sector timers, value-oriented managers, asset allocation specialists, plus various pools of fixed-income funds, usually including a market-timing fund or two.[28] Nothing is left out. As the kid said when he left the candy store, "Oh gosh, I ate the whole thing."

- *S&P 500: buy high, sell low.* The S&P 500 is the plain vanilla, most popular index, because managers know that they will, in any event, be graded by comparison with it. But unlike the Dow industrials, for example, the S&P 500 is a dollar-weighted index, and that creates problems. Each of the 500 stocks is weighted by the market value of its capitalization, so that someone buying into the index would buy more of a large company than a small one and—this is the problem—more of each company's stock when high than when low. For pension funds that are continually investing new money—CalPERS, for one, receives $20 million of new money (net of disbursements) every day—indexing meant buying rather less of, say, Capital Cities/ABC in the early 1980s, when it was cheap, and loading up on it in the late 1980s, when it was dear. For those who believe that the stock market is a genius and that the price is always just right—or as right as can be—that result may be acceptable. But it would come as a surprise to the rest of us who would instead prefer, as in a dollar-averaging technique, to buy more of a stock when it's down than up.

- *Indexing has ceased to be conservative.* In the early 1970s, it was common wisdom that investors could not do better than to buy the so-called nifty-fifty, the blue chip growth stocks of the day. It was the ultimate one-decision strategy, and so price did not matter. Even at eighty or ninety times earnings, it was considered conservative to buy Kodak, Avon, and Polaroid.

The underlying error was that what may have been a good strategy for a few initial investors and tolerable for some few imitators became absurd for the crowd. Something like that same phenomenon can be seen in indexing. It has not been nearly as egregious as the nifty-fifty, but it is not trivial either. In a recent study, Barrie A. Wigmore calculated that only about 35 percent of the dramatic 1980s' increase in the S&P 500 can be explained by earnings growth and interest rate changes.[29] The price of Blockbuster Entertainment, which became part of the S&P 500, jumped 9 percent on the announcement day, when the market generally was declining.[30] The very success of indexing produces a self-fulfilling prophecy. Those who stay out are made to feel foolish because they are unable to match the index's performance, which makes the index even more attractive, which encourages still other funds, and so on, until one day someone spoils the fun, saying that maybe the emperor has very little clothing on. The nifty-fifty lost more than half its value overnight.

At some future date, also not announced beforehand, money managers will gag on the fact that collectively they own over two-thirds of the stock of Bethlehem Steel, a dismal investment by any standard. Or they will prefer to invest abroad. Or they will simply need to raise cash. For any of these or a myriad of other reasons that we cannot now glean, they will begin to sell the S&P 500 with all the enthusiasm with which they first bought it.

To buy and hold stocks rather than to continually trade makes obvious sense. But where is it written that the best buy-and-hold strategy must be devoid of any judgment or insight or that diversification is not useful unless it is done on a massive scale?[31] One of the major benefits of being a long-term value investor, one genuinely willing to hold for five or ten years, is that it should force a fund manager to think long and hard about where the money goes. Just because large sums of new money are showing up on the doorstep every day does not force a pension fund to buy the whole market *regardless of price and value*.

These, then, are some of the reasons that a corporation might not accept at face value the assertion that indexers will stay the course, loyal and true. For the moment, they are steadfast, and a number of major claims have been built on that fact. Only with time, and perhaps a market break, will we test the strength of their conviction.

Indexers as Good Owners
Indexing has always struck me as something good professional investors would not do with their own money.[32] But the fact is that index-

ing is more popular than ever. CalPERS, the New York State pension funds, and others all use indexing for most of their equity investments, and that may not change. As a recent study showed, in the civil service culture of a public pension fund, indexing is very congenial. With small and modestly paid staffs, there are no rewards for superior performance and there is a high potential for criticism from politicians and the press for poor performance.[33] The chief executive of one public fund called indexing the easiest decision he ever made.

CalPERS, for one, has been working strenuously to overcome the skepticism of corporate managers. Being largely an indexer, it has an average holding period of about eight years, and at various companies it is taking an active interest not just in matters that will immediately affect stock prices but in executive compensation and other, longer-term issues as well.

Even at its best, however, the institutional voice we have been hearing in the debate on corporate governance has been almost solely that of CalPERS and a few other public employee pension funds, which as a group account for less than 20 percent of the institutional dollars. Public pension funds are the segment that, until now, has been the most exempt from the pressures of the marketplace and so is freer to invest time and money in such matters. (Competition works well, but not among standard setters, where, as we know, it lowers all boats.) In truth, the other 80 percent or more remain asleep.

We do not know yet how many of these sound sleepers have any immediate desire for a wake-up call. Insurance companies, with their liability structure and high degree of independence, *ought* to behave more like public pension funds, or so it seems, but clearly they do not. The remote causes are the laws adopted early in the century in various states, notably New York, restricting insurance company holdings of stocks, particularly large holdings in any single company. The laws reflected a deep-rooted populist fear of these rich financial institutions, many of which had no shareholders and seemed particularly free of checks and balances.[34] By now, of course, we have bred several generations of insurance company managers who see their role and their responsibilities in very constricted terms, and that culture is not likely to change soon. As for banks, they are even less likely to adopt an aggressive posture, constrained as they are by the desire of the commercial side of their business to stay on the good side of the corporate community. Even if the Glass-Steagall Act is eventually rescinded, as the Bush Administration recommends, it would be foolish to expect Bank of America or Citibank to behave much like CalPERS. With a few modest exceptions, such as the Fidelity group, the same is true of money managers, who have shown almost no interest in matters of corporate oversight. Here, too, there are legal constraints, but we should not make too much of them. Fund managers would in any event fear that if they become too activist, corporations will retaliate by pulling back pension monies. Being particularly concerned about the army of consultants that is continually looking over their shoulders—an army that will starve in the trenches if it does not find something that needs fixing—money managers tend to ignore anything that will not produce an immediate score or might chill their access to corporate information.

Let's assume that indexing is here to stay. Even so, CalPERS and a few others like it may only be the exception to the rule, with most other indexers preferring to sit on their hands.

- *Efficient market theory and intelligent shareholder activism.* The conceptual basis for indexing ruptures the link that, for an ordinary shareholder, exists between owning shares and the success of the underlying business. An individual shareholder often buys a stock because he or she likes the product and believes in the company; Peter Lynch, the extraordinarily successful manager of the Fidelity Magellan Fund and now retired, wrote rhapsodically about this sort of "bottom-up" investing.[35] Indexing, on the other hand, is largely an outgrowth of the efficient market hypothesis and other modern financial theories that make it unnecessary for investors to be concerned at all with the underlying enterprise. As some of the more enthusiastic believers have said, stocks should be bought and sold like pork bellies.[36] While, of course, nothing specifically prohibits a fund from behaving thoughtfully, the economic theory that spawned indexing suggests that most of them will not have the inclination to do so.
- *Two basic points worth of monitoring.* Wells Fargo Institutional Trust, the leading index fund manager, has about $60 billion in various equity index portfolios. Of that, about $40 billion is in the S&P 500, and the rest is in various small-company or foreign stock indexes. It owns in all 5,000 stocks. On the S&P 500 portion, the fund gets paid as little as two basis points a year. Wells Fargo is typically one of the six or seven largest shareholders of an S&P 500 company, but two basis points, or even four, do not buy much corporate oversight. William L. McEwan, the now retired director of proxy voting services, said to me, "Since we invest by formula, we vote by formula."

Wells Fargo never initiates a shareholder proposal, and for the proposals put forward by others it has a written set of guidelines. The guidelines enable Wells Fargo to demonstrate that it has met its fiduciary duties under ERISA and the like, which is important for managers, but the guidelines are rather crude. (Some of them, such as the one on stock option plans, can easily be circumvented.) They do not pretend to distinguish well-run companies from the rest. Still, I was told, they are broken only rarely because of the burden involved and because clients fear that Wells Fargo might be favoring customers of the bank or other friends. At many large institutions there is a certain amount of posturing about their profound concern for proxy voting. But McEwan was candid. Voting proxies, he said, "is a production job."

Part of the difficulty is that it is not clear who truly owns the shares that Wells Fargo has bought and who, therefore, is most concerned about the voting process. Is it Wells Fargo, which gets paid not for picking stocks but for its computerized skills in tracking the market, or is it the plan sponsor that hired Wells Fargo, or, more remote, the beneficiaries of the plan? If the ownership rights are diffused and ambiguous, it is hardly surprising that the responsibility for voting is seen as nothing more than a chore.

- *Like hitting singles, with no one on base.* A pension fund that creates its own index portfolio, rather than using a Wells Fargo, might be willing to invest a bit more in corporate governance matters. But even so, it would be impossible for it to know much about the operations and management of hundreds of companies. Given this pervasive ignorance, how thoughtful can a fund be when it comes to scrutinizing a company's business, making suggestions, and otherwise exercising influence? It can do the quick-and-dirty stuff, such as voting against certain stock option plans, but that's about all. CalPERS, for example, owns about $250 million of GM stock, a tidy sum. But even large improvements at any one company will have only trivial consequences in a portfolio of over 1,000 companies. It's like hitting only singles, with no one on base—ever.

- *Too much smile, not enough cat.* Indexers sometimes talk about their commitment to a company and their desire to build enduring relationships.[37] They have sworn off the Wall Street Rule and will not sell out in the face of bad news. But they have also taken a solemn "oath" not to invest in the relationship. If an emergency arises and financing is required, don't call on them. Unlike a du Pont when GM was in distress, they cannot supply it. Indexers speak of their buy-

and-hold strategy, but their resemblance to a du Pont stops there. Like the Cheshire cat, there is more smile than cat.

INDEXING AS A METAPHOR

Efficient market theorists like to assume that money managers are doing their job.[38] But indexing is a metaphor for much of what ails institutional investors generally in the United States. Indexing as such may be relatively new, but it is only a latter-day version of a run-with-the-crowd attitude that itself runs old and deep.

A study of pension fund management recently conducted under the auspices of the Institutional Investor Project at Columbia Law School by John M. Conley of the University of North Carolina and William M. O'Barr of Duke University found that at almost every level of fund management, people are eager to displace responsibility. For the portion of their money that is managed actively, and not through an index, the funds use outside managers, who can then be shuffled in and out.[39] They use consultants to monitor and advise on how best to shuffle, thus insulating themselves still further. If the investments are administered in-house, there is typically an elaborate system of committees, again so that responsibility is diffused and cannot be pinned on any one or few individuals. Even without indexing of a formal kind, therefore, we see massive diversification. No decision matters very much, and so no one can be blamed very much. On a more personal and emotional level, no one will experience any significant sense of failure or regret.[40]

"Our knowledge," as Keynes said, "of the factors which will govern the yield of an investment some years hence is usually very slight and often negligible."[41] In the face of an assignment so beset by ambiguity and uncertainty, "choosing not to choose," as Richard Thaler put it, is a predictable and normal outcome.[42] But it is not a happy outcome, least of all for American industry. *Investors who are running from responsibility make poor shareholders.* A senior officer at one of the largest corporate pension funds described proxy voting as "a miserable job." Their hearts are not in it.

CAPITALISM WITHOUT CAPITALISTS

Some leaders of the business community believe that shareholders ought to be disenfranchised, leaving corporate managers to watch themselves. Even the largest of shareholders should not be allowed to nominate a director, they say, arguing that it is a job best left to the incumbent board. They resist so much as meeting with a CalPERS, dismissing public pension funds as "special-interest" shareholders. At the state level, business groups persuaded a number of legislatures to adopt new antitakeover statutes that discourage not only takeovers but also shareholder participation and managerial accountability at almost every level, even when no takeover is threatened.

The monarchs of *ancien régime* Europe claimed that God was the source of their power. Modern-day CEOs are only slightly more humble. They recognize that, under law, the shareholders are supreme, but they then nullify that supremacy, saying that investors lack the competence to give advice about the business. CEOs assume that they have the right to determine whether those owners are as gifted and knowledgeable as they themselves are. But the assumption does not stand up. The owners' excellence or experience is not the issue. Power without accountability to someone *in particular* is not accountable at all, and our entire economic system is organized in a way that makes shareholder interests primary. Over the short run, stock prices should not mean much, but over a sustained period they mean a great deal. If through a complete business or industry cycle a company's stock has performed poorly relative to the appropriate industry and other yardsticks and if, as is then likely, the operating performance has also been poor, the shareholders, *because they own the company*, are entitled to hold management to task.

In a capitalist system, there is no substitute for the capitalists. In chapter 7, we saw how easy it is for, say, a mining company management to keep digging new holes, despite an almost unbroken history of losses and inadequate returns. A mining executive's whole life is built around copper, silver, and the like. That is what he knows and loves and, given free rein, will dig forever. Worse yet, the board of directors may allow it to go on. The alternatives are clear enough. One solution would be to pay larger dividends. But it's up to shareholders to focus their energies and attentions on those readily identifiable companies, in whatever industry, that have demonstrated a "superior" talent for dissipating capital. They need to read financial statements and to ask hard questions, not episodically, but on a continuing basis. Only shareholders, or directors truly chosen by them, can bring to bear the necessary pressure.

WHAT TO DO WITH YOUR COMPANY'S SHAREHOLDERS?

Some of those institutional shareholders are quite thoughtful and know a good deal about their portfolio companies. To what extent have corporate managers tried to attract that better class of investor? Probably very little. "Investor relations" programs are popular, but they are a misnomer. Usually they consist of courting security analysts at brokerage houses, whose livelihood is buying and selling shares, not holding them. Except for an occasional meeting hosted by a broker, and except in special circumstances, such as when a wolf is at the cottage door, companies do not routinely meet with the major investors who already own their stock. One would think that, if a CEO could, by getting together just twenty people, have in one place the holders of one-third of the shares of the company, some of whom have demonstrated a continuing interest and loyalty, he or she would jump at the chance (or better yet, six to eight of those investors at a time, over a quiet dinner). But that is not what happens.

The usual investor relations program is designed to attract the *most* investors rather than the *best* investors, as if the company needed them all. Why do that, when it may have only 50,000 shareholders in all, if that, and only two dozen important ones? In chapter 9, we saw that a stock split or large stock dividend might attract additional support for your stock, but it would come from investors who think that two shares of a $60 stock are "cheaper" than one share of a $120 one. Are those the investors that management wants—those who before long will sell out and will sell for reasons no better than the one that attracted them in the first place?

Wonderful things happen when companies stop overaggregating, as economists like to say, about shareholders. Glossy annual reports, written by a hired gun, rarely appeal to intelligent money managers. Studies show that they are too long on four-color photographs and short on candor. The select few investors whom a company really and truly would like to encourage are surely turned off. My own (limited) experience was that writing the letter to shareholders myself produced one that was less superficial and, so I was told, more credible. Better yet, the process of explaining to shareholders what I thought were the major issues and events was a useful discipline.

A few years ago, I put forward the idea that institutional investors should be represented on the board by allowing them to nominate a few directors, not just elect those who have been nominated by management, and without having to fight their way in. It would, I said, provide "a bridge between owners and managers, and it just might turn a we-they conflict into a continuing dialogue about how best to satisfy the interests of both. Not that the [differences] would disappear. In mature companies, for example, shareholders almost surely are seeking higher payouts than managers would prefer. But the boardroom is the appropriate place to work it out."[43]

The ability to communicate at close hand, and not through a megaphone, with a director who might be a retired CEO but who would have been nominated by investors, would provide for corporate managements more loyalty from the major shareholders, where it now counts. That loyalty can pay off in a variety of ways. Why scorn it?

While shareholder-nominated directors still seem like a good idea, I recognize that the battle lines may be hardening. For the moment, rather than this or that legislative solution, the best we can do may be to understand the complexity of the problem. Many more companies have been poorly managed than the business community cares to admit.[44] Some visible examples were mentioned in earlier chapters: American Express, General Motors, Hecla, and my "worst favorite," National Intergroup, to name a few. Poorly run, often lacking in candor, there seemed to be no prompt way of changing the management short of force.

It is not hard to write a better script, and there is a major role in it for shareholders. Still, it is true that as we search among those shareholders, we have yet to find many who have the discipline and training to play Hamlet or even the good friend and counselor, Laertes.

234 / *Sense and Nonsense in Corporate Finance*

Appendix 11a:
A Program for Pension Fund Management

Corporations tempted to criticize institutional money managers might look to their own houses first. CEOs who would keep a watchful eye on a billion-dollar investment in a widget factory, with detailed reporting and accountability, are likely to do just the opposite with their billion-dollar pension fund, relying on committees, consultants, and outside managers to splinter the fund into so many parts, with so many bit players, that there is no coherent whole. A large pension fund might hire as many as fifty different money managers, *all at the same time*.[45] The General Motors pension fund, which owns in all over 4,000 stocks, typifies this sort of mind-numbing diversification. By making so many choices, they have made none at all except to pay a small ransom in trading and management costs.

Encouraged by the news media and a blizzard of statistics, companies put their pension fund managers under the same immediate performance pressures of which they are then so fond of complaining. They talk about using three-year goals for fund managers, and they talk vaguely about the "long term," but anyone can see that if, after a year or so, a segment of the fund is below par, the manager of that segment had best shape up and do something radical, or he or she is on the way out.[46] Three years, which should be the barest minimum for a value-oriented strategy, becomes the de facto maximum. An untutored outsider examining large pension funds, with billions of dollars in hand, would expect to have found some independence of judgment or at least a consistent economic rationale, but it's not there, according to Conley and O'Barr.[47] Instead, they saw a steady shedding of responsibility, with no time out to formulate a coherent set of investment policies. Not surprisingly, the outside money managers who are asked to supply the "lyrics" to this ever-changing tune make sure to keep in step.

The failure of even these professional investors to beat the averages is sometimes taken as powerful evidence of the efficiency of the stock market. Having turned back the corners a bit and looked in some detail at how money is managed, however, we can now see a very different explanation for the failure. "Even" professional investors fail to beat the averages *because so few of them are "even" trying.* They go with the flow.

Companies could themselves take useful steps to produce the better class of investor they profess to seek—and achieve some better investment results to boot—because there would be a better alignment of the interests of the fund managers and the beneficiaries of the pension fund. Three guidelines would be useful so that fund managers get a clearer signal of what is expected.

1. *Eating your own cooking.* First, any outside fund managers would have to agree to "eat their own lunch" by investing a minimum of, say, one-third of their personal financial assets in the fund they run. (It would be interesting to hear the explanations that would surely follow as to why that is not "practical.")

2. *Patience and selectivity.* The second rule, adapted from a suggestion by Bill Ruane, chairman of the Sequoia Fund, is that a manager would be eligible only if the firm agreed to invest in no more than twenty stocks and, except for arbitrages, to keep them on average for at least two years. To be sure, a plan sponsor would not fix the rule so strictly that a manager would be unable to get a waiver, but the rules are to be taken seriously. The premise is that the management of a company's pension monies is not much different from the operation of its core businesses. With a limited number of good opportunities, the corporate sponsor should insist on the same high degree of selectivity as it does in its capital budgeting.

Until now, money managers have survived and prospered by hiding in the middle of the pack, chasing the crowd regardless of where it took them. Wildebeests know to stay with the herd. For a money manager, that is equally safe because so many corporate sponsors do what, for their chief financial officers, is also safe: fire each year or so the manager who, like an aging wildebeest, has been lagging behind. Only by imposing a ceiling on the number of stock positions—and Ruane would set it even lower—will managers be forced to do what they should have been doing all along: deciding whether they want to be a significant owner of a particular business for at least a considerable part of one business cycle. They would now have to think more about the fundamentals of Ford's business, not just guess whether Ford's sales this year will be (slightly) up or down.

A handful of managers are known for their patience and commitment,[48] and others might also find this second rule congenial, as if to say, "You should have told us sooner." There is evidence, for example, that fund managers typically hold an average of four times as many stocks in their clients' accounts as in their own.[49] The general sense is that there would be no shortage of applicants. Still, like it or not, managers would quickly adjust, and their new sense of commitment, both personal and intellectual, should help enormously.

3. Fewer managers, please. The third rule may be the most difficult because it requires a commitment by the pension plan sponsor itself, not just the hired hands. It requires that the pension fund not hire so many managers that it achieves in the aggregate the massive diversification and flip-flopping that was forbidden to the separate managers individually. Twenty rotating managers, like twenty cooks, spoil the broth, because their efforts nullify one another. The effect of this third rule, taken in conjunction with rule 2, is that very large plans, with billions of dollars in equities, would be forced to invest significantly larger sums in fewer stocks than at present. But even a very large corporate pension fund, one with, say, $10 billion just in the equity portion of its portfolio, could hire five managers to invest $2 billion each. With aggregate holdings of about 100 stocks, no one position would be so large as to raise serious legal or other concerns. The S&P 500 index alone had an aggregate market value in January 1991 of about $2.2 trillion. Even if this $10 billion fund confined its choices to the S&P 500, five portfolio managers would still have the freedom to weed out at least four of five stocks in the index. Assuming that the 100 stocks are a cross-section of the index measured by market values, the fund sponsor would, on average, own only slightly more than 2 percent of the outstanding shares of the 100 companies, a level often seen even now.

Lawyers have occasionally suggested that it might be imprudent for a pension fund to hold "only" a few dozen stocks, but no court or administrative agency has so said or even so intimated. In any event, one additional rule might be useful. Because the individual managers are not, and should not be, checking with each other, the plan sponsor might see to it that its aggregate holdings of any one stock, at cost, do not exceed 10 percent of the plan's total portfolio.

The benefits of such a program would be enormous. By requiring critical judgment and patience in the selection of investments, the rule would produce greater judgment and patience in the holding and monitoring of them. That is precisely what the corporate plan sponsors have allegedly been seeking all along—from other corporations whose pension funds are their own company's shareholders.

The proposed program would go a long way toward easing some of the tensions that now exist among labor, suppliers, middle management, and other so-called stakeholders in the corporate enterprise. Modern financial theory taught pension fund managers to diversify widely and to think of stocks as interchangeable commodities. The scholarly explanation was that corporate executives would then feel freer to embark on new ventures and take other large risks. What it produced, however, was a tragic mismatch in which workers and middle managers, for example, are heavily invested in, and committed to, a company owned by investors who, by design, don't take any interest in the workings of the business, its plans and prospects. (Senior management was also heavily invested, but, realizing their predicament, they opted for golden parachutes to let them bail out in safety, if need be.)

This was the fundamental error of modern portfolio theory, the error that the proposed program is designed to undo. A company will be better managed, its workers and suppliers will be more motivated and loyal, if the major shareholders know something about the company and share some measure of that loyalty. That can hardly happen, however, unless they have a continuing stake in the company and that stake is significant, not just in absolute dollars but as a proportion of their wealth.

Almost forty years ago, Ben Graham captured this now-forgotten principle when he wrote that investing "is most intelligent when it is most *businesslike*."[50] Investing should be done, he cautioned, in accordance with several business principles, of which the most important for our purposes was " 'Do not let anyone else run your business unless (1) you can supervise his performance with adequate care and comprehension or (2) you have usually strong reasons for placing implicit confidence in his integrity and ability.' " The importance of investor care and comprehension has not diminished over time, but they have been woefully neglected.

Recently Peter Drucker urged on us much the same concept by resurrecting the notion that investors should be thinking not in the usual but narrow terms of maximizing shareholder values but instead should be seeking to maximize the wealth-producing capacity of the enterprise.[51] The idea is not a simple one, but Drucker was driving at the need for investors to see the operational impact of their behavior and to understand that the corporate-investor objective must be one that integrates the goals of all the important constituencies—shareholders, suppliers, and employees.

By holding fewer stocks, a pension plan will have lost some market liquidity. Hooray! With a bit less freedom to move out of a stock, fund managers will exercise more thoughtful, patient, and independent judgment on the way in. That is what investing is all about.

Some companies already run their pension funds along the lines recommended here and feel quite comfortable doing so. Others could too. The impetus, however, will have to come from CEOs. Otherwise, the bureaucratic pressures to shed responsibility will overwhelm even the best of intentions.

Notes

INTRODUCTION

1. E. Gerald Corrigan, remarks before the Institute of International Bankers, May 23, 1989, New York, 4.

2. Carolyn K. Brancato and Patrick A. Gaughan, *The Growth of Institutional Investors in U.S. Capital Markets* (New York: Columbia University School of Law, Institutional Investor Project, November 1988), p. 13.

3. Ira M. Millstein, ed., *Our Money's Worth: The Report of the Governor's Task Force on Pension Fund Investment* (New York: New York State Industrial Cooperation Council, 1989), 1, 8.

4. W. T. Grimm & Co.

5. Benjamin Graham, *The Intelligent Investor*, 4th ed rev. (New York: Harper & Row, 1973), xi.

6. Fred Schwed, Jr., *Where Are the Customers' Yachts?* (Burlington, Vt.: Fraser Publishing, 1985), 39; see also Benjamin Graham, David L. Dodd, and Sidney Cottle, *Security Analysis*, 4th ed. (New York: McGraw-Hill, 1962), 720.

7. John M. Keynes, *The General Theory of Employment, Interest and Money*, Royal Economic Society edition (New York: Cambridge University Press, 1973), 152.

8. Linda Sandler, "Heard on the Street: Cloud Cast on 'Junk' IOUs by Integrated Resources," *Wall Street Journal*, June 28, 1989, p. C1, col. 4.

CHAPTER 1

1. Arthur Stone Dewing, *The Financial Policy of Corporations* (New York: Ronald Press, 1926), 120.

2. RJR Holdings Corp., prospectus dated May 12, 1989, for $250,000,000 Subordinated Floating Rate Notes due 1999.

3. Metropolitan Life Insurance Company v. RJR Nabisco, Inc., 716 F. Supp. 1526 (SDNY, 1989).

4. The last of the traditional books on finance were Harry G. Guthmann and Herbert E. Dougall, *Corporate Financial Policy*, 4th ed. (Englewood Cliffs, N.J.: Prentice-Hall, 1962), and Pearson Hunt, Charles M. Williams, and Gordon Donaldson, *Basic Business Finance*, 5th ed. (Homewood, Ill.: Richard D. Irwin, 1975).

5. Thomas E. Copeland and J. Fred Weston, *Financial Theory and Corporate Policy*, 3d ed. (Reading, Mass.: Addison-Wesley, 1988).

6. James C. Van Horne, *Financial Management and Policy*, 7th ed. (Englewood Cliffs: Prentice-Hall, 1986), 2 (italics added).

7. Gordon Donaldson, *Strategy for Financial Mobility*, rev. ed. (Boston: Harvard Business School Press, 1986), 30–31.

8. Paul Marsh, Patrick Barwise, Kathryn Thomas, and Robin Wensley, *Managing Strategic Investment Decisions in Large Diversified Companies*, Centre for Business Strategy Report Series (London: London Business School, 1988), 3.

9. Lawrence J. Gitman and Vincent A. Mercurio, "Cost of Capital Techniques Used by Major U.S. Firms: Survey and Analysis of *Fortune*'s 1000," *Financial Management* 11 (Winter 1982): 21.

10. Alfred Rappaport, *Creating Shareholder Value: The New Standard for Business Performance* (New York: Free Press, 1986), quoted in Quaker Oats, *1988 Annual Report*, p. 2; see also David W. Mullins, Jr., "Does the Capital Asset Pricing Model Work?" *Harvard Business Review* (January–February 1982): 105.

11. Telephone conversation with Paul E. Price, senior vice-president of finance, Quaker Oats Company, August 7, 1989.

12. Marsh et al., *Managing Strategic Decisions*, 23–24.

13. Michael E. Porter, "From Competitive Advantage to Corporate Strategy," *Harvard Business Review* (May–June 1987): 43.

14. The Quaker Oats Company, *1988 Annual Report*, p. 5.

CHAPTER 2

1. Carol J. Loomis, "The Biggest Looniest Deal Ever," *Fortune*, June 18, 1990, 48, 49 (quoting William Mayer).

2. Writing after the bankruptcy filing, Professor Steven N. Kaplan, relying largely on market prices and efficient market theory, concluded that the LBO *increased* the real value of Federated's assets by $1.8 billion. Kaplan, "Campeau's Acquisition of Federated: Value Destroyed or Value Added," *Journal of Financial Economics* 23 (1989): 191.

3. The decline in capital expenditures by LBO companies has been documented in Steven N. Kaplan, "The Effects of Management Buyouts on Operating Performance and Value," *Journal of Financial Economics* 24 (1990): 217; see also Michael C. Jensen, Steven N. Kaplan, and Laura E. Stiglen, "Effects of LBOs on Tax Revenues of the U.S. Treasury," in *The High Yield Debt Market*, ed. Edward I. Altman (Homewood, Ill.: Dow Jones–Irwin, 1990), 285, 292.

4. Louis Lowenstein, "Ignorance Isn't Bliss: Lack of Disclosure by Junk-Bond Funds Is Shameful," *Barron's*, May 29, 1989, p. 11.

5. See, e.g., Frederick H. Joseph, "A Wall Street View of the High-Yield Debt Market and Corporate Leverage," in *High Yield Debt*, 115; Michael C. Jensen, "The Eclipse of the Public Corporation," *Harvard Business Review* (September–October 1989): 61, 72 (unlike public companies, LBOs are likely to be reorganized speedily, without a Chapter 11 filing, and at lower cost).

6. The inability to reorganize informally was commonplace. John J. Curran, "Hard Lessons from the Debt Decade," *Fortune*, June 18, 1990, 76; see also Roger Lowenstein and George Anders, "No Picnic: Firms that Default Find Their Troubles May Have Just Begun," *Wall Street Journal*, April 17, 1991, p. A1, col. 6. See also Steven N. Kaplan and Jeremy C. Stein, "The Evolution of Buyout Pricing and Financial Structure in the 1980s." Working paper, Graduate School of Business, University of Chicago, 1991.

7. Subrata N. Chakravarty, "The Benefits of Leverage," *Forbes*, May 1, 1989, p. 42.

8. Amy Dunkin, "The Year's Best Sale at Macy's: Itself," *Business Week*, January 12, 1987, p. 136.

CHAPTER 3

1. Sidney Cottle, Roger F. Murray, and Frank E. Block, *Graham and Dodd's Security Analysis*, 5th ed. (New York: McGraw-Hill, 1988), 559.

2. Salomon Brothers, Inc.

3. Federal Reserve Bank of New York. According to the Federal Reserve Board, the figure was higher still, $130 billion. Federal Reserve Board, *Balance Sheets for the U.S. Economy, 1949–88* (Washington, D.C.: Federal Reserve Board, 1989).

4. *Economic Indicators, May 1989, Prepared for the Joint Economic Committee by the Council of Economic Advisers* (Washington, D.C.: Government Printing Office, 1989), 8.

5. *Economist*, November 25, 1989, p. 14.

6. Debt-to-equity ratios in Japanese nonfinancial companies have shrunk almost to the vanishing point. "Corporate Japan: Escape from Debt," *Economist*, July 21, 1990, p. 84. But even when they were higher, the risks were far less than in the more market-based financial system of the United States because of the stable network in Japan of shareholdings and other ties with banks and affiliated companies. See Robert N. McCauley and Steven A. Zimmer, "Explaining International Differences in the Cost of Capital," *Federal Reserve Bank of New York Quarterly Review* (Summer 1989): 7. In effect, there was always more "equity" in Japanese companies than met the eye.

7. *Grant's Interest Rate Observer*, August 4, 1989, p. 3; Simplicity Holdings, Inc. Report on Form 10-Q for quarter ended April 30, 1989, filed with SEC June 12, 1989.

8. Barrie A. Wigmore, "The Decline in Credit Quality of New-Issue Junk Bonds," *Financial Analysts Journal* (September–October 1990): 53, 54.

9. Salomon Brothers, *Composite Financial Statements of the S&P Industrials: 1989* (October 1989). Despite the overall decline in the coverage of interest charges from 1984 to 1988, there was a wide disparity from one industry to another. Aluminum improved; publishing and autos deteriorated. Ibid.

10. Not surprisingly, it was not just the ousted managements that were tempted by the trappings of the good life. See Connie Bruck, *The Predators' Ball: The Junk Bond Raiders and the Man Who Staked Them* (New York: American Lawyer/Simon & Schuster, 1988), 144–45, 236–37 (describing the corporate jets and Paris residences of Nelson Peltz and Ronald Perelman).

11. Revlon, Inc. v. MacAndrews and Forbes Holdings, Inc., 506 A.2d 173 (Del. 1986); see generally Ralph C. Ferrara, Meredith M. Brown, and John H. Hall, *Takeovers: Attack and Survival* (Stoneham, Mass.: Butterworth, 1987), pt. III.

12. Warren Law, "A Corporation Is More Than Its Stock," *Harvard Business Review* 64 (May–June 1986): 80, 83.

13. In the LBO negotiations management may also arrange for guaranteed reimbursement of their group's fees and expenses. Randall Smith, "In Failed Bid for UAL, Lawyers and Bankers Didn't Fail to Get Fees," *Wall Street Journal*, November 30, 1989, p. A1, col. 6 (airline reimburses management group bidders for $58.7 million of fees incurred in failed takeover bid).

14. We sometimes forget that corporations are a creature of the state. The laws on corporate operations and capital used to be much more restrictive. They could be changed again.

15. The vice-chairman and senior financial officer of General Mills, F. Caleb Blodgett, said that the company was intent on maintaining a single-A bond rating, not so much to reduce interest costs but to ensure access to financial markets in the event of a financial crisis. To do that, it targeted a coverage of interest charges by earnings before interest and taxes of six times.

16. Graham, *Intelligent Investor*, 37–38.

17. Ibid.

18. For a discussion of Gillette, see Louis Lowenstein and Ira M. Millstein, "The American Corporation and the Institutional Investor: Are There Lessons from Abroad?" *Columbia Business and Law Review* (1988): 739, 744–45. The continuing success of Gillette is described in Subrata N. Chakravarty, "We Had to Change the Playing Field," *Forbes*, February 4, 1991, p. 82.

19. See, e.g., Peter G. Peterson, "A Wall Street Perspective of Restructuring" (speech before the Business Council, Hot Springs, Virginia, May 13, 1989), 8–9.

20. Ibid. At the time he was giving this self-serving lecture, Peterson's banking firm was negotiating a white knight takeover of the Chicago & North Western Railroad for about $1.2 billion. Being "pro-active" has its costs, however. Fees and expenses in connection with the takeover and the

related financing, primarily for the two banking firms that would control the railroad, totaled $112 million. See Chicago & North Western Acquisition Corp., prospectus, October 20, 1989, for $475,000,000 14⅜% Senior Subord. Debentures due 2001, cover page, p. 20. Having burdened a cyclical railroad with seemingly excessive ($1 billion) debt, Peterson appeared keen on learning first-hand how to "manage leverage." See also *Grant's Interest Rate Observer*, July 23, 1989, p. 3.

21. In 1989 the United States was faced with the sale to a Japanese buyer of Perkin-Elmer, the last major domestic producer of tools for producing future generations of computer chips. The business is very capital-intensive, but it was widely agreed that without a domestic source of tools, American chip producers would operate at a significant disadvantage. David E. Sanger, "Chip Operation in U.S. May Go to the Japanese," *New York Times*, November 27, 1989, p. A1, col. 1. The decision by Perkin-Elmer was beset with externalities of grave national concern but which were not the responsibility of the company's shareholders. See also Stephen S. Cohen and John Zysman, *Manufacturing Matters: The Myth of the Post-Industrial Economy* (New York: Basic, 1987). The absence of a ready solution to the problem does not diminish its importance.

22. See, for example, American Medical International, which in 1989 was highly leveraged and trying to sell its acute-care centers; See also Glenn Ruffenach, "Charter Medical Will Post Yearly Loss of $210 Million; Restructuring Possible," *Wall Street Journal*, December 31, 1990, p. A2, col. 5. Hospital, heal thyself.

23. There is a debate over whether pension funds should "maximize" their returns, in the sense of generating relatively predictable financial returns, or whether they should instead "optimize." *Optimization* is shorthand for including (along with immediate gains) consideration of the longer-term economic interests of the plan beneficiaries, such as the vitality of the plan sponsor and the strength of the local and national economies. For a controversial proposal in favor of greater optimization, see *Our Money's Worth: The Report of Governor Cuomo's Task Force on Pension Fund Investment* (New York: State Industrial Cooperation Council, June 1989), 19–26.

24. For a criticism of state "multiconstituency" laws that dilute management's accountability to shareholders, see Statement of Bevis Longstreth before the Subcommittee on Securities of the Senate Banking Committee, 101st Congress, first session, October 3, 1989.

CHAPTER 4

1. I wrote several pieces on the LBO bubble. See, e.g., "Three New Reasons to Fear Junk Bonds," *New York Times*, August 24, 1986, sec. 3, p. 3, col. 1; "Junking the Junk-Bond Market," *New York Times*, November 16, 1987, p. A19, col. 1; "Ignorance Isn't Bliss"; "Lessons for Wall Street from Main Street," *Columbia, the Magazine of Columbia University* (October 1989): 24.

2. G. Bennett Stewart III, "Remaking the Public Corporation from

Within," *Harvard Business Review* (July–August 1990): 126, 131; see also Jensen, "Eclipse."

3. Stewart, "Remaking," 131.

4. Graham Dodd, and Cottle, *Security Analysis*, 286.

5. Merrill Lynch, *Mergerstat Review 1989*, p. 72.

6. Ibid., 72.

7. Kaplan, "Management Buyouts." For more recent evidence that investment spending is squeezed by reductions in cash flow, see Richard B. Berner, *The New Profit Cycle II: Leverage Works Both Ways* (Salomon Brothers, October 4, 1990).

8. Roger Lowenstein, "Still Disbelieving, a Highflying Yuppie Tastes Unemployment," *Wall Street Journal*, July 17, 1990, p. A1, col. 6.

9. Roger Lowenstein, "Heard on the Street: Bonds with Resettable Interest Rates Face Major Test with Western Union Note Issue," *Wall Street Journal*, May 2, 1989, p. C2, col. 3.

10. August 31, 1988, semiannual report of the T. Rowe Price High Yield Fund.

11. Constance Mitchell, "Junk-Bond Defaults Expected to Multiply," *Wall Street Journal*, January 2, 1991, p. R6, col. 4.

12. George P. Baker and Karen H. Wruck, "Organizational Changes and Value Creation in Leveraged Buyouts: The Case of the O. M. Scott & Sons Company," *Journal of Financial Economics* 25 (1989): 163, 183.

13. Vincent P. Carosso, *The Morgans: Private International Bankers, 1854–1913* (Cambridge: Harvard University Press, 1987), 225–30.

14. This summary of the Morgan Stanley investment in Burlington is based on George Anders's account, "Captive Client: Morgan Stanley Found a Gold Mine of Fees by Buying Burlington," *Wall Street Journal*, December 14, 1990, p. A1, col. 6.

15. The academic debate over the efficacy of LBOs is summarized in Ben S. Bernanke, John Y. Campbell, and Toni M. Whited, "U.S. Corporate Leverage: Developments in 1987 and 1988," *Brookings Papers on Economic Activity* 1:1990 (1990): 255, 272.

16. For a more systematic criticism of economic methodology, see Daniel M. Hausman, "Economic Methodology in a Nutshell," *Journal of Economic Perspectives* 3 (1989): 115 (the value of rough generalizations, e.g., aspirin cures headaches, even when difficult to test empirically).

17. For a discussion of financial disturbances and debt deflations, see Hyman P. Minsky, "Comments and Discussion," *Brookings Papers on Economic Activity* 2:1989 (1989): 173, 174.

18. Graham, *Intelligent Investor*, 302.

19. Graham, Dodd, and Cottle, *Security Analysis*, 542.

20. For a more extensive discussion, see Louis Lowenstein, "Management Buyouts," *Columbia Law Review* 85 (1985): 730. For a more sanguine view of management's role, see Ronald J. Gilson, "Market Review of Interested Transactions: The American Law Institute Proposal on Management

Buyouts," in *Leveraged Management Buyouts,* ed. Yakov Amihud (Homewood, Ill.: Dow Jones–Irwin, 1989), 217.

21. Randall Smith, "Buy-Out Bomb: In Failed Bid for UAL, Lawyers and Bankers Didn't Fail to Get Fees," *Wall Street Journal,* November 30, 1989, p. A1, col. 6.

CHAPTER 5

1. Kenneth S. Most and Lucia S. Chang, "How Useful Are Annual Reports to Investors?" *Journal of Accountancy,* Sept. 1979, p. 111.

2. Financial Accounting Standards Board, "Qualitative Characteristics: Criteria for Selecting and Evaluating Financial Accounting and Reporting Policies" (Exposure Draft, August 9, 1979), in Ted J. Fiflis, Homer Kripke, and Paul M. Foster, *Accounting for Business Lawyers,* 3d ed. (St. Paul, Minn.: West, 1984), 127.

3. Kidder, Peabody & Co. Inc., *Pension Expense: A Hidden Source of Past Profit Growth Is Fading* (newsletter, April 7, 1990); Roger Lowenstein, "Heard on the Street: Pension Expense May Drag Down '90s Corporate Profits," *Wall Street Journal,* August 14, 1990, p. C1, col. 4.

4. Gary Hector, "Cute Tricks on the Bottom Line," *Fortune,* April 24, 1989, p. 193.

5. Bear, Stearns & Co., *Accounting Issues,* March 2, 1990, p. 1.

6. Tatiana Pouschine, "Malled," *Forbes,* October 30, 1989, p. 46. The Rouse Company disputed the claim that its properties were overvalued. Letter to shareholders and analysts, October 23, 1989. In 1990, the company reduced its current-value net worth back to the level of 1988, but arguably that was still much too high. "Wounded Bear: But Jim Chanos Is Still There Shorting Stocks," *Barrons,* June 3, 1991, pp. 16, 17.

7. Joseph A. Grundfest, "What the SEC Should Do for Investors," *Fortune,* April 9, 1990, p. 113 (seeking current value data).

8. This account is based on an article by Carol J. Loomis, "How Fireman's Fund Stoked Its Profits," *Fortune,* November 28, 1983, p. 99; see also Loomis, "The Earnings Magic at American Express," *Fortune,* June 25, 1984, p. 58. A good review of sham transactions is contained in Ted J. Fiflis, *Accounting for Business Lawyers,* 4th ed. (forthcoming), chap. 3.

9. Arthur R. Wyatt, "Efficient Market Theory: Its Impact on Accounting," *Journal of Accountancy* (February 1983): 56, 59–60 (summarizing the results of an FASB research report).

10. Bear, Stearns, *Accounting,* 3.

11. Roger Lowenstein, "Heard on the Street: Prime Motor Inns' Stock Slump May Be Tied to Bearish View of Firm's 'Quality,' " *Wall Street Journal,* March 21, 1989, p. C2, col. 3.

12. "U.S. Lists Top Pension Plans at Risk," *New York Times,* February 26, 1991, p. D9, col. 4.

13. Carol J. Loomis, "Will 'Fasbee' Pinch Your Bottom Line?" *Fortune,* December 19, 1988, p. 93.

14. SEC release 33–6835, May 18, 1989, contained in *Federal Securities Law Reports* (CCH), para. 72,436.

15. "Blowing the Whistle on Accountancy," *Economist*, December 22, 1990, p. 15.

16. Debbie Galant, "The Hazards of Negative Research Reports," *Institutional Investor* (July 1990): 73; Jeffrey M. Laderman, "How Much Should You Trust Your Analyst?" *Business Week*, July 23, 1990, p. 54.

17. Jeffrey M. Laderman, "Did Donald Trump Shoot the Messenger?" *Business Week*, July 23, 1990, p. 56.

18. Galant, "Negative Research."

19. Thornton L. O'glove, *Quality of Earnings* (New York: Free Press, 1987), 7.

CHAPTER 6

1. Martin Ricketts, "Why Do Corporations Distribute Assets? An Analysis of Dividends and Capital Structure," *Journal of Institutional and Theoretical Economics* 143 (1987): 52.

2. In a study of the financial policy of various companies, Gordon Donaldson found that the "overwhelming justification of whatever payout obtained at a given time was the factor of precedent." *Strategy for Financial Mobility*, rev. ed. (Boston: Harvard Business School Press, 1986), 248.

3. James S. Ang, *Do Dividends Matter? A Review of Corporate Dividend Theories and Evidence*, Monograph Series in Finance and Economics, No. 1987-2 (New York: New York University, Salomon Brothers Center for the Study of Financial Institutions, 1987).

4. Merton Miller and Franco Modigliani, "Dividend Policy, Growth, and the Valuation of Shares," *Journal of Business* 34 (1961): 411; see also Merton Miller and Franco Modigliani, "Corporate Income Taxes and the Cost of Capital: A Correction," *American Economic Review* 53 (1963): 433, at 439.

5. Franco Modigliani and Merton Miller, "The Cost of Capital, Corporation Finance and the Theory of Investment," *American Economic Review* 48 (1958): 261.

6. See generally Stephen A. Ross and Randolph W. Westerfield, *Corporate Finance* (St. Louis: Times Mirror/Mosby, 1988), chap. 15.

7. Richard Brealey and Stewart Myers, *Principles of Corporate Finance*, 3d ed. (New York: McGraw-Hill, 1988), 888.

8. Some corporate finance texts do add a section to the theoretical analysis in order to "consider some *practical* things," as one of them said. See, e.g., Van Horne, *Financial Management*, 353.

9. Miller and Modigliani, "Dividend Policy," 424–25.

10. Carol Loomis, "A Case for Dropping Dividends," *Fortune*, June 15, 1968, 181. As one investment banker said, "If you want to find out whether the institutions want dividends, for God's sake, go and . . . ask them!" He did ask, and the replies he got were yes, yes, yes. Donald H. Chew, ed., *Six*

Roundtable Discussions of Corporate Finance with Joel Stern (New York: Quantum Books, 1986), 81–82.

11. Brealey and Myers, *Principles*, 350; see also Van Horne, *Financial Management*, 349. Merton Miller describes the preference for dividends as "an optical illusion," much as a stick in water seems to be bent. "Can Management Use Dividends to Influence the Value of the Firm?" in Joel M. Stern and Donald H. Chew, Jr., eds., *The Revolution in Corporate Finance* (New York: Basil Blackwell, 1986), 299.

12. Stephen A. Ross, "Comment on the Modigliani-Miller Propositions," *Journal of Economic Perspectives* 2 (1988): 127.

13. Martin Feldstein and Jerry Green, "Why Do Companies Pay Dividends?" *American Economic Review* 73 (1983): 17. Or as the former president of the American Finance Association said, "I think dividends that remain taxable will gradually vanish." Fischer Black, "Editorial Viewpoint," *Institutional Investor* (May–June 1990): 5.

14. *New York Stock Exchange 1989 Fact Book*, 78.

15. See, e.g., Terry A. Marsh and Robert C. Merton, "Dividend Behavior for the Aggregate Stock Market," *Journal of Business* 60 (1987): 1.

CHAPTER 7

1. National Intergroup, Inc. *1988 Annual Report*, cover page, 4.

2. Bruck, *Predators' Ball*, 213.

3. *Economic Report of the President, January 1989* (Washington, D.C.: U.S. Government Printing Office, 1989), 377.

4. Robert L. Rose, "Currency Squeeze: Caterpillar Sees Gains in Efficiency Imperiled by Strength of Dollar," *Wall Street Journal*, April 6, 1990, p. A-1, col. 6.

5. Graham and Dodd, *Security Analysis*, 1st ed., 349.

6. Dewing, *Financial Policy*, 1926 ed., 636–37.

7. Jensen, "Eclipse," 61 (criticizing Ford's accumulation of cash).

8. Paul Ingrassia and Neal Templin, "Cash Crunch: Hemorrhaging Money, Ford Cuts Spending and May Sell Assets," *Wall Street Journal*, January 24, 1991, p. A1, col. 6.

9. Guthmann and Dougall, *Corporate Financial Policy*, 532–33. To be "traditional" is not a good thing in the lexicon of modern financial theory. Brealey and Myers, for example, state flatly that "with hindsight we see that [traditionalists] did not think too clearly." *Principles*, 393. Only in their rigorously mathematical world would one be so certain.

10. Berkshire Hathaway Inc., *1984 Annual Report*, 16. Some economists use a test similar to Buffett's, *except* that their cost of capital fluctuates directly with the market price of the company's shares and so is too volatile. Thus, if a company's shares are trading at a price such that the earnings yield, say, is 6 percent, then all internal investments should yield at least 6 percent. See Victor Brudney and Marvin A. Chirelstein, *Corporate Finance:*

Cases and Materials, 3d ed. (Mineola, N.Y.: Foundation Press, 1987), 483–84 (quoting W. G. Lewellen).

11. Berkshire Hathaway, *1984 Annual Report*, 17 (italics partially added).

12. CDA Investment Technologies, Inc.

13. Brealey and Myers, *Principles*, 126 (citing the Ibbotson studies).

14. Martin L. Leibowitz, Stanley Kogelman, and Terence C. Langetieg, *"Equity Risk Premiums and the 'Volatility Drag,'"* (Salomon Brothers Research Department, April 1989); Charles P. Jones and Jack W. Wilson, "Is Stock Price Volatility Increasing," *Financial Analysts Journal* (November–December 1989): 20. At least one financial text, however, suggests that for capital budgeting purposes, the arithmetic average result is preferable. Brealey and Myers, *Principles*, chap. 9.

15. For an excellent account of such behavior, see Joseph L. Bower, *Managing the Resource Allocation Process: A Study of Corporate Planning and Investment*, rev. ed. (Boston: Harvard Business School Press, 1986), pt. II.

16. Quaker Oats Co., *1988 Annual Report*, 33.

17. See Capital Cities/ABC, Inc., *1988 Annual Report*, for an excellent explanation and application of the available cash flow concept. Ross and Westerfield, *Corporate Finance*, 29–31, is the rare corporate finance text that makes a worthwhile effort to reconcile accounting earnings and cash flow.

18. For an analysis of the impact of inflation on available cash flow, see Warren Buffett, "How Inflation Swindles the Equity Investor," *Fortune* (May 1977): 250; see also Robert N. McCauley and Steven A. Zimmer, "Explaining International Differences in the Cost of Capital," *Federal Reserve Bank of New York Quarterly Review* (Summer 1989): 7, 15.

19. Hersh M. Shefrin and Meir Statman, "Explaining Investor Preference for Cash Dividends," *Journal of Financial Economics* 13 (1984): 253.

20. Graham, Dodd, and Cottle, *Security Analysis*, 484–85.

21. See Louis Lowenstein, *What Wrong With Wall Street* (Reading, Mass: Addison-Wesley, 1988), 99 (note 11).

22. Richard J. Maturi, "The Allure of Reinvesting Dividends," *New York Times*, August 7, 1988, p. F8, col. 3. Companies that issue new shares for their dividend reinvestment plans, rather than buying stock in the open market, are diluting a shareholder's position, even while urging him to build it up.

23. Graham, Dodd and Cottle, *Security Analysis*, 4th ed., 500–501; see also Buffett, "Inflation Swindles."

CHAPTER 8

1. Salomon Brothers, Inc.

2. See, e.g., O'glove, *Quality of Earnings*, 149.

3. Artur Nussbaum, "Acquisition By a Corporation of Its Own Stock," *Columbia Law Review* 35 (1935): 971, 973, 976–77.

4. Brudney and Chirelstein, *Corporate Finance: Cases and Materials*, 489–90.

5. Arlene Hershman, "The Spreading Wave of Stock Buybacks," *Dun's Business Month* (August 1984): 40, 45 (quoting Theo Vermaelen). See also Louis Uchitelle, "Business Scene: Stock Buybacks vs. Risky Outlays," *New York Times*, January 1, 1990, p.32, col. 1 ("Buybacks provide instant gratification; capital investment takes longer to pay off," said Stephen S. Roach, an economist at Morgan Stanley.).

6. See Francis A. Lees, *Repurchasing Common Stock*, Research Bulletin 147 (New York: Conference Board, 1984).

7. Telephone conversation with Philip Bradtmiller, director of investor relations, Tandy Corp, September 4, 1989.

8. Victor Brudney's articles—"Equal Treatment of Shareholders in Corporate Distributions and Reorganizations," *California Law Review* 71 (1983): 1072; "A Note on Materiality and Soft Information Under the Federal Securities Laws," *Virginia Law Review* 75 (1989): 723—offer an excellent summary of the law and the moral risks of stock repurchases.

9. Charles M. Nathan and Marilyn Sobel, "Corporate Stock Repurchases in the Context of Unsolicited Takeover Bids," *Business Lawyer* 35 (1980): 1545, 1546.

10. Comprehensive Care Corp., *Annual Report*, year ended May 31, 1987.

11. Swedish Parliamentary Commission on Stock Ownership and Efficiency, *Corporate Control and Corporate Power in the Business Sector of Sweden* (November 1988, English Summary), supp. 1.

12. Companies Act of 1985, pt. V, ch. VII, sec. 162–70. See generally, "Share Repurchase by Quoted Companies," *Bank of England Quarterly Bulletin* (August 1988), 382 (study prepared by the City Capital Markets Committee) for a summary of various restrictions on share repurchases imposed by the Companies Act, the Stock Exchange, the Takeover Panel, and the Investment Committee of the Association of British Insurers.

13. Compare Van Horne, *Financial Management*, 380 (rejecting the treatment of a share repurchase as an investment).

14. Berkshire Hathaway Inc., *1984 Annual Report*, pp. 3–4. See also comments by Buffett in Carol Loomis, "Beating the Market by Buying Back Stock," *Fortune*, April 29, 1985, p. 42.

15. In the fall of 1988, for example, the management of RJR Nabisco announced its desire to buy the company in a leveraged buyout. But earlier that same year, the company had repurchased 21 million shares without, it is alleged, disclosing the fact that significant discussions of a buyout had already taken place. Brown v. RJR Nabisco, 88 Civ. 7905 (JMW) (SDNY, amended complaint December 15, 1988).

16. See, e.g., Robert J. Shiller, "Investor Behavior in the October 1989 Stock Market Crash: Survey Evidence," Discussion Paper 853 (New Haven: Cowles Foundation, November 20, 1987); Robert J. Shiller and William J. Feltus, "Revisiting Oct. 13: Fear of a Crash Caused the Crash," *New York Times*, October 29, 1989, p. F3, col. 1 (noting the impact of psychological factors).

17. Teledyne Inc., Offer to Purchase 5,000,000 Shares of Common Stock, May 14, 1984.

18. James W. Wansley and Elayan Fayez, "Stock Repurchases and Securityholder Returns: A Case Study of Teledyne," *Journal of Financial Research* 9 (1986): 179.

19. Brudney, "A Note on Materiality and Soft Information," 738–40.

20. See, e.g., Ross and Westerfield, *Corporate Finance*, 433.

21. John L. Grant, "There's Nothing Wrong with Being in the Money," *Wall Street Journal*, May 20, 1985, p. A26, col. 3.

22. Audio/Video Affiliates, Inc., Offer to Purchase 4,500,000 shares, February 7, 1989.

23. On a similar note, when General Mills sold its specialty retail businesses in 1988, it was, according to the chief financial officer, part of a plan whereby the proceeds would be used to pay down debt and buy back 7 million shares.

24. CDA Investment Technologies, Inc.

25. In announcing a $1 billion stock buyback in October 1989, IBM also characterized the program as a good "long-term investment." Paul B. Carroll, "IBM's Board Votes $1 Billion Stock Buy-Back," *Wall Street Journal*, October 19, 1989, p. A3, col. 1.

26. Peter Lynch, *One Up on Wall Street* (New York: Penguin, 1989), 146.

27. See, e.g., Ross and Westerfield, *Corporate Finance*, 434.

28. Joint Committee on Taxation, Staff Report, *Federal Income Tax Aspects of Corporate Financial Structures* (Washington, D.C.: Government Printing Office, January 18, 1989), 55, n.90.

29. See, e.g., Tandy Corp., *1977 Annual Report*, 48–54 ("A Statement of Financial Philosophy").

30. Value Line Investment Survey.

31. For an analysis of the effect of share repurchases on stock prices, see Loomis, "Buying Back Stock."

32. Copeland and Weston, *Financial Theory*, 600; Theo Vermaelen, "Common Stock Repurchases and Market Signalling," *Journal of Financial Economics* 9 (1981): 139; Paul Asquith and David M. Mullins, Jr., "Signalling with Dividends, Stock Repurchases, and Equity Issues," *Financial Management* (August 1986): 27.

33. Loomis, "Buying Back Stock," 44.

34. Roger Lowenstein, "Heard on the Street: Exxon Views Big Outlays, Rather Than Buying Own Stock, as Better Way to Help Its Holders," *Wall Street Journal*, May 12, 1982, p. 55, col. 3

35. Morgan Stanley & Co., Inc., materials (n.d.).

36. See the discussion of Hyman P. Minsky's financial instability hypothesis in his comments in *Brookings Papers on Economic Activity* 2:*1989* (1989): 173.

37. Price Communications Corp., Prospectus for $50 Million 10% Conv. Debs., September 15, 1989, p. 26.

38. Ibid., 18.

39. George Anders, "Price Communications Ask Bondholders to Approve

a Possible Chapter 11 Filing," *Wall Street Journal*, October 15, 1990, p. B6, col. 3.

40. Marvin A. Chirelstein, "Optional Redemptions and Optional Dividends: Taxing the Repurchase of Common Shares," *Yale Law Journal* 78 (1969): 739; Robert I. Keller, "Revamping the Tax Treatment of Stock Redemptions: A Two-Transaction Approach," *Arizona State Law Journal* 20 (1988): 989. There is almost no limit to these "as if" arguments. For example, if redemptions of some shares are treated as if a dividend had been paid on all, perhaps retained earnings should be treated as if a dividend had been paid and then reinvested.

CHAPTER 9

1. *New York Stock Exchange Fact Book 1989*, p. 35, 79; see also Graham, Dodd, and Cottle, *Security Analysis*, 495.

2. Graham and Dodd, *Security Analysis*, chap. 30.

3. Graham, Dodd, and Cottle, *Security Analysis*, 499.

4. For a summary of the rules, see Brudney and Chirelstein, *Corporate Finance*, 524–28. See New York Stock Exchange Listed Company Manual, Sec. 703.02(a).

5. Being so "cheap," penny stocks have been the subject of widespread and persistent abuse by brokers, leading Congress to adopt the Securities Enforcement Remedies and Penny Stock Reform Act of 1990.

6. See, e.g., Van Horne, *Financial Management*, 373–76, for a summary of the research.

7. Hechinger and Selective Insurance each declared stock splits in 1983, only to see their shares sell, within eighteen months, at prices 30 percent or more below the price immediately before the announcement of the split, despite a generally rising market.

8. They were the first twelve companies in a list published by the New York Stock Exchange, excluding one, a cigar company, that by 1983 had been liquidated. The finding that there are no significant, better-than-the-market *long-term* price gains anticipated by a stock split is consistent with an earlier, more systematic study. Eugene F. Fama, Lawrence Fisher, Michael C. Jensen, and Richard Roll, "The Adjustment of Stock Prices to New Information," *International Economic Review* 10 (1969): 1.

9. Graham, Dodd, and Cottle, *Security Analysis*, 498.

10. Ibid., 499. An exception was GEICO, in which Graham's investment company held a significant interest.

11. See Berkshire Hathaway, *1983 Annual Report*, 12–13.

12. Warren E. Buffett, chairman, to shareholders of Berkshire Hathaway Inc., August 5, 1988 (announcing listing on the New York Stock Exchange).

13. True, roughly half of the shares are closely held, but even so the institutional ownership was far below the average for large New York Stock Exchange companies. See chapter 11.

14. Lowenstein, "Other Voices: Regulate the Wall Street Casino," *Fortune*,

(February 27, 1989, p. 125. See also Lowenstein, *What's Wrong With Wall Street,* chapter 3.

15. Benjamin Graham, "Stock Dividends," *Barron's,* August 3, 1953, p. 3; August 10, 1953, p. 5. The current popularity of dividend reinvestment programs, in which shareholders do not even get to put the dividends in their checking account, reinforces Graham's comments. See page 141, in chapter 7.

16. Loomis, "Dropping Dividends."

CHAPTER 10

1. The idea that the cost of capital should be adjusted for risk is not recent. See Guthmann and Dougall, *Financial Policy,* 126.

2. Ibbotson Associates, cited by Brealey and Myers, *Principles,* 130–31.

3. Brealey and Myers, *Principles,* 136.

4. Tom Copeland, Tim Koller, and Jack Murrin, *Valuation: Measuring and Managing the Value of Companies* (New York: Wiley, 1990), 183–87.

5. Anise C. Wallace, "Issues of 'Junk Bonds' Off Sharply in Quarter," *New York Times,* March 29, 1990, p. C2, col. 5.

6. See, e.g., Ross and Westerfield, *Corporate Finance* 213–14.

7. According to Ibbotson Associates, over a sixty-year period the average (adjusted for inflation) excess return of common stocks over the risk-free, T-bill rate has been 8.4 percent, the figure used in the text.

8. Brealey and Myers, *Principles,* 137.

9. CAPM usually assumes—a company's beta assumes—that the distribution of returns from stocks is a normal one, resembling a bell curve, and not a skewed one. Diana R. Harrington, *Modern Portfolio Theory and the Capital Asset Pricing Model* (Englewood Cliffs: Prentice-Hall, 1983), 24–25, 51–53. Whatever the value of such an assumption in looking at a broadly based group of stocks, there is far less reason to accept it for internal corporate budgeting, where there may not be many look-alike investment opportunities.

10. Finance scholars tend to say exactly the reverse: it's not the assumptions of an economic model that matter but how well it works in practice. See, e.g., David W. Mullins, Jr., "Does the Capital Asset Pricing Model Work?" *Harvard Business Review* (January–February 1982): 105, 110.

11. Brealey and Myers, *Principles,* 143 (italics added); see also William F. Sharpe, *Investments,* 3d ed. (Englewood Cliffs, N.J.: Prentice-Hall, 1985), 168.

12. Brealey and Myers, *Principles,* 134.

13. Sharpe, *Investments,* 168. Sharpe also discusses two-factor and other models in which, for example, major, pervasive factors, such as oil price changes, also enter into the calculation. Even these factors, however, are not firm-specific risks.

14. Brealey and Myers, *Principles,* 174.

15. While the finance texts typically add some reservations, such as that CAPM cannot be mechanically applied, the concerns arise only at the margin of the analysis and do not diminish at all their enormous enthusiasm for it.

See, e.g., Sharpe, *Investments*, 170; Mullins, "Capital Asset," 113; and particularly, Ross and Westerfield, *Corporate Finance*, chap. 9. What they preach, corporate practitioners then adopt as gospel, with no reservations at all. See, e.g., Morgan Guaranty Trust Co., *Corporate Finance and Value Creation* (New York, 1988).

16. Harrington, *Modern Portfolio*, 119.

17. An exception is Harrington, ibid., 118–21.

18. Rajnish Mehra and Edward C. Prescott, "The Equity Risk Premium: A Puzzle," *Journal of Monetary Economics* 15 (1985): 145.

19. See generally Martin L. Leibowitz and William S. Krasker, "The Persistence of Risk: Stocks versus Bonds over the Long Term," *Financial Analysts Journal* (November–December 1988): 40; see also Rappaport, *Shareholder Value*, 58.

20. Lowenstein, *What's Wrong with Wall Street*, 47.

21. Phyllis Berman, "The Fanjuls of Palm Beach: The Family with a Sweet Tooth," *Forbes*, May 14, 1990, 56, 69.

22. While not as severely as Homestake's, the betas of Quaker Oats and Caterpillar, two companies discussed in chapter 7, also fluctuated by 25 percent or more during the 1980s.

23. Sharpe, *Investments*, 167.

24. Brealey and Myers, *Principles*, 188–89.

25. Harrington, *Modern Portfolio*, 128.

26. Friedrich von Hayek, "The Pretence of Knowledge," *American Economic Review* 79 (December 1989, special issue): 3. See also Albert O. Hirschman, *Rival Views of Market Society* (New York: Viking, 1986), 122.

27. von Hayek, "Pretence," 3.

28. See chapter 7.

CHAPTER 11

1. See, e.g., Graham and Dodd, *Security Analysis*, 508.

2. Brett Duval Fromson, "The Big Owners Roar," *Fortune*, July 30, 1990, pp. 66, 78; Jay Palmer, "Itching to Buy," *Barron's*, December 3, 1990, p. S3.

3. According to the same SEC filings, the median aggregate holdings of the top twenty institutions were a slightly lower 30 percent of the outstanding shares of these S&P 500 companies, and institutional investors as a whole accounted for an average of 54 percent.

4. For a history of the du Pont–GM relationship, see Alfred P. Sloan, Jr., *My Years with General Motors* (New York: Doubleday, 1963); Alfred D. Chandler and Stephen Salsbury, *Pierre S. du Pont and the Making of the Modern Corporation* (New York: Harper & Row, 1971).

5. Sloan, *My Years*, 67.

6. U.S. v. E.I. du Pont de Nemours & Co., 126 F. Supp. 235 (D. Del., 1954), rev'd, 353 U.S. 586 (1957).

7. Letter from Thomas Murphy to the author, December 18, 1990.

254 / Sense and Nonsense in Corporate Finance

8. Sloan, *My Years*, 410 (italics added).

9. Letter from Murphy, December 18, 1990.

10. The convertible preferred stocks that Berkshire bought from some of these companies, such as Salomon, Gillette, and USAir, have been criticized because they were purchased at a time when the companies were the subject of takeover rumors or threats. The premiums over market at which the preferreds issued to Berkshire were convertible into common stock were, however, larger than appeared because the market price had been inflated by the rumors and also because the price did not yet reflect the dilutive effects of the transaction, as would have been the case with a public offering of convertible securities. While the Berkshire management believes that the operating companies will, like GM, benefit from such a relationship, still it is true, in general, that stock issuances under such circumstances represent a potential source of abuse.

11. Fred R. Bleakley, "Paper Losses: Some Savvy Investors Bought Bank Stocks, Now Look Less Savvy," *Wall Street Journal*, December 5, 1990, p. A1, col. 6 (Corporate Partners buys 16 percent of First Bank System of Minneapolis). Cummins Engine has sold a 27 percent block of its stock to three customers, two American and one Japanese. Jerry Flint, "A Very Japanese Solution," *Forbes*, August 6, 1990, p. 38.

12. Anders, "Captive Client."

13. Mark J. Roe, "A Political Theory of American Corporate Finance," *Columbia Law Review* 91 (1991): 10, 25–29; see also Bernard S. Black, "Shareholder Passivity Reexamined," *Michigan Law Review* 89 (1990): 520. Roe and Black together paint an impressive picture of the legal impediments to acquiring large blocks of stock and to the exercise of block voting power. Many of the impediments are there by political design or as a matter of public policy.

14. Bennett Harrison and Maryellen R. Kelley, "The New Industrial Culture: Journeys toward Collaboration," *American Prospect* (Winter 1991): 54, 59.

15. Salomon Brothers, Inc. Forty-five percent of individual investors don't trade even once a year, and another 25 percent trade only once or twice. New York Stock Exchange, *Shareownership 1990* (1991), 19.

16. "Pension Forum: Dipping into Derivatives," *Institutional Investor* (December 1990): 173; "Pension Forum: Dismay Over Short-termism," *Institutional Investor* (March, 1991): 139. (Fifty-six percent of surveyed pension officers think pension funds are too short term–oriented.)

17. Werner F. M. De Bondt, *Some Thoughts on the Shefrin-Statman View of Investment Advice* (Madison: University of Wisconsin, February 1989), 4.

18. Tom Heyes, "A Problem of Communication," *Treasurer* (September 1990): 20, 22; see also "Management of UK Equity Portfolios," *Bank of England Quarterly Bulletin* (May 1987): 253, 258. For a wide-ranging analysis of the impact of the stock market on corporate control in England, see Jonathan Charkham, "Corporate Governance and the Market for control of Companies," *Bank of England Panel Paper No. 25* (March 1989).

19. Randall Smith and Bridget O'Brian, "Trump Bid Might Find Some

Support among AMR Shareholders; Stock Rises," *Wall Street Journal*, October 9, 1989, p. A3, col. 2. One large public pension fund, critical of Trump's bid for AMR, did speak to other shareholders about the possibility of standing by the AMR management, but it does not appear that their views were communicated to either the target company or the bidder. John M. Conley and William M. O'Barr, *The Culture of Capital: An Anthropological Investigation of Institutional Investment* (forthcoming).

20. Roe, "Political Theory." See also Edward B. Rock, "The Logic and (Uncertain) Significance of Institutional Shareholder Activism," *Georgetown Law Journal*, 79 (1991): 445; John C. Coffee Jr., "Liquidity Versus Control." Working paper, Columbia Law School, 1991, p. 19.

21. De Bondt, *Some Thoughts*, 1–2 (n.1).

22. "Wall Street's New Musclemen," *Newsweek* , June 5, 1989, p. 46; see also William Taylor, "Can Big Owners Make a Big Difference?" *Harvard Business Review* (September–October 1990): 70; *Our Money's Worth—The Report of the Governor's Task Force on Pension Fund Investment* (New York: State Industrial Cooperation Council, 1989), 36–43.

23. Jonathan R. Laing, "Insidious Indexing," *Barron's*, January 15, 1991, pp. 8, 9 (quoting Professor James Lorie that "indexing remains a great idea . . . for the small retail investor seeking professional [sic] management [and there's] plenty of room for growth").

24. New York Stock Exchange, *Institutional Investor Fact Book 1990*, 5–6.

25. Warren Buffett, "You Pay a Very High Price in the Stock Market for a Cheery Consensus," *Forbes*, August 6, 1979, p. 25.

26. Salomon Brothers, *Prospects for Financial Markets: Structural Changes in a Capital-Short World* (December 1990), 4. (Pension funds load up on real estate in 1980s.)

27. Edward A. Wyatt, "Avidly Average: Indexing Enjoys a Surge in Popularity," *Barron's*, May 22, 1989, p. 17.

28. Jay O. Light and André F. Perold, "The Institutionalization of Wealth: Changing Patterns of Investment Decision Making," in Samuel L. Hayes III, ed., *Wall Street and Regulation* (Boston: Harvard Business School Press, 1987), 97, 104.

29. Barrie A. Wigmore, "How Can We Explain the Growth of the S&P 500 in 1980s?" *Goldman Sachs Investment Research*, May 23, 1991.

30. "Market Indicators," *New York Times*, January 10, 1991, p. D11, col. 1.

31. Studies show that at about fifteen stocks, the benefits of diversification are virtually exhausted. James H. Lorie, Peter Dodd, and Mary T. Hamilton, *The Stock Market: Theories and Evidence*, 2d ed. (Homewood, Ill.: Dow Jones–Irwin, 1985), 85. Oblivious to the sorry results experienced in real estate syndications, some economists believe that investors in real estate should buy a diversified national portfolio instead of parcels they can see and manage. See Kenneth R. French and James M. Potoba, "Investor Diversification and International Equity Markets," *American Economic Review* (May 1991): 222.

32. Lowenstein, *What's Wrong With Wall Street*, 64–66.

33. Conley and O'Barr, "Culture of Capital."

34. Roe, "Political Theory," 25–29.

35. Lynch, *One Up on Wall Street*, 78–80.

36. Frank H. Easterbrook and Daniel R. Fischel, "Limited Liability and the Corporation," *University of Chicago Law Review* 52 (1985): 89, 96.

37. Richard Koppes, "What Drives the Informed Institutional Investor Activist" (speech before the Institution for International Research, New York, September 10, 1990).

38. Brealey and Myers, *Principles*, 289.

39. Sequoia Fund, *1990 Annual Report*, 2.

40. De Bondt, *Some Thoughts*.

41. Keynes, *General Theory*, 149.

42. Richard H. Thaler, "Toward a Positive Theory of Consumer Choice," *Journal of Economic Behavior and Organization* 1 (1980): 39.

43. Lowenstein, *What's Wrong With Wall Street*, 211.

44. See, e.g., W. W. Adams, "Remarks" CEO Roundtable Conference Panel, Naples, Florida, January 19, 1991, p. 3. Adams said to institutional investors: "Trust us. We deserve it."

45. Roger G. Clarke, Michael T. FitzGerald, Philip Berent, and Meir Statman, "Diversifying among Asset Allocators," *Journal of Portfolio Management* (Spring 1990): 9.

46. The same pressures are visible in the United Kingdom. Bank of England, *Management of UK Equity*.

47. Conley and O'Barr, "Culture of Capital." See also "Pension Forum: Dismay." (Ninety-seven percent of all pension officers surveyed review their managers quarterly or constantly).

48. Mary Lowengard, "Corporate America's Favorite Shareholders," *Institutional Investor* December 1990): 63 (naming several money managers selected by investor relations people).

49. Arnold S. Wood, "Manager vs. Client: What's the Difference?" *Journal of Portfolio Management* (Summer 1988): 63, 64.

50. Graham, *Intelligent Investor*, 3d ed., 263.

51. Peter F. Drucker, "Reckoning with the Pension Fund Revolution," *Harvard Business Review* (March–April 1991): 106, 112.

Index

257